CANOEING MICHIGAN RIVERS

A Comprehensive Guide to 45 Rivers

Text by

JERRY DENNIS

Maps and Photographs by

CRAIG DATE

Friede Publications

TO GAIL

Friede Publications
2339 Venezia Drive
Davison, Michigan 48423

First Printing, June 1986
Second Printing, August 1986
Third Printing, June 1987
Fourth Printing, September 1988
Fifth Printing, February 1990
Sixth Printing, February 1991
Seventh Printing, May 1992
Eighth Printing, July 1993
Ninth Printing, April 1995
Tenth Printing, February 1997

Printed in the United States of America

ISBN 09608588-4-9

OTHER GUIDEBOOKS BY FRIEDE PUBLICATIONS

A Guide to 199 Michigan Waterfalls

Michigan State and National Parks: A Complete Guide

Natural Michigan

Fish Michigan — 50 More Rivers

Fish Michigan — 50 Rivers

Fish Michigan — 100 Upper Peninsula Lakes

Fish Michigan — 100 Northern Lower Michigan Lakes

Fish Michigan — 100 Southern Michigan Lakes

Ultimate Michigan Adventures

A Traveler's Guide to 116 Michigan Lighthouses

A Traveler's Guide to 100 Eastern Great Lakes Lighthouses

A Traveler's Guide to 116 Western Great Lakes Lighthouses

ACKNOWLEDGMENTS

The authors wish to express their gratitude to the Sawyer Canoe Company for generously assisting in equipment needs during the research of this book.

We would also like to thank the many people who helped and supported us, especially Mike and Marcy McCumby, Mark and Denise Wilkes, Gerald and Eva Dennis, Paul Maurer, Dick and Tricia Armstrong, Elaine Dennis, Wayne Overberg, Bob and Daisy Kostus, Barry and Terry Barto, Jerry Weese and Andy Willey.

Cover Design: Gail Dennis

Cover Photo: Presque Isle River by Craig Date

All black and white photos are by Craig Date unless otherwise noted.

INTRODUCTION

This book was conceived on a February weekend on the Pine River. That trip — our antidote to cabin fever — began and ended so inauspiciously that it has earned an honored listing in our personal archives under "Chalk It Up to Experience."

It began early Saturday morning in a search for Edgetts Bridge — lost on roads with names like 50 and 48 1/2, guided by a vague hand-drawn map and even vaguer local advice. It ended Sunday evening when we found our way back to that remote bridge and discovered that our vehicles had been broken into and ransacked.

During the drive home that night we decided something had to be done. There had been too many trips marred by insufficient and inaccurate information. There had been too many hours spent driving in circles on unfamiliar roads, too much confusion over access sites and bridge names, and too many days spent hauling canoes over logjams and fallen trees on rivers we would never have attempted had we been warned ahead of time. Obviously it was time to invest in a good guide to Michigan rivers.

But there was no such guide. So, to make a long story short, we decided we would create one, and — two years and about 1500 miles of canoeing later — you are holding the result in your hands.

For us, though, the story goes far beyond the pages of this book. It, itself, is enough reward for those two years work, but there have been so many bonuses along the way that several more volumes would be necessary to give them their due. Our friends and families and the many people we met on the rivers have been a continuous source of pleasure and surprise. What we learned about canoes and canoeing — especially whitewater canoeing —

has added immeasurably to our enthusiasm for a sport we had already enjoyed for many years. And all of those out-of-the-way corners of Michigan we stumbled into have given us a new appreciation for a state we thought we knew pretty well.

But the greatest bonus — and the one we will carry with us the longest — has to do with the rivers themselves. We would never have begun this book if we did not care for rivers, and in candid moments we have been willing to admit that the entire project was designed to give us an excuse to be near them more. Even after the hundreds of hours afloat, the miles of driving, the long days and too-short nights, the bad jokes and worse food, the rain, the snow, the mosquitoes and deerflies, and the mornings when all we wanted to do was stay curled up in our sleeping bags — but dragged ourselves to the canoe anyway — our appreciation for the rivers has not abated. It has, in fact, grown.

If there is one thing we hope for *Canoeing Michigan Rivers* it is this: That everyone who reads it and uses it will find his or her appreciation for Michigan rivers growing too.

PREFACE

We have made every effort to compose this guidebook in a manner that will make it a useful — and enjoyably useful — tool. Following are some explanations of the logic behind our terms and methods:

RIVERS

It is already apparent to us that there are going to be some readers who will be disappointed or even angered to learn that a favorite river or section of river has been omitted from this book. All blame or credit has to be placed squarely on the authors' shoulders.

We began, determined to include only those rivers we found to be particularly appealing to us. Our standards are simple. We prefer not to paddle on polluted water, or through long stretches of crowded, dirty, noisy surroundings, or in the company of too many powerboats and waterskiers. We looked for rivers that offer beauty, variety and challenge, and that, if not remotely situated, had qualities that were interesting and appealing in their own right.

That is not to say that every river we omitted is dull or tainted with industrial waste. We have left out some fine rivers — perhaps enough for a second volume of this book — and very probably simply missed some others. In the end, our decisions were based on our own prejudices but resulted, we hope, in a good representation of the best moving water in Michigan's two peninsulas.

COUNTIES

County names are listed at the beginning of each river description and appear in the order of the river's passage. The first county listed, then, contains the upstream or beginning reaches of the described river; the last county contains the end of the river or the final section we describe.

START/END

This refers only to the initial put-in and final take-out of the portion of the river described.

MILES

All river miles given are the result of our own measurements using a map measurer to trace each winding mile of every river on U.S. Geological Survey topographical maps. This is the most careful measurement system we could devise and is, we believe, quite accurate. Discrepancies with other sources are somewhat baffling. For instance, the length of the Au Sable from Grayling to Oscoda is variously reported as 180 to 240 miles. Repeated measurements of 1:24,000 scale topographical maps convinced us that the actual length is 114 miles. Perhaps what is most relevant is that all miles listed in this book resulted from the same method and will, therefore, be consistent from one river to the next.

HOURS

Because paddling time varies greatly according to ability, river character, water conditions and weather, we have included a range of times for each section of river only as a general guide. In a section listed as, say, a 3-5 hour trip, three hours is the time it took us at a steady, moderately fast pace. Five hours is the time we estimate casual paddling and floating will take. We have tried to remain consistent from river to river, but again, the times should be regarded as general references only.

GRADIENT

Gradient is the measure of a river's descent and is expressed in feet per mile. A 10 ft/mile gradient means that the river drops 10 feet for each mile of lateral distance. We arrived at the gradient of each river by counting contour lines on topographical maps. On rivers where gradient varies greatly from section to section, we have listed the section gradients separately; otherwise, the figure listed is a good average for the entire river.

The gradient of a river is a fairly good gauge of its speed and difficulty, although other factors such as water volume, bottom type and number of obstructions also have to be considered. Generally, a descent of 10 feet/mile will create rapids. Anything over 15/feet mile is certain to have some exciting water. A gradient over 20 feet/mile demands careful planning and preparation.

CAMPGROUNDS

All streamside campgrounds that we know of — both public and private — are marked on the maps or are listed in the descriptions. In some cases, campgrounds in the general vicinity are noted, but usually only when there are few on the rivers themselves.

CANOE LIVERIES

Canoe liveries are not usually noted in our descriptions. A list of Michigan liveries can be obtained from the Recreational Canoeing Association. (See Appendix IV, page 131.)

SKILL REQUIRED

This, again, is intended as a general guide. The numerals I, II, III and IV refer to the river rating system devised by the American Whitewater Affiliation. Level I, for example, is used to recommend the ability of paddlers to negotiate rapids designated as Class I in the International Scale of River Difficulty (see Appendix I, page 127). Level I, therefore, could be considered beginner or novice, level II intermediate, and level III and higher advanced or expert.

TOPOGRAPHICAL MAPS

We have listed the quadrant names of maps that cover rivers we consider remote enough, fast enough, or otherwise challenging enough to warrant special attention. Those who want maps of other rivers can get an index from the U.S. Geological Survey and other agencies where topos are available. (See Appendix IV, page 131.)

MISCELLANEOUS

This is a book for paddlers and is written from a paddler's perspective. Therefore, all directions — such as right and left, up and down, and above and below — unless otherwise noted, are based on usual downstream progress.

MAP LEGEND

Legend of symbols used on maps included with individual river descriptions.

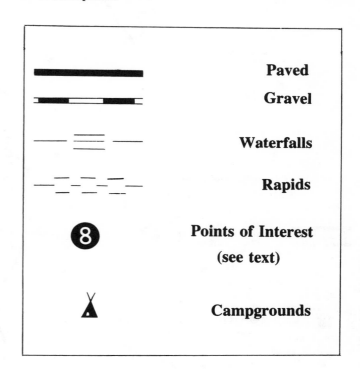

Although we have made every effort to ensure that the information contained in this book is accurate, it is entirely possible that we have made an occasional mistake. We would be grateful to receive corrections, suggestions or comments of any kind. Please write care of: Friede Publications, 2339 Venezia Drive, Davison, Michigan 48423.

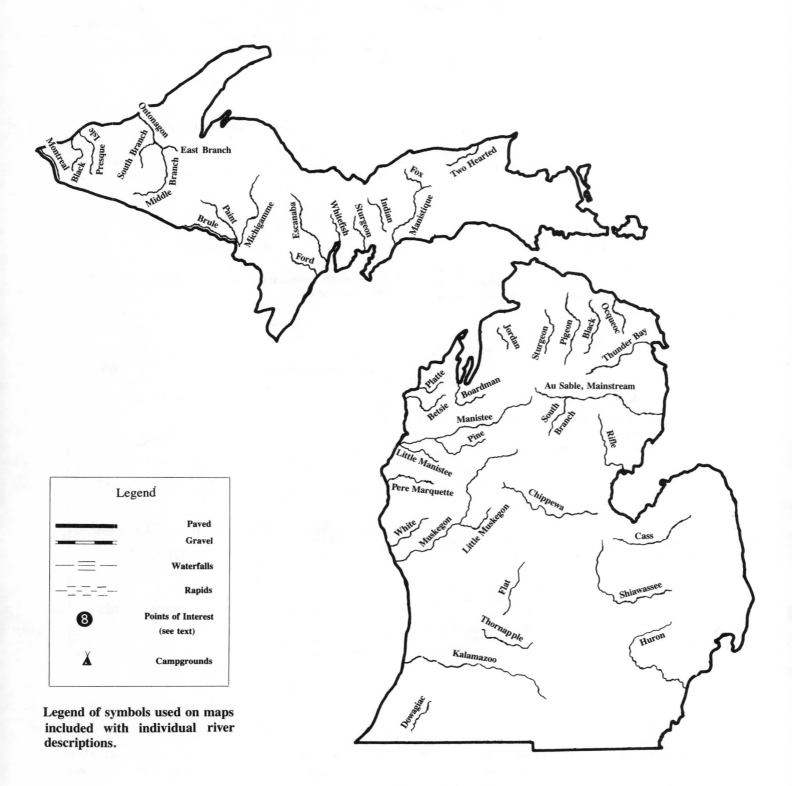

Montreal
Black
Presque Isle
Isle
South Branch
Ontonagon
East Branch
Middle Branch
Brule
Paint
Michigamme
Escanaba
Ford
Whitefish
Sturgeon
Indian
Manistique
Fox
Two Hearted

Jordan
Sturgeon
Pigeon
Black
Ocqueoc
Thunder Bay
Platte
Betsie
Boardman
Au Sable, Mainstream
Manistee
Pine
South Branch
Rifle
Little Manistee
Pere Marquette
Chippewa
White
Muskegon
Little Muskegon
Cass
Flat
Shiawassee
Thornapple
Huron
Kalamazoo
Dowagiac

Legend

▬▬▬▬	**Paved**
▬▭▬▭▬	**Gravel**
‒‒ ═ ‒‒	**Waterfalls**
‒ ‒ ═ ‒ ‒	**Rapids**
⑧	**Points of Interest** (see text)
⚑	**Campgrounds**

Legend of symbols used on maps included with individual river descriptions.

CONTENTS

LOWER PENINSULA RIVERS

UPPER PENINSULA RIVERS

—Photo by Gail Dennis—

LOWER PENINSULA

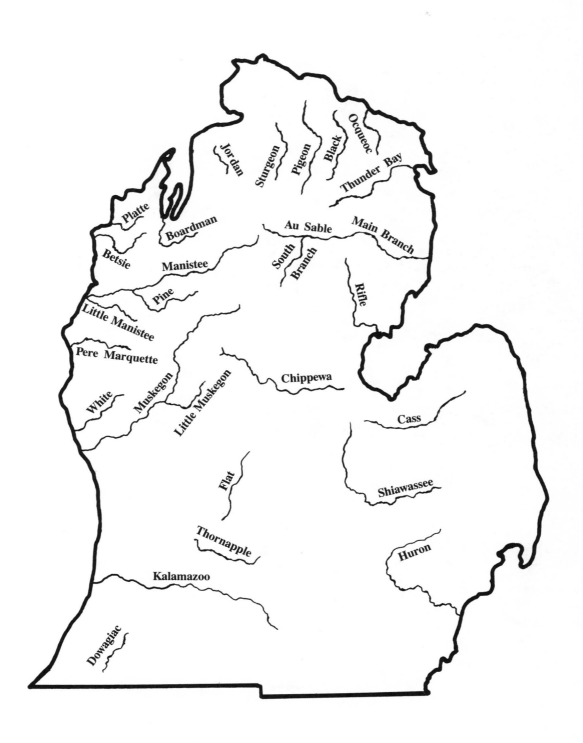

AU SABLE, MAINSTREAM

Counties:	**Crawford, Oscoda, Alcona, Iosco**
Start/End:	**Grayling to Oscoda**
Miles:	**114**
Gradient:	**Grayling to Parmalee Bridge — 5.2 ft/mile**
	Parmalee Bridge to Oscoda — less than 3 ft/mile
Portages:	**6 dams, fairly easy**
Rapids/Falls:	**None**
Campgrounds:	**Numerous**
Canoe Liveries:	**Numerous**
Skill Required:	**I**

Long famous as one of the finest trout streams in the Midwest, the Au Sable is undoubtedly the best-known Michigan river. It first gained the attention of sportsmen in the mid-19th century when its abundant grayling population became known. By the early 20th century, overfishing and years of bottom-scouring log drives had contributed to the extinction of the grayling, but brook, brown and rainbow trout — introduced in the 1890s — flourished and have continued to attract anglers.

Today the Au Sable's popularity among fishermen is nearly matched by its popularity among canoeists. Clear water, consistent flow, easy access and attractive surroundings make it a nearly ideal river for beginners and families. Although the series of dams beginning at Mio hinder progress, portages are clear and well-marked, and numerous campgrounds and long stretches of state and national forests make the Au Sable a good choice for extended camping/ canoeing trips.

Fishermen should note that special regulations apply to certain sections of the river, including flies-only in the Holy Water from Burton's Landing to Wakeley Bridge.

MAP #1: GRAYLING to McKINLEY BRIDGE —

57.5 Miles
Grayling to Wakeley Bridge
14 Miles
5 1/2 - 6 1/2 Hours

Although the Au Sable's beginnings are 20 miles north of Grayling, the river above the town is usually considered too small and brushy for enjoyable canoeing. It is interesting that, near the town of Frederick, the upper Au Sable comes within a few miles of the upper Manistee River, and for centuries, that area was the site of portages by native Americans using the two rivers as a cross-state canoe route.

1 Access in **Grayling** is not as simple as you might imagine. There is a city park on the upstream side of the M-72 Bridge, but a water-control dam under the bridge makes it necessary to portage the busy highway. Canoe liveries just downstream will usually grant permission to launch non-rental canoes from their property; the one we asked charged a modest fee for overnight parking. An alternative is to put in at any one of numerous access sites and campgrounds a short distance downstream from Grayling.

The river in town is small, shallow and narrow — with sand and gravel bottom — and is shaded by maples and willows. Current is steady and moderate — typical of most of the river all the way to Lake Huron. After the little East Branch of the Au Sable joins the mainstream, just outside of the Grayling city limits, the river widens. From here to Wakeley Bridge the river is 25-40 feet wide and one to three feet deep, with sand or gravel bottom and beds of aquatic vegetation lining the shore areas. The water is remarkably clear and cold. Terrain is low hills of hardwoods with cedars and occasional tag alders near the river. Homes and cottages are frequent but scattered.

② Access and parking are good at **Burton's Landing State Forest Campground, Keystone Landing State Forest Campground** and **Au Sable River Canoe Campground** — all 1-1/2 to 2-1/2 hours below Grayling. Camping facilities are primitive (water, toilets and picnic tables), but the sites will often be fairly crowded on summer weekends. Canoe Campground, especially, is very popular and is used as a take-out by canoe liveries.

③ Access and parking are good at the public site 200 yards downstream and on the right, below **Stephan's Bridge.**

④ The access site at **Wakeley Bridge** is a few hundred yards downstream on the right and has good access and parking.

Wakeley Bridge to Parmalee Bridge
16.5 Miles
4 1/2 - 5 1/2 Hours

Below Wakeley Bridge the river deepens and slows somewhat and enters a series of turns and switchbacks with deep pools at the bends. There are likely to be fewer canoes than in the section above. Cottages are frequent, but they tend to be fairly widely spaced. The bottom is predominantly sand and silt, and large numbers of drowned logs and stumps line the banks.

A short distance downstream is **Whitepine Canoe Forest Campground,** a good choice for an overnight trip from Grayling (five to 6 1/2 hours of paddling time). It is considered a "group" campground because of the large size of its sites, and offers only primitive facilities—toilets and potable water but no picnic tables. Access is limited to canoeists only, since the road leading to the campground is privately owned and posted. **⑤**

The junction with the South Branch of the Au Sable occurs a mile or two below Whitepine Campground. From here to Rainbow Bend Campground is a long stretch of wide, slow, relatively deep (three to six feet) water known as Conner's Flats or the Stillwater. Conner's Flats Public Access is reached off Conner's Flats Road and is about 1 1/2 to two hours below Wakeley Bridge.

Rainbow Bend State Forest Campground is shortly after **⑥** Conner's Flats Public Access. It is a small, primitive five-site campground and is likely not to be marked from Conner's Flats Road. It is also difficult to spot from the river. Look for a sandy landing and trail on the left bank.

McMasters Bridge, with good access and parking, is a short **⑦** distance downstream. From here to the junction with the North Branch of the Au Sable, expect faster current — though still far from difficult paddling conditions — gravel bottom, and some wide riffles with medium-size stones to avoid. Below the North Branch is another stretch of wide, slow flats followed by fairly fast, wide, interesting water, with gravel bottom and occasional large rocks the rest of the way to **Parmalee Bridge.** **⑧**

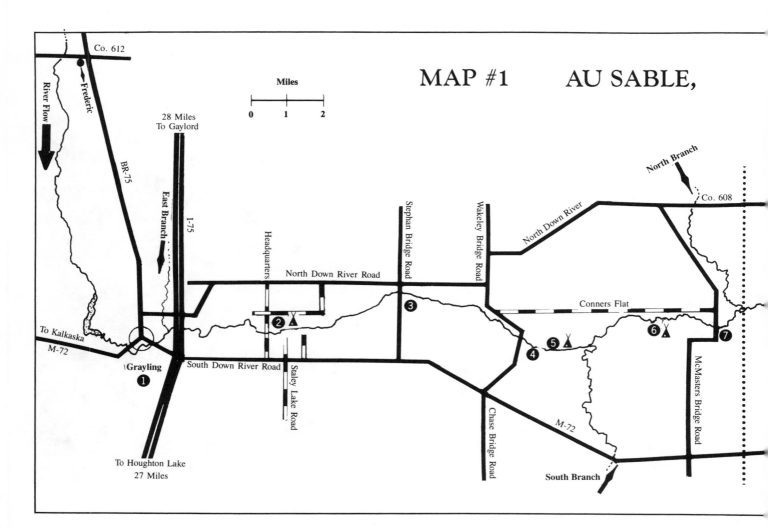

The access and parking site at Parmalee is on the right, before the bridge. Parmalee Campground, with seven modern sites near the road and an area of primitive sites for canoeists on the river, is directly across from the public access.

Parmalee Bridge (Red Oak Road) to Mio Dam
12 1/2 Miles
3-6 Hours

We made this trip in a little more than two hours of steady paddling, with a tail wind that helped greatly in crossing Mio Pond. In fact, prevailing west winds are an aid on all of the Au Sable's impoundments, in contrast to the Manistee, Muskegon and other west-flowing rivers, where winds seem always to be a hindrance.

Below Parmalee Bridge are several miles of fine water, with wide, fairly shallow riffles — some fast enough to create broken water — alternating with narrow, deep, slow pools. Bottom is generally gravel- to grapefruit-size stones with occasional large rocks to avoid.

9 There is camping and access at **Luzerne Free Park**, a short distance below Parmalee Bridge.

10 Good access and parking are found at **Camp 10 Bridge**. From here to Mio Pond are several miles of slow water and uninhabited marshlands leading into the backwaters.

The Mio Pond crossing is not especially long or difficult.
11 There is a **state-forest campground**, picnic area and boat-launching ramp on the left (north) shore halfway to the dam. On the opposite shore is Sportsman's Park, a county-maintained site with modern facilities and a large number of campsites.

Portage Mio Dam just right of the dam, using the steel platform to step up and over the concrete face. Watch for a black-and-yellow "barber pole," the portage sign used on impoundments throughout the entire Au Sable system.

Mio Dam to McKinley Bridge
14.5 Miles
4-5 Hours

Put in below Mio Dam or just downstream at the access site below the **M-72/M-33 Bridge**. Expect lots of company on summer weekends. The river is wide (75-100 feet) and often fairly fast as it repeats the riffle/pool pattern of the water above Mio. There is much public land along the way as the river passes through the Huron National Forest, and camping is permitted. Posted signs read: "Required for Camping: Shovel, Ax, Bucket." Excellent streamside campsites are abundant. Gradient is fairly quick with some wide, shallow riffles and occasional channels of fast, lightly broken water. Terrain varies from open meadows to forests of oak, ash and especially jack pine. This is Kirtland's Warbler country —the colorful, endangered bird nests only in jack pines in northern Michigan and has the excellent sense to spend the winters in the Bahamas. **12**

Take out at **McKinley Bridge**, where access and parking are good, or continue downstream to Alcona Pond. **13**

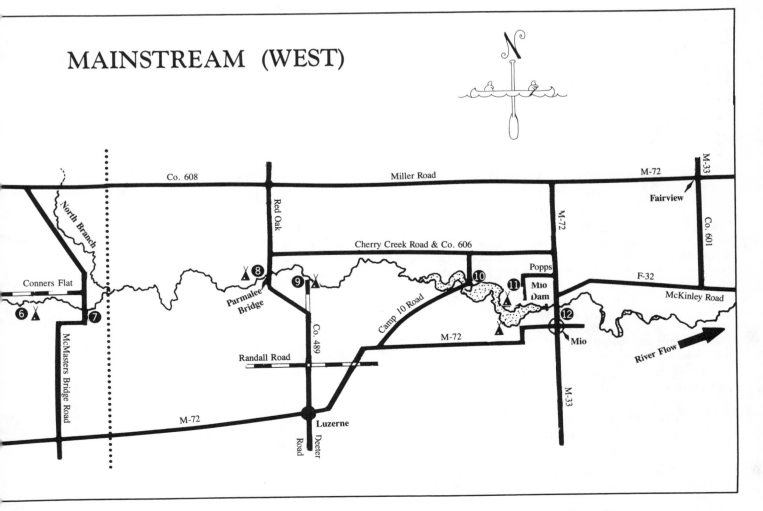

MAINSTREAM (WEST)

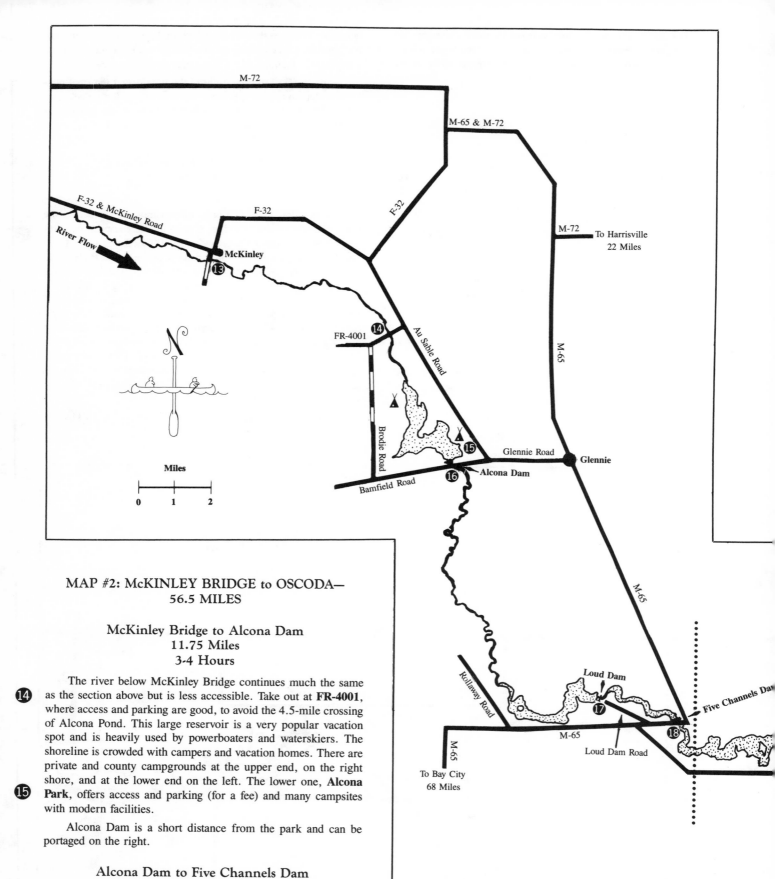

River Flow

F-32 & McKinley Road

M-72

M-65 & M-72

F-32

F-32

M-72   To Harrisville
22 Miles

McKinley

⑬

N

Miles

0   1   2

⑭   FR-4001

Au Sable Road

M-65

Brodie Road

⑮

Glennie Road   Glennie

⑯   Alcona Dam

Bamfield Road

M-65

Rollaway Road

Loud Dam

⑰

Five Channels Dam

M-65   Loud Dam Road   ⑱

To Bay City
68 Miles

M-65

MAP #2: McKINLEY BRIDGE to OSCODA— 56.5 MILES

McKinley Bridge to Alcona Dam
11.75 Miles
3-4 Hours

⑭ The river below McKinley Bridge continues much the same as the section above but is less accessible. Take out at **FR-4001**, where access and parking are good, to avoid the 4.5-mile crossing of Alcona Pond. This large reservoir is a very popular vacation spot and is heavily used by powerboaters and waterskiers. The shoreline is crowded with campers and vacation homes. There are private and county campgrounds at the upper end, on the right shore, and at the lower end on the left. The lower one, **Alcona**
⑮ **Park**, offers access and parking (for a fee) and many campsites with modern facilities.

Alcona Dam is a short distance from the park and can be portaged on the right.

Alcona Dam to Five Channels Dam
17.75 Miles
4 1/2 - 7 Hours

⑯ Put in below **Alcona Dam** or at the public access site below the Bamfield Road Bridge a short distance downstream. Watch for

MAP #2   AU SABLE,

sudden water rises of up to three feet. A siren announces discharge from the dam. From here to Loud Dam is a 15-mile stretch of wide (80-100 feet), deep water with medium current. The water is likely to be discolored. There are few houses or other streamside development, including access sites. Terrain is mostly high hills of hardwoods and pines, with high sand and clay banks common near the river. Much of the land is within the Huron National Forest, and there are frequent, often-used campsites.

(17) **Loud Pond** is smaller than Alcona Pond and much less populated. Portage the dam on either the right or the left. The right portage is a 250-yard carry down a gravel road. The left portage is much shorter but very steep; take out at the steel platform (below the "barber pole") to climb over the concrete dam face.

From here to Five Channels Dam is a three-mile stretch of backwaters. Suitable campsites are frequent. Portage the dam on the right at the ledge platform. There is a steep climb down to the docksite of one of the paddle-wheel excursion boats *Au Sable Queen*. There is good access and parking below the **M-65 Bridge** **(18)** on the left.

Five Channels Dam to Foote Dam
15.5 Miles
5 1/2 - 8 1/2 Hours

Almost immediately below Five Channels Dam are the backwaters of Cooke Dam. This is another large impoundment, and high waves can be a problem. The water, which has been discolored since Alcona Dam, is clear in Cooke Pond. Its shores are largely undeveloped, with many good campsites — some at the feet of tremendous wooded hills that come down to the shore.

There is a campground midway on the right shore at Lumberman's Monument; access, however, is very poor up 100-foot banks.

Portage **Cooke Dam** on the left. The river below is lovely. **(19)** The water remains crystal clear, and current is strong and steady as it opens into channels and bays with beds of weeds that offer cover for large numbers of bass and pike. Many good campsites can be found along this undeveloped stretch.

Foote Pond, the largest of the Au Sable reservoirs, is a short distance downstream. Wind and waves can create problems on the huge pond, and crossing can be discouraging for beginners. There is camping at Old Orchard Park, midway on the pond on the right shore, and supplies are available at the right of the dam at **Foote Site Village**, where there are docking facilities for another *Au* **(20)** *Sable Queen*. Portage Foote Dam on the left.

Foote Dam to Oscoda
11.5 Miles
2 1/2 - 3 1/2 Hours

The river below Foote Dam is wide (80-150 feet) and deep. Current is slow to moderate except immediately below the dam, where it can be quite swift and heavy. There are a few very wide, very shallow stretches of wadable water and some beaches and sandbars where good picnicking is possible. But most of the way the river meanders through lowlands and hardwood forests, where there are only occasional suitable camp and picnic sites. Bottom is generally sand, and water tends to be discolored. This is very popular steelhead- and salmon-fishing water and can be crowded in the spring and fall.

In **Oscoda** there is good access and parking at the public **(21)** boat-launching site near the mouth of the river.

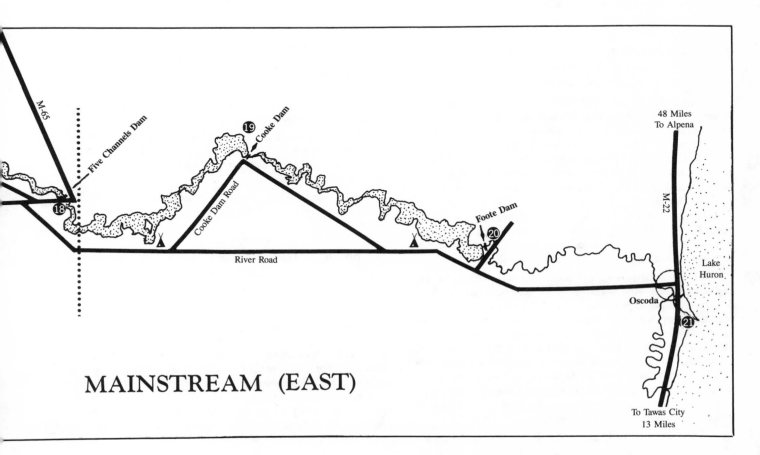

MAINSTREAM (EAST)

AU SABLE, SOUTH BRANCH

Counties:	**Roscommon, Crawford**
Start/End:	**Roscommon to junction with Mainstream**
Miles:	**21.5**
Gradient:	**2.5 ft/mile**
Portages:	**None**
Rapids/Falls:	**None**
Campgrounds:	**One**
Canoe Liveries:	**Numerous**
Skill Required:	**I**

Like the Mainstream of the Au Sable, the South Branch is rich in historic associations and has long been famous for classic flyfishing for trout. Also like the Mainstream, it is popular with canoeists seeking gentle family-suited water and near-wilderness settings.

The heart of the river flows through the Mason Tract, a several-thousand-acre sanctuary bequeathed to the state in 1954 by automobile-manufacturing-magnate George Mason. According to the dictates of the bequeathal, the land in the Mason property has been left to revert, as closely as possible, to the natural state of a Michigan forest. What few buildings that once existed have been removed, camping and picnicking are forbidden, and the numbers of roads and trails are kept at a minimum. The remains of Durant's Castle, Mason Chapel, and the foundations of one or two homes and cottages are nearly the only signs of human interference in the Mason Tract, which extends from Chase Bridge nearly to Smith Bridge.

Unlike the Mainstream, water levels on the South Branch are quite variable. It is unusual for levels to vary more than 12 inches from spring to summer on the Mainstream, but the South Branch will vary by as much as several feet and will often flow high and discolored during the spring or after heavy rains.

Camping is limited to a state-forest campground at the end of the Mason Tract. Special fishing regulations include flies-only from Chase Bridge to the mouth, with no kill of trout allowed in the first four miles of that section.

Steckert Road Access to Smith Bridge
12.5 Miles
4-6 Hours

Many paddlers, especially canoe-livery customers, put in at Roscommon, 3.5 miles above Steckert Road Access. However, access is difficult in Roscommon unless you get permission to launch from one of several liveries that are on the banks near the M-18 Bridge. **Steckert Road Access**, also known as **Mead's Landing**, has good parking and access. The river to here is 30-75 feet wide and one to four feet deep, with gentle current, mostly sand bottom and no serious obstructions. From Roscommon to Chase Bridge (six miles, two to three hours) there are a fair number of homes and cottages. But the banks are wooded for the most part, and even here, there is a feeling of serenity and isolation that peaks in the Mason property downstream.

There is good parking and access at **Chase Bridge**, at the beginning of the Mason Tract. On summer weekends we have found it advisable to put in here early in the morning to get ahead of canoe-livery customers. Immediately below the bridge the river enters wooded hills of hardwoods, pines and cedars. Some tag alders line the banks. Bottom is sand and silt at the edges with gravel and occasional larger stones at midstream. Century-old drowned logs remain from the lumbering era, when log drives were heavy on the entire Au Sable system. There are a few survivors of those days: red pines and white pines three feet or more in diameter that tower over the river valley.

A few miles below Chase Bridge is a landing and sign announcing Durant's Castle. The 42-room mansion was built for William Durant (who founded General Motors in 1908) and included gables, turrets and separate servant's quarters. It burned in 1931 and was never rebuilt; nothing remains today except the foundation and basement. Downstream one-half mile, the Mason Chapel commemorates George Mason.

Canoe Harbor State Forest Campground is a short distance upstream from Smith Bridge at the end of the Mason property. It is a primitive campground with 45 sites, and canoe pick-up is prohibited.

Access and parking are good at **Smith Bridge** (M-72, or South Downriver Road) at the public site just downstream on the right.

Smith Bridge to Conner's Flats Public Access
(Mainstream)
7.5 Miles
2-3 Hours

From Smith Bridge to the confluence with the Mainstream is 5.5 miles of slow, winding, quite-deep water. Cottages and homes are scattered most of the way, and virtually all of the bordering land is private. The river is 60-85 feet wide and two to five feet deep with very deep holes. Still water begins before the junction and extends downstream on the Mainstream in Conner's Flats. Access and parking are good at **Conner's Flats Public Access** or **Rainbow Bend State Forest Campground**, both about two miles below the junction of the Mainstream.

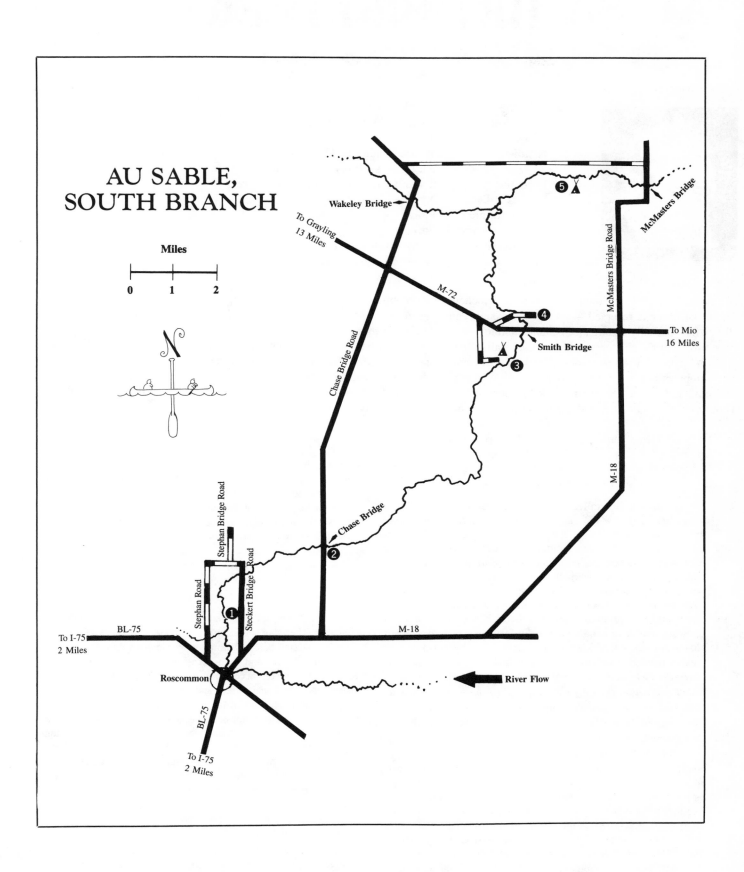

AU SABLE,
SOUTH BRANCH

Miles

0   1   2

Wakeley Bridge

To Grayling
13 Miles

M-72

Chase Bridge Road

Chase Bridge

Stephan Bridge Road

Steckert Bridge Road

Stephan Road

BL-75

To I-75
2 Miles

M-18

Roscommon

BL-75

To I-75
2 Miles

McMasters Bridge Road

McMasters Bridge

To Mio
16 Miles

Smith Bridge

M-18

River Flow

BETSIE RIVER

Counties:	**Benzie, Manistee**
Start/End:	**Grass Lake to Elberta**
Miles:	**45**
Gradient:	**Wallin Bridge to Thompsonville Dam — 5.6 ft/mile**
	All other sections — less than 4 ft/mile
Portages:	**2 small dams, occasional fallen trees**
Rapids/Falls:	**None**
Campgrounds:	**Few**
Canoe Liveries:	**Several**
Skill Required:	**Above Wallin — I**
	Below Wallin — I-II

From its source in Green Lake, near Interlochen, to its mouth, at Elberta, the Betsie River provides an interesting variety of water. The usual order is reversed — expect the easiest canoeing in the upper reaches. There, current is slow to nearly nonexistent, and the river winds casually through marshlands and low wooded hills. Farther downstream, tight bends and moderate to moderately fast current create some fairly challenging water. Especially during high water, beginners will have difficulty negotiating quick turns and occasional fallen trees and other minor obstacles that occur much of the way from Wallin to Betsie Lake, above Elberta.

Campgrounds are limited, but state land along much of this Michigan Wild-Scenic River opens up possibilities for streamside camping. Fishing is for warm-water species above Wallin and for brown and rainbow trout below it. Salmon and steelhead run to Thompsonville Dam, and fishing pressure can be heavy, especially below Homestead Dam.

Grass Lake State Forest Campground to Thompsonville Dam
10.5 Miles
3-5 Hours

There are four miles of slow water between Betsie River Road Bridge (below the outlet at Green Lake) and Grass Lake, but private property makes access and parking so difficult at Betsie River Road that we recommend putting in at **Grass Lake Campground**, where access and parking are good. The campground has primitive facilities and is usually uncrowded, partly, no doubt, because the roads leading to it are poorly marked. The river below Grass Lake is shallow and warm enough in summer for swimming (though it tends to be rich with aquatic weed growth), and there is little current. In fact, strong winds can halt downstream progress. Like much of the Betsie, this upper section passes through uninhabited countryside of hardwood forests, meadows and occasional marshlands.

Downstream from the dam is a mile or two more of shallow, slow water. The river gradually quickens, however, until, upstream from Wallin, it becomes a gravel-bottomed, fairly fast trout stream.

There is good access and parking at **Wallin Road Bridge**, and from here to Thompsonville Dam is a fine seven-mile float. The river remains small — 25-35 feet wide in most places —and is quick but not difficult for paddlers with basic skills. During summer's low water stay near the outside of bends to utilize the most depth. Expect to scrape bottom or run aground occasionally in this section, especially where the river widens over gravel riffles. The countryside remains largely undeveloped, with only occasional streamside houses. Meadows and upland forests of hardwoods alternate, and there are frequent moss-covered clay-banks feeding the river with cold spring-water.

There is fair access and roadside parking at Carmen Road Bridge and at Thompsonville Road Bridge. After King Road Bridge, also with fair access and roadside parking, there is about a mile of sand bottom and slow water winding through marshland before the backwaters of **Thompsonville Dam**. The actual pond is quite small, and crossing to the portage trail on the right side of the dam, where there is good access and parking, is easy.

Thompsonville Dam to County Line Road Bridge
11.5 Miles
3 1/2 - 5 Hours

From Thompsonville Dam, the river begins to change in character. There are several miles of moderately quick water similar to the stretch below Wallin but with more volume. The riverbed is gravel and sand with occasional large rocks. By Kurick Road Bridge, where access and parking are fair, the current has slowed and the river is wider and deeper. There remain stretches of quick, fairly shallow riffles, but they become increasingly less frequent. The more usual characteristic — and the one that predominates throughout the remainder of the river — is sand bottom dropping away into deep holes at every bend. Current is moderate and water tends toward cloudiness. Watch for logs and snags just below the surface and for fallen trees that can sometimes be a nuisance. Beginners might have difficulty with some of the frequent, very sharp bends. Much of this section is lined with thickets of tag alders and cedars, and there are fewer suitable resting places than in the upper reaches.

Fair access and roadside parking are available from the bridges on Kurick Road and Psutka Road. There is no access at Lindy Road or M-115.

Access and parking are good at **County Line Road Bridge**.

County Line Road Bridge to Homestead Dam
11.5 Miles
4-5 Hours

From County Line Road, expect much of the same kind of water and terrain as in the section above. Hardwood forests rise in intersecting ridges above the river valley, and cedars and tag-alder thickets line the banks.

About halfway to Homestead Dam, one-quarter mile before M-115 Bridge, is **Dair's Mill Landing**. Access and parking are good, although the site is not marked. Follow Dair's Mill Road to the parking area beside the creek at the old mill site; the river is through the alders just beyond the parking area. From here to Homestead Dam, the river winds tightly through lowlands and low wooded hills. Deadfalls, sweepers and small logjams are fairly frequent in the first several miles. Current is moderate to fairly quick. A few houses near M-115 diminish quickly, and most of the way to Homestead Dam is uninhabited. Depths are one to six feet; bottom is sand with sections of gravel and stone and very occasional larger rocks. Good campsites can be found, but they are not common.

The backwaters of Homestead Dam were once a reservoir and a floodplain of marshes, but the demolition of the dam (and replacement with a low-head dam) drained the area. Now the river winds between sandbars and low banks overgrown with willows, cattails and marsh grasses.

Access and parking are good at **Homestead Dam**. Portage the dam on the right at the developed landing.

Homestead Dam to M-22 Bridge (Elberta)
11.5 Miles
3 1/2 - 5 Hours

From Homestead to Elberta is a popular summer float, but keep in mind that in spring and fall the Betsie River is heavily fished. Extended seasons are open from Kurick Road Bridge downstream to the mouth, but 90 percent of the fishermen seem to congregate below Homestead Dam, making it risky business to pass by in a canoe. The river is slow to moderate, is 35-50 feet wide, and passes mostly through lowland forests with cedars near the banks. Water is often discolored.

At US-31 Bridge, there is a private landing and campground with supplies, but there is no public access.

There is good access and parking at the public site at **Smith Bridge**, the first of two bridges on River Road. The second, Lewis Bridge, has fair access and roadside parking.

In Elberta, take out at the **M-22 Bridge** at Betsie Lake, where there is good access and parking.

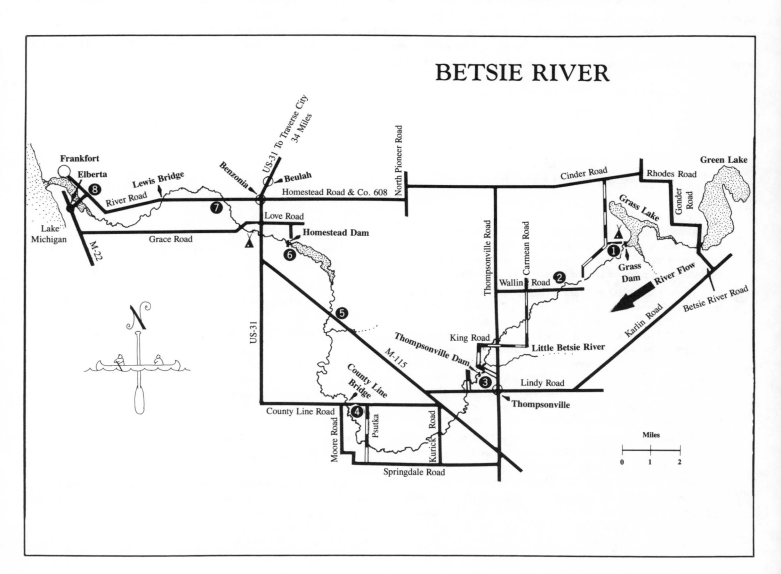

BLACK RIVER

Counties:	**Cheboygan, Presque Isle**
Start/End:	**Clark Bridge to Black Lake**
Miles:	**32.25**
Gradient:	**4 ft/mile**
Portages:	**Two dams, fairly difficult**
Rapids/Falls:	**Crocket Rapids, just above South Black River Road, — Class I**
Campgrounds:	**None**
Canoe Liveries:	**None**
Skill Required:	**I**
Topo. Maps:	**Hetherton, Tower, Atlanta (15 min.)**

Better known for outstanding brook-trout fishing than fine canoeing, the Black River is the most remote and least-often paddled of Cheboygan County's major rivers. A generally slow-paced river, it meanders through long stretches of undeveloped woods and lowlands. Paddlers with basic maneuvering skills should have no trouble during normal water levels. During high water the stretch of fast current above Crockets Bridge (South Black River Road) requires some caution.

There are sufficient access sites, especially above Tower Pond, but no on-bank campgrounds. State-forest campgrounds are found near the river, above the sections described here, at Round Lake and Town Corner Lake. Public land in the Black Lake State Forest has the potential for streamside camping, although low ground and thickets of tag alders reduce the number of good sites.

Fishing is excellent for brook trout, with 18-inchers not uncommon, and to a lesser degree for brown trout. Northern pike and other warm-water species are found in the impoundments and in the lower section below Kleber Dam.

Clark Bridge to
Crocket Bridge (South Black River Road)
6 Miles
2-3 Hours

Although there is some canoeable water above Clark Bridge, a large area of private property at Black River Ranch limits access, and a locally infamous "spreads" below Main River Bridge (not shown on map) makes for discouraging prospects.

1 Access is excellent at **Clark Bridge**, with plenty of parking space available near the river. The river is 25–40 feet wide and two to four feet deep with much deeper holes. Water is clean but stained dark brown. Current is slow in the vicinity of the bridge but speeds up gradually as you move downstream. As the current increases, sand and silt bottom changes to gravel and stone. This section flows almost entirely through state-forest land, and most of the bordering land is low, with tag alders and marshes backing up to lowland forests. Higher ground above Crocket Rapids is mostly privately owned and has scattered homes and cottages.

Crocket Rapids is an easy Class I series of riffles over gravel and rocks up to bushel size. They should offer little challenge except during very high water, when standing waves develop, and very low water, when rocks will have to be avoided.

2 Access and parking are good at **Crocket Bridge**, on South Black River Road. There is public land for about a quarter-mile upstream, with several often-used campsites on the high bank above the river.

Crocket Bridge to Tower Dam
14 Miles
5-7 Hours

From Crocket Bridge the river slows and widens somewhat. Width is 40-60 feet; depth is two to five feet. Terrain is mostly lowlands of hardwoods and tag alders.

Milligan Road Bridge has poor access and parking.

There is parking and fair access at the public site at the end of Wigglesworth Road.

Errat Road Bridge has fair access and limited roadside parking.

County Line Road Bridge is immediately below Errat Road and has no access or parking. Watch for large rocks under the bridge — they create a narrow chute that can be easily run at midriver.

Black River Road Bridge, just above Tower Pond, has poor access and parking.

Tower Pond is about a mile long and quite narrow. Access at the M-68 Bridge is fair at best, with poor roadside parking. It is **3** better to take out at **Tower Dam**, where there is better roadside parking and access is good. Portage the dam on the left, down a steep but hospitable stairway.

BLACK RIVER

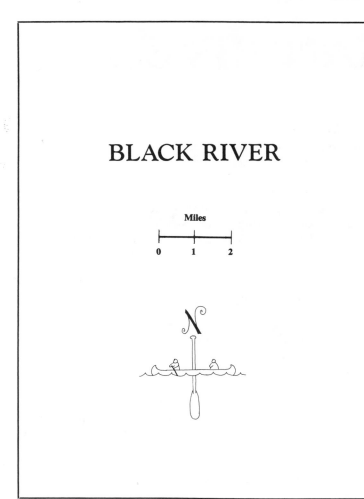

Miles

0   1   2

Tower Dam to Black Lake
12.25 Miles
4-6 Hours (est.)

We have not paddled this section, but we drove the roads to determine access sites. The river appears to be slow to moderate and, generally, 50-80 feet wide. The general area is within the Black River State Forest, but much of the bordering land is private. Most of the terrain is lowlands and swamps.

Kleber Pond begins almost immediately below Tower Dam and is a 2.5-mile crossing. Just before the pond is Barkley Avenue Bridge with fair access and roadside parking.

Kleber Dam is a fairly difficult portage on either the left or the right, down a steep bank. From here to Black Lake the river meanders through continuous lowlands, and there appears to be little or no streamside development. There is intermediate access at Red Bridge Road; however, when we were there, the road was closed, and we have no information about access at the bridge.

④ Shortly before Black Lake there is a **bridge at Upper Black River Road**. Access is poor, and parking is very limited along the narrow roadside.

BOARDMAN RIVER

County:	**Grand Traverse**
Start/End:	**Supply Road Bridge to Traverse City**
Miles:	**25.25**
Gradient:	**Supply Road to Brown Bridge Dam — 3 ft/mile**
	Brown Bridge Dam to Boardman Pond — 9.6 ft/mile
Portages:	**4 dams, fairly easy; occasional fallen trees in upper section**
Rapids/Falls:	**Beitner Rapids, directly below Beitner Road Bridge — Class I-II**
Campgrounds:	**Several in upper section**
Canoe Liveries:	**Few**
Skill Required:	**Upper section — I**
	Lower section to Boardman Pond — I-II

One of Michigan's finest and best-known trout streams, the Boardman is as highly esteemed by canoeists as it is by fishermen. It is not a heavily used river, however, and even on summer weekends will not usually be crowded.

Dams divide it into an upper section, a middle section, and a lower section of slow river and backwaters before the mouth at Grand Traverse Bay in Traverse City. The upper section is designated a Wild-Scenic Michigan Natural River and is the river's remotest and least-developed section. It passes through Fife Lake State Forest and has several streamside state-forest campgrounds. The river below Brown Bridge Dam is designated Country-Scenic but, since it flows mostly through private property, has few camping opportunities. This lower section is faster than the upper and requires slightly more advanced paddling skills. Beitner Rapids, especially, will challenge inexperienced paddlers.

Fishing is for brook and brown trout above Brown Bridge Dam and primarily for brown trout below it. In the impoundments, bass and northern pike predominate, and salmon and steelhead run up the lower river to the Union Street Dam.

Supply Road Bridge to Brown Bridge Dam
7 Miles
2-4 Hours

Originating in Kalkaska County, the North and South Branches of the Boardman are generally too small and brushy for enjoyable canoeing. They meet at the Forks, immmediately above Supply Road Bridge in western Grand Traverse County, and from there to Brown Bridge Dam the mainstream is large enough for clear passage, although there may be occasional fallen trees to bypass, especially in early spring.

 Access at Supply Road is fairly good, although parking is limited to the roadside. Many paddlers put in instead one-half mile downstream at **Forks Forest Campground**, where primitive sites are on the riverbank and access and parking are good. The river in the upper section varies from 20-40 feet wide and one to three feet deep with many pools over five feet. Current varies from moderate to fairly quick over bottom of alternating gravel and sand. The river passes through a largely undeveloped valley of mixed hardwoods and conifers, including many large pines and hemlocks, especially near Forks Campground. Water levels are usually sufficient, although some stretches of light riffles may be shallow in summer. Cedars line the banks in many places, some leaning or fallen into the river to become the "sweepers" famous as trout habitat in Michigan angling lore. In the close confines of the small upper river, they also create minor hazards to canoeists.

About midway through the section is **Scheck's Place Forest Campground**. Facilities are primitive; access to the river is good. Just upstream is the only significant development along this section, with access, lodging and supplies available. Scheck's

Place Campground is the last easy access before Brown Bridge Pond, one to two hours downstream. Much of the final mile or so of river before the pond is slow and relatively wide through lowlands and marshes. Portage **Brown Bridge Dam** on the left at the public site.

Brown Bridge Dam to Boardman Dam
12.5 Miles
3 1/2 - 4 1/2 Hours

This middle section is generally swift with gravel and sand bottom and occasional riffles over fist-size to pumpkin-size stones. Width is 30-45 feet; depths are one to four feet with pools over five or six feet common. Many submerged and half-buried logs, remnants of early log drives, are visible on the bottom. Water quality here and in the upper section is excellent, with water generally clear. Levels fluctuate moderately and are not, at least at the time of this writing, affected by discharges from Brown Bridge Dam. There are scattered stretches of undeveloped land, but cottages and homes are frequent and most streamside property is private. Numerous private bridges, some low enough to require caution or portaging, cross to residences. Stands of hardwoods and thickets of cedars and tag alders alternate with occasional meadows and farmlands.

Six miles below Brown Bridge Dam is **Shumsky Road Public Access** with the best intermediate access in this section.

Bridges at Brown Bridge Road, Garfield Road, and two on River Road have fair to good access with limited roadside parking.

5   **Beitner Road Bridge** has good access and parking at the roadside park on the downstream side of the bridge. Light rapids begin immediately below the bridge and become more intense a few hundred yards downstream. Although these rapids will never rate more than Class II, standing waves, occasional bushel-size boulders and several abrupt turns make this half-mile stretch fairly challenging, especially during high water. The best water is at the site of the washed-out Keystone Dam, where the river channel narrows to 15 feet and waves are high enough to wash into an open boat. Experienced paddlers will not find Beitner Rapids difficult; beginners may find them well beyond their ability.

Toward the end of the fast water there is access and parking near a recently built footbridge. Take out here to avoid crossing Boardman Pond or take out at the public site just before the pond where there is a dock at the river and a stairway on the right bank.

6   **Boardman Pond** is about one mile across. Take out at the public site to the left of the power station, where parking and access are good. Portage across Cass Road and follow the marked portage trail left of the dam.

Boardman Dam to the Mouth (Traverse City)
6 Miles
2-4 Hours

Sabin Pond begins almost immediately below Boardman Dam. There is good parking and access at **Sabin Dam**, although the climb is steep. Portage the dam on the right. The river below passes for 2.5 miles through an undeveloped and, considering its proximity to Traverse City, surprisingly remote valley. Thickets of cedar and tag alders near the bank and mixed stands of hardwoods and conifers away from the river alternate with meadows and grassy banks. Current is slow to moderate over bottom of sand and silt. **7**

Near South Airport Road, there is fairly heavy streamside development that makes access difficult at the bridge. Immediately downstream is **Boardman Lake**, with good access and parking at a public site to the right of the rivermouth. Boardman Lake is about a two-mile crossing and leads into Traverse City, where there is a dam to portage at Union Street. The final mile of river passes through residential neighborhoods and the downtown area before emptying into Grand Traverse Bay. Good access and parking are found at Union Street Dam and at a public boat-launching site a few hundred yards before the mouth of the river. **8**

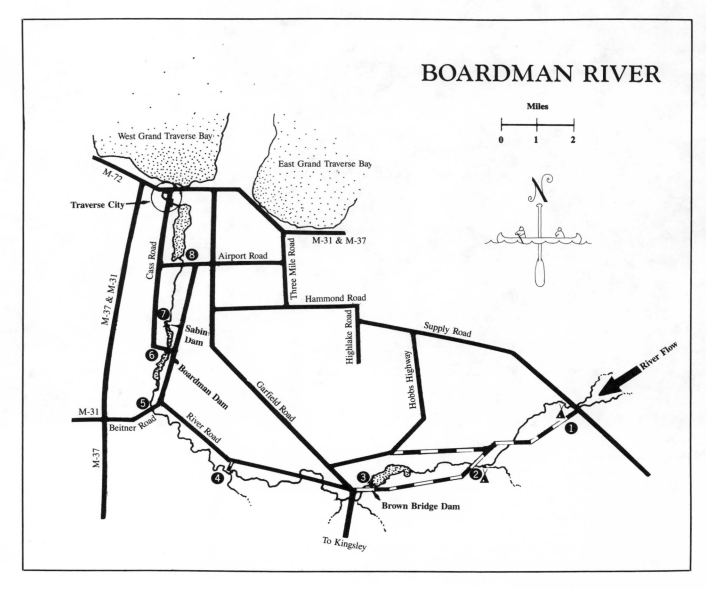

BOARDMAN RIVER

—Photo by Gail Dennis—

CASS RIVER

Counties:	**Tuscola, Saginaw**
Start/End:	**Cass City to M-13 Bridge**
Miles:	**59**
Gradient:	**2.5 ft/mile**
Portages:	**Two dams, easy**
Rapids/Falls:	**None**
Campgrounds:	**None**
Canoe Liveries:	**None**
Skill Required:	**I**

Anyone familiar with the lower Cass River where it crosses M-13 just before joining the Saginaw River — and where it is wide, slow and muddy — is likely to be surprised by the upper river. Rock and gravel bottom, pools of still water alternating with stretches of riffles, and quiet, wooded terrain are reminiscent of northern rivers. Canoeing and fishing pressure is light, and the Cass will seldom be crowded. Water quality is only fair, with visibility barely reaching three feet.

In summer, low water will make many short riffles impassable. Even at the end of a wet September, we did a lot of scraping and bumping, especially in the upper section between Cass City and Caro. Flow is supplemented by ground springs and tributaries, so midsummer trips are usually possible between Caro and Frankenmuth and are probably never a problem between Frankenmuth and the junction with the Saginaw.

Long stretches of river pass through Defoe, Tuscana and Vassar state game areas, where the chances are excellent of sighting deer, beaver and other wildlife. Camping potential is limited. Fishing is for warm-water species including smallmouth bass and northern pike.

Cemetery Road Bridge (Cass City)
to Chippewa Landing (Caro)
17 Miles
5-7 Hours

① A short distance upstream from Cass City, the North, East and Middle branches of the Cass converge, creating a mainstream large enough to be navigable. **Cemetery Road Bridge** is the farthest upstream access to the mainstream; access is fair, and parking is limited to one or two vehicles. The river ranges from 30-60 feet wide with depths of six inches to three feet.

Short runs of moderately fast water spill over reefs of fist-size to bushel-basket-size stones and boulders. In the alternating slow stretches, the bottom is paved with gravel and stones over bedrock slabs with frequent boulders to dodge. Many stretches require careful maneuvering through rock gardens. Note that with the clouded water, many submerged rocks, especially in slow water, are difficult to detect. The chutes, riffles and light rapids should not create problems even for beginning paddlers, although in extremely high water in spring, some could require caution and fairly complex maneuvering.

Hardwoods, poplars, and occasional cedars fill the shallow river valley, and thick beds of aquatic weeds line the water's edges. In this section, as along much of the river to Frankenmuth, there are occasional suitable campsites on public land.

Dodge Road Bridge has poor access and parking.

② **Hurd's Corner Road Bridge** has fair access and parking.

Deckerville Road Bridge has fair access and roadside parking.

Water volume increases gradually, due to ground springs and small tributaries, so that by Hurd's Corner Road, levels are noticeably increased. Summer passage is more conceivable from here downstream, although there may still be some sections that require walking through. Generally, the stretches of riffles and quick water through rock gardens — although they are found all the way to Frankenmuth — diminish in frequency and duration the farther downstream you progress. A few larger tributaries — most notably White Creek, just upstream from Deckerville Road — add substantial amounts of water. Not far below Deckerville Road, slow, deep water precedes the backwaters of Caro Dam. Take out at East Dayton Road Bridge, where access and parking are fair, or, better, go to **Chippewa Landing** public park and boat ramp next to the M-24 Bridge in Caro.

③ The dam is approximately 1.5 miles downstream from Chippewa Landing and can be portaged either right or left; use caution in the vicinity of the dam, where there is no barrier at the spillway. There is very poor access to the dam and river off Wireline Road. Access to the next section is better at Chambers Road Bridge, four miles downstream. About one-half mile before Chambers Road there is access and parking at Indian Fields Township Park (no camping).

Chambers Road Bridge to Frankenmuth
22 Miles
6 1/2 - 8 Hours

The topography of this section varies little from that of the section above. A few scattered homes are visible, especially near bridges, and occasionally the valley deepens and banks become

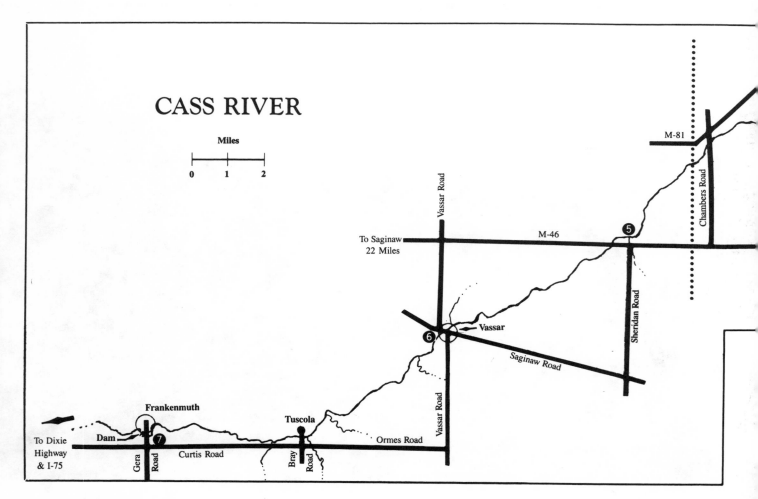

steeper. The river also is similar, although it widens in some stretches to 90-100 feet. Shallow riffles are common, but, as mentioned, they diminish in frequency. Stretches of slow water are longer and deeper.

4 Access and parking at **Chambers Road Bridge** are fair.

5 There is good access and parking at the **roadside park at M-46**.

6 In Vassar, there is good access and parking at the **community park below Saginaw Road** (Huron Avenue in town). Caution should be used at the old mill dam site here — the three-foot

drop over a concrete spillway is runnable on the right but is potentially hazardous, especially in high water, when the hydraulic at the bottom becomes significant. Portage through the park on the right if in doubt.

The bridge in Tuscola at Bray Road offers poor access and roadside parking.

In Frankenmuth, there is fair access and parking at both the park near the **bridge on Gera Road** and just downstream at the **7** flood-control dam. The dam must be portaged on right or left.

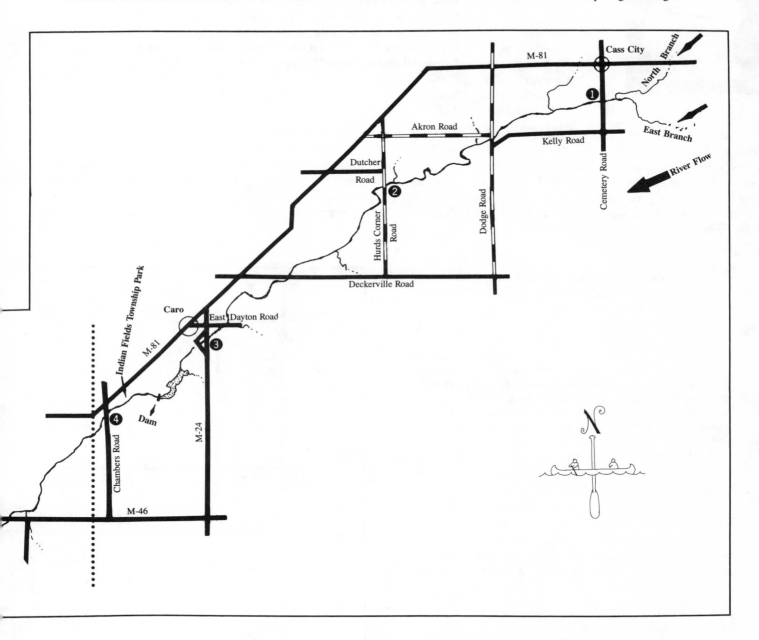

Frankenmuth to M-13 Bridge
16 Miles
5-7 Hours (est.)
(Not on map)

We ended our trip in Frankenmuth, but paddlers continuing downstream will find the water becoming consistently slow and

deep and the terrain low and marshy. There are bridges at Dehmel Road (poor access and parking) and Dixie Highway (no access or parking). Fort Road in Bridgeport has fair access and limited parking at the bridge and good access and parking (no overnight) at the township park immediately below the bridge. Access and parking at Sheridan Road are poor. M-13, the final bridge before the Cass joins the Saginaw River, has good access and parking just below the bridge on the right.

CHIPPEWA RIVER

Counties:	**Mecosta, Isabella, Midland**
Start/End:	**Barryton Dam to Midland**
Miles:	**88.5**
Gradient:	**Barryton Dam to Lake Isabella — 4.8 ft/mile**
	Lake Isabella to Mt. Pleasant — 6 ft/mile
	Mt. Pleasant to Midland — 2 ft./mile
Portages:	**Four dams, easy; occasional fallen trees**
Rapids/Falls:	**Unnamed rapids near Deerfield County Park — Class I**
	Unnamed Rapids below Chippewa Rd. — Class I-II
Campgrounds:	**Few**
Canoe Liveries:	**Several**
Skill Required:	**I-II**

The Chippewa is one of many rivers in the Saginaw Valley that were important during the logging boom that centered around Saginaw in the second half of the 19th century. Canoeists will find the Chippewa the best of the lot. Its gravel and rock bottom, moderate to fast current, and mostly undeveloped banks make it a pleasant and popular float. Low water can be a problem during dry seasons, especially in the sections above M-20. High water in spring can make some stretches, especially the rapids below Chippewa Road, inadvisable for paddlers without experience and good basic skills.

Camping possibilities are somewhat limited, although there is a good campground about midway on the river at Deerfield County Park. Fishing is primarily for smallmouth bass.

Barryton Dam to Coldwater Road Bridge
19.5 Miles
5-7 Hours

❶   The **dam at Barryton** gathers the two upper branches (the North and the West), and only below here is there enough width and depth for easy navigating. There is good access and parking at the dam. Put in either down the short, steep bank at the tailrace or follow one of several two-tracks a short distance downstream for lower banks and easier access. The river here is 30-50 feet wide and one to two feet deep and flows moderately fast over gravel and stones. The slightly tea-colored river passes through low woodlands of maples and willows with tag alders at the banks. There are few houses and cottages.

There is fair access and roadside parking at 20th Avenue Bridge, where the river slows and deepens.

Fair access but poor parking are at 10th Avenue Bridge.

Nineteen Mile Road Bridge has poor access and parking.

Between 10th Avenue and 19 Mile Road, much of the river is lined with cottages on both banks. There are sections of fairly fast water over shallow gravel bottom scattered with occasional large rocks. The riffles alternate with sections of slow water — a pattern repeated through most of the length of the Chippewa. A few spots in this stretch combine quick current with tight bends and obstacles to make good maneuvering abilities an advantage.

After 19 Mile Road Bridge, there is much slow water punctuated by unusual low reefs of rocks and boulders. The current is forced back by the damming action of the reefs, then spills over them into what amounts to tiny rapids. They should present no difficulty, even to inexperienced paddlers, unless low water makes the rocks a hindrance. There are also sections of slow, deep sand-bottomed river winding through lowlands, woods, and picturesque and well-used cow pastures. The first large pasture has a low-strung wire across the river to avoid. Also, several fallen

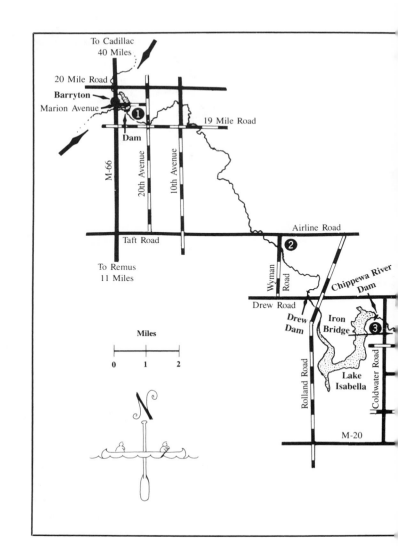

trees and logjams might require short portages. Just before the bridge at Airline Road, the cattle farm has two neck-high, nearly invisible wires stretched across the river.

The river is accessible at Airline Road, but parking is on the roadside and very limited. Access is better at **Wyman Road Bridge**, where there is roadside parking for several vehicles. Supplies are available at the small store within sight of the bridge.

Below Wyman Road is more water similar to above — slow sections alternating with fairly fast riffles and one or two of the reefs and short drops. Shortly before Drew Road is a stretch of slow, deep tag-alder-lined water leading to Drew Dam. This is a jumble of large boulders with a narrow chute of fierce water through the center. The drop is severe — five or six feet — and may be runnable by experts in high water, but we strongly recommend portaging on either right or left.

Access and parking are poor and limited at Drew Road. Rolland Road, a short distance downstream, is not much better but is a less-busy road and probably a better choice for access. It is the last access site before Lake Isabella, a large, popular impoundment about three miles long. Portage Isabella Dam at the golf course on either the right or the left.

Coldwater Road Bridge to Deerfield County Park
12.5 Miles
4-7 Hours

There is no access at Lake Isabella Dam because of private property; however, **Coldwater Road Bridge**, with adequate access and fair roadside parking, is a short distance downstream. The river here is 30-50 feet wide and one to three feet deep and runs slow to moderate over sand and gravel bottom. Not far downstream is Iron Bridge, now closed, at the end of an unnamed gravel road. Because the bridge is quite low, local canoe liveries often put in here during the early season when high water makes passage under the bridge difficult. Access is fair, and parking is not bad but remote. The river to M-20 flows through low country, with tag alders common along the banks and occasional meadows punctuating forests of young hardwoods. There are a few scattered houses, with more appearing just before M-20. The streambed is generally gravel and occasionally shallow, especially in summer, with bushel-size rocks common.

Access is fair at River Road Bridge; parking is on the roadside.

Littlefield Road Bridge has good access and roadside parking.

Access and parking are good just downstream on the left of the **M-20 Bridge**.

Below M-20 are more stretches of slow water alternating with wide, shallow riffles. Not far downstream, the river opens into a wide pond formed by a gravel pit. Paddle nearly straight across to find the outlet. There is a well-worn access site and parking area on the point beside the outlet. Broomfield Road Bridge follows immediately with fair access and parking.

Winn Road Bridge has fair access and roadside parking. During periods of low water, the livery at M-20 often puts in here rather than at Lake Isabella to avoid the shallow riffles in that upper section.

From Winn Road to the county campground and picnic area at Deerfield Park are remote, low hills of hardwoods and pines. The river runs somewhat faster and deeper over gravel and rock, with some riffles breaking into light rapids. About half a mile after the swinging foot bridge (part of a network of footpaths in the county park), look for a small sign in a tree on the right bank announcing the **Deerfield County Park Campground**. On the bank are unnumbered, lightly developed campsites with water and restrooms but no picnic tables.

Downstream from the campground is a covered bridge followed by a short stretch of Class I rapids. The rapids are minor, with some maneuvering around rocks required, but should not be difficult even for inexperienced paddlers. Just downstream, the river enters a natural pond, and there is access and parking at either the landing in the bay or the lagoon to the left. Continue to the right, beneath another swinging bridge, to proceed downstream.

Deerfield County Park to Mt. Pleasant
11 Miles
2 1/2 - 4 Hours

This stretch is similar to the water above, with the slow, deep water near Deerfield giving way to sections of riffles. Water levels from here downstream are usually adequate, even in late summer. Slow sections have sand bottom and are more prevalent than above. The river is somewhat larger, with average width 40-60 feet. Houses appear in greater numbers — scattered near bridges at first, becoming more prevalent closer to Mt. Pleasant.

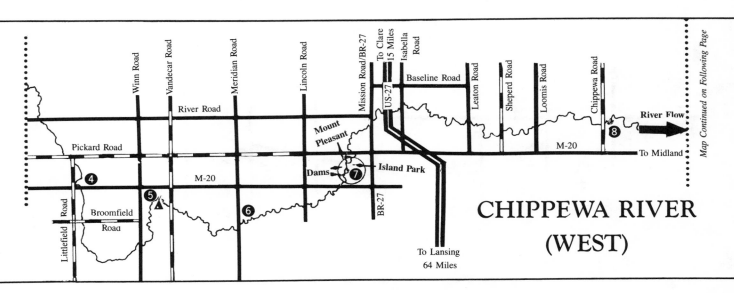

Vandecar Road Bridge has access on the left upstream side, but parking is limited to the roadside.

6 The river is accessible from Meridian Road, but parking is forbidden — use the **landing** at the park a few hundred yards downstream, where there is good parking and access.

Lincoln Road Bridge has fair access, but parking is poor along the side of the busy road.

Winding through a golf course and woodlots choked with underbrush, the river slows as it approaches the city. There is a city park 15-30 minutes below Lincon Road Bridge, where access and parking are good.

Mt. Pleasant to Geneva Road Bridge
23.5 Miles
5-7 Hours

There are several parks in Mt. Pleasant, each of which has good access to the river and good parking, although in most cases overnight parking is forbidden. Not far into the city is a low dam. Portage either on the right or continue along a channel to the right until you come to the twin sister of the first dam; portage this one on the right as well.

7 About in the center of Mt. Pleasant is a large community park appropriately named **Island Park**. The river splits to form the island, with the left channel falling into a 30-foot rapids that might be runnable during high water. Most paddlers go to the right side of the island, where the current is slow and there are many grassy banks suitable for access or picnicking.

Below Mt. Pleasant the river remains slow and deep as it meanders through an almost entirely undeveloped valley of lowland with large maples, oaks and willows predominating. The water picks up sediment from mud banks here and in the city and is clouded, with visibility about 1 1/2 - 2 1/2 feet. Bottom is sand through the slow stretches below Mt. Pleasant. Fallen trees are common as are well-established logjams at the bends and against fallen trees; expect several short, easy portages.

Access is possible at BR M-27 Bridge (Mission Road), but parking is poor; at Isabella Road Bridge, where parking is poor; at Leaton Road Bridge, where parking is poor; and at Shepherd Road Bridge, where parking is at the roadside and poor. Loomis

Road Bridge has fair access and limited roadside parking.

By Loomis Road, the river has gained momentum, current is faster, bottom is gravel and rock, and some sections are shallow. The terrain has opened up into farmlands and low wooded hills. Shallow riffles alternate with long, slow stretches most of the way to Midland.

8 Just below the **bridge at Chippewa Road**, where access and parking are good, are rapids that rate a solid Class II in high water. This run is only about 100 feet long, but the drop is sudden and pronounced and there are surprisingly substantial standing waves at the bottom. Run them straightforward, down the middle.

Coleman Road Bridge has fair access and poor parking.

There is no access or parking at M-20 Bridge. Below here is another long section of slow, winding river through lowlands of hardwoods and underbrush. Expect a few fallen trees and logjams.

Geneva Road Bridge has fair access with limited roadside parking.

Geneva Road Bridge to Midland City Park
22 Miles
4 1/2 - 6 1/2 Hours

Most of the river in the lower section is wide — up to 150 feet — shallow and quite slow. Bottom remains gravel and stone, studded with boulders that rise above the water level most of the year. A few shallow riffles glide around bends. Houses are frequent but scattered.

MacGruder Road Bridge has fair access and roadside parking.

Eight Mile Road Bridge has fair access but poor parking.

9 **Meridian Road Bridge** has fairly good access and good parking for several vehicles. It is the last good access site before Midland. There is one more bridge, at Homer Road, but access and parking are so poor we recommend ending the trip at Meridian or continuing two to three hours into Midland and ending at **10** the **city park** at the junction with the Tittabawassee. This final stretch, after the junction with the Pine River, is big water. The city park in Midland has good access and parking. Supplies are within easy walking distance.

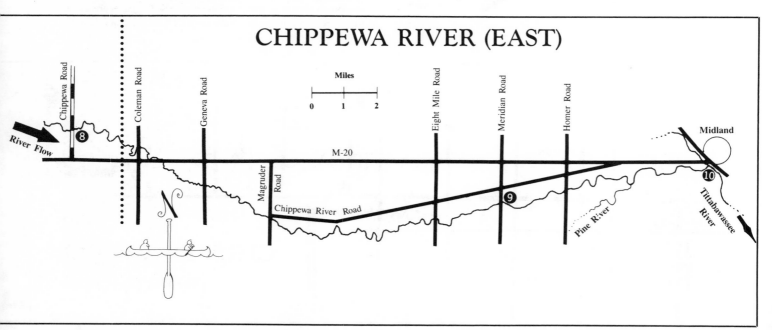

CHIPPEWA RIVER (EAST)

DOWAGIAC RIVER

Counties:	**Cass, Berrien**
Start/End:	**M-62 Bridge (Dowagiac) to US-31 Bridge (Niles)**
Miles:	**13.5**
Gradient:	**4.4 ft/mile**
Portages:	**One dam, fairly easy**
Rapids/Falls:	**None**
Campgrounds:	**Few**
Canoe Liveries:	**Several**
Skill Required:	**I**

A small, mild-tempered tributary of the St. Joseph River, the Dowagiac offers one of the most interesting trips in southwest Michigan. It flows through a variety of terrain, much of it wooded and nearly all of it undeveloped and surprisingly remote. As with many rivers in the southern third of the state, camping opportunities are limited, and there are not nearly enough good access sites and parking areas. But, in spite of such limitations, the Dowagiac remains an attractive and pleasant river, well-suited for beginners and families seeking a casual one- or two-day trip. Water in the Dowagiac is clouded, but quality is good and supports brown trout as the predominant gamefish.

M-62 Bridge (Dowagiac) to US-31 Bridge (Niles)
13.5 Miles
5-7 Hours

1 The initial **put-in at M-62** presents something of a problem: There are two bridges to consider. The western one is over the Dowagiac River; the eastern structure is over Dowagiac Creek. Neither offers very good access or parking, other than at the roadside. Both streams are about the same size — 25-30 feet wide — and both are plagued with fallen trees. We put in on Dowagiac Creek, which is clear, shallow and sandy with a moderate but steady current. Trees form an almost continuous canopy overhead; where they have fallen, they reach easily from bank to bank. Don't despair — the downed trees last less than a quarter-mile until the junction with the Dowagiac River.

Water volume doubles with the addition of the clouded water of the mainstream, and from here to the end of the river there are few obstructions. The river after the junction of the two branches flows uncannily straight, between banks 12-15 feet high. Dense woods of black willow, silver maple, poplar, sycamore, oak, beech and other hardwoods crowd the banks and form the overhead canopy. Some trees are remarkably large. The bottom is sand with occasional patches of gravel and rocks. Depth at midsummer is two to five feet, but high-water marks in the trees suggest spring floods of considerable depth.

There is a private bridge and landing shortly below the junction of the river and Dowagiac Creek. The next bridge is at Peavine Road with no access and parking.

2 **Sink Road Bridge**, 1 1/2 - 2 1/2 hours below M-62 Bridge, has good access and parking. County maps show camping both here and at Rogers Lake Recreation Area; the facilities, however, are in private ownership and can be used only by club members.

From Sink Road the river continues much the same — straight and through a wooded valley.

Crystal Spring Road Bridge has poor access and parking.

Indian Lake Road Bridge has fair access, but parking is on the roadside only and very limited. Watch for a low-hanging cable below Indian Lake Road Bridge. There is a **county park** one-half **3** mile below the bridge with access, parking and picnic grounds. The river from here begins to increase in current speed, and tight bends, logs, and leaning or fallen trees require basic maneuvering skills to negotiate. This stretch could be tricky for beginners, especially in high water.

At Kinzie Road Bridge, there is fair access and roadside parking. The river slows here and enters the backwaters of **Niles Dam**. If water is being discharged from the dam, expect the backwaters to be a maze of sandbars and mud flats. Look for the **4** deepest channels and wind your way across. Take out on the right bank just before the bridge. Portage 200 yards over Pucker Street across the circle drive on the right side of the dam to the wooden foot bridge. The trail leads to a small community park with access to the river below the dam.

From the dam to US-31 is a one- to 1-1/2-hour float past the outskirts of the city of Niles. The current is fairly quick but subject to dam discharges. The bottom remains sand and gravel, though gravel is more prevalent than upstream. There is a private campground at Nub Lake, near the river, with supplies and modern camping facilities. Access is fair at **US-31**, and parking is **5** limited to the roadside.

We did not continue the three miles downstream to the St. Joseph but were told it is a popular trip from US-31 down the St. Joseph River 6.5 miles to the town of Buchanan.

DOWAGIAC RIVER

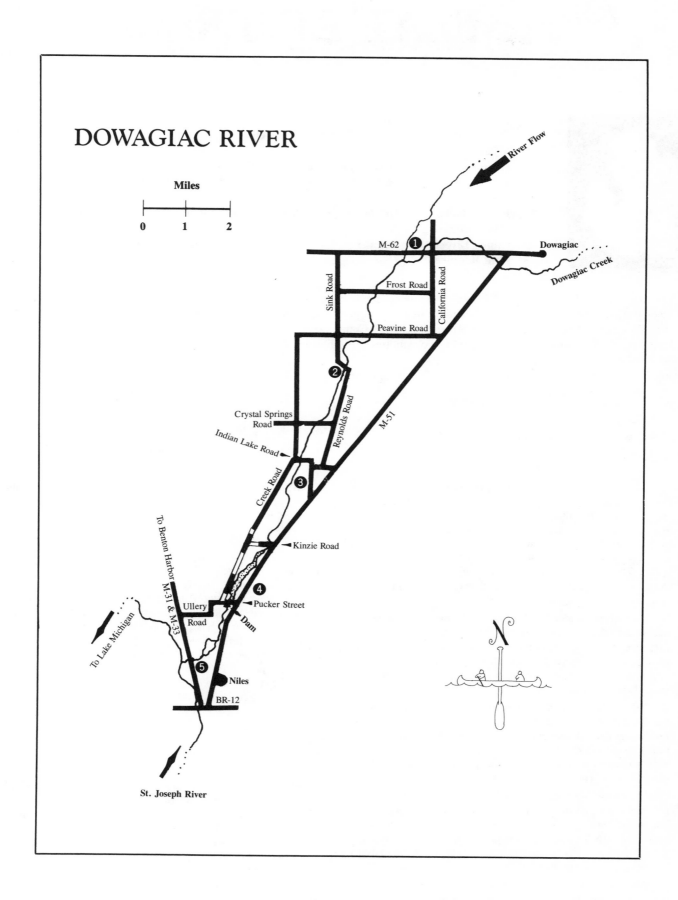

Miles

0 1 2

River Flow

M-62 ① Dowagiac

Dowagiac Creek

Sink Road

Frost Road

Peavine Road

California Road

②

Crystal Springs Road

Reynolds Road

M-51

Indian Lake Road

Creek Road

③

Kinzie Road

To Benton Harbor

M-31 & M-33

④ Pucker Street

Ullery Road

Dam

To Lake Michigan

⑤

Niles

BR-12

St. Joseph River

N

FLAT RIVER

Counties:	**Montcalm, Ionia, Kent**
Start/End:	**Greenville Dam to Lowell**
Miles:	**32.5**
Gradient:	**Greenville to Fallasburg Park — 3.2 ft/mile**
	Fallasburg Park to Lowell Dam — 6.25 ft/mile
Portages:	**Four dams, fairly easy**
Rapids/Falls:	**Unnamed rapids before Ingall's Bridge (Smyrna) — Class I**
Campgrounds:	**None**
Canoe Liveries:	**Several**
Skill Required:	**I**

A serene and gentle river, the Flat is one of the many fine tributaries of the Grand River that spread a network across the center of the Lower Peninsula. Generally quite wide and shallow with consistently slow to moderate current, it is a good choice for families and beginning canoeists. A Michigan Natural River designated Country-Scenic, it passes through several stretches of state land, where streamside camping is possible. Other camping possibilities are quite limited. Fishing is for smallmouth bass and other warm-water species.

Greenville Dam to Belding Dam
12.5 Miles
3-5 Hours

Although there are many miles of river above the city of Greenville, we found the upper sections extremely small, shallow, and obstructed by fallen trees and logjams. We recommend putting in at Greenville, either at the **Greenville Dam** (where there is good parking and access at a community park), or at Jackson's Landing, below the M-57 Bridge (where access and parking are good). The river here is 50-75 feet wide and one to three feet deep with current steady to fairly quick over gravel and rock bottom. The water is slightly discolored.

Baker Road Bridge has fair access and roadside parking for one or two vehicles. This is the beginning of the Flat River Game Preserve, an uninhabited area of hardwoods and pines, where the river is wide and generally quite slow. It is a pleasant, relaxing two- to four-hour float through the preserve and is rightfully considered the prime water on a Flat River canoe trip.

Bricker Road Bridge, a steel truss bridge on a gravel road, has fair access and limited parking. A short distance below it, Long Lake Road Bridge, with fair access and parking, marks the end of the Flat River Game Preserve. There is much slow, somewhat deeper water from here to Belding and the narrow backwaters of Belding Dam.

In Belding, several bridges have no access or parking. Portage the **dam** — where there is a community park with good access and parking — on either the right or the left. The water below the dam is fairly fast over gravel. Take the right channel around the small island immediately downstream to take advantage of the most water flow.

Main Street Bridge is a few minutes below the dam and has good access and parking downstream on the right.

Belding Dam to Fallasburg Park
12 Miles
5-6 Hours

Below Belding the river widens to 60-80 feet with depths from three to six feet. It flows through largely uninhabited countryside of low hardwood hills with tag alders at the banks among scattered meadows. There is no access or parking at the M-44 Bridge just below the town. Downstream stretches of gentle riffles alternate with slow water. The riffles flow over gravel with some rocks to bushel size.

The bridge at Button Road has fair access and roadside parking. Below it there is a quite long stretch of riffles with a climax of sorts in a short rapids at the site of a washed out dam just before **Ingalls Road Bridge** near Smyrna. Take the rapids through the center to best avoid rocks or portage on the left if in doubt. It is not difficult water by most whitewater standards, but high spring flows could create some fairly high standing waves. There is fair access and good parking at the dam site before the bridge. Riffles continue downstream a short distance before the river enters the backwaters of White's Bridge Dam. The reservoir is fairly long and narrow and winds through wooded hills. Portage the dam on the left.

A short distance below the dam is one of Michigan's few original wooden covered bridges, **White's Bridge**, with fair access and limited parking downstream on the left. The river is wide (80-150 feet), rocky, and shallow with moderate current. From here to Fallasburg Park there are a few scattered homes, but much of the distance is through the low wooded hills and meadows of the Lowell Game Area. The current remains moderate to fairly quick over shallow riffles, where large rocks are frequent and where low-water canoeing is sure to result in some bottom-dragging.

McPherson Road Bridge has good access and parking below the bridge on the left. **Fallasburg Park** is just downstream and has extensive picnic grounds and good access and parking at the lower end of the park just before Covered Bridge Road (site of the Flat River's second covered bridge).

Fallasburg Park to Lowell
8 Miles
2-4 Hours

The lower end of the river has two medium-size reservoirs with sections of moderately paced river between. Below Covered Bridge are about two miles of backwater behind the first dam. Houses near the bridge give way to high wooded hills and isolated forests in the Lowell State Game Area. The reservoir is formed by two dams. Paddlers intending to continue downstream to Lowell should bear to the right (west) to the dam, visible from the wide body of the impoundment. Portage on the right. Access to this dam is poor — limited to two-track dirt trails that circumvent power-company property — making it an unlikely choice for a put-in or take-out. The alternative is a channel visible on the left (east) end of the impoundment. The channel is narrow, and the M-91 Bridge (Flat River Drive) is visible from the pond. Take out at the bridge. Fenced power-company property — with a very difficult portage at the small power dam there — is immediately downstream. Access at the bridge is fair, and parking is limited to the roadside.

Continuing downstream from the west dam, the river is shallow and rocky until below the Borroughs Road Bridge, where there is poor parking and access. Below the bridge the river slows and deepens and remains that way as it winds through farmland and hills before entering the backwaters of Lowell Dam.

Take out at the **dam in downtown Lowell** on the left upstream shore. The junction with the Grand River is less than a mile downstream.

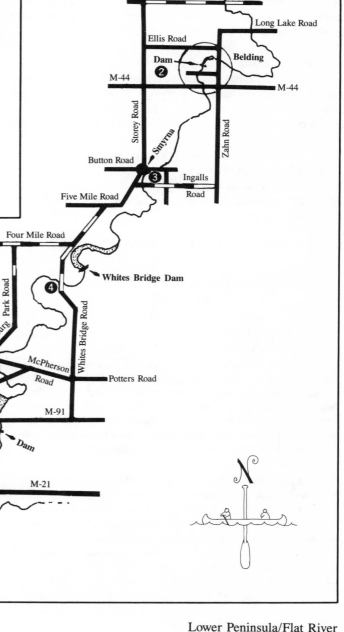

HURON RIVER

Counties:	Oakland, Livingston, Washtenaw, Wayne
Start/End:	Proud Lake to Mouth
Miles:	100
Gradient:	Hudson Mills to Ann Arbor — 3.6 ft/mile
	All other sections — less than 2 ft/mile
Portages:	9 dams, easy; 2 dams, difficult
Rapids/Falls:	Unnamed rapids at Territorial Road Bridge — Class I
	Delhi Rapids, above Delhi Road Bridge — Class I-II
Campgrounds:	Numerous
Canoe Liveries:	Numerous
Skill Required:	I-II

Of all southern Michigan rivers, there is probably none that has been promoted more for canoeing and other recreational uses than the Huron. A large and extensive system of parks has been arranged to make the river accessible and attractive to large numbers of people in Ann Arbor, Ypsilanti and Detroit. It is not only its proximity to metropolitan areas that has inspired this kind of development.

With its clear water, rock and gravel bottom, and attractive and unspoiled surroundings, this Country-Scenic designated Natural River would be a favorite with canoeists wherever it happened to be located. Generally, it has slow to moderate current and few hazards or obstructions that cannot be easily avoided. There are, however, several stretches of fast water that can be difficult for beginners. At least one short rapids is challenging enough during high-water stages to attract kayakers and other whitewater enthusiasts. Although never quite out of earshot of freeways, the Huron flows through mostly undeveloped country, much of it wooded. Except in the cities, of course, there are few houses on its banks, and wildlife is as abundant as on many far northern rivers. We were surprised to see otters, herons, osprey and a variety of waterfowl.

Fishing is primarily for warm-water species, especially smallmouth bass, although a put-and-take trout fishery has been established in the section below Proud Lake.

Wilderness enthusiasts will perhaps find the large number of reservoirs and the fee-oriented park system too civilized, but for large numbers of city residents the Huron provides a quick and convenient getaway. Certainly most of them come away, as we did, surprised and delighted by a fine river.

MAP #1: PROUD LAKE to BASELINE LAKE— 33 MILES

Proud Lake to Kent Lake Dam
13.5 Miles
4 1/2 - 5 1/2 Hours

❶   **Proud Lake** is the upstream limit of good canoeing water. Above here is a series of lakes and impoundments threaded together by narrow, shallow river. Access and parking are good at Proud Lake, where a state vehicle permit is required. Get used to it, because virtually every service in the state and metropolitan park systems along the Huron requires fees. Proud Lake is small, narrow and bordered by marshlands. Stay to the right to find the outlet. A state park and campground is on the south shore midway down the lake. At the outlet, portage the water-control dam on the right.

The river from here to the dam at Milford is clear and slow, with sand bottom punctuated by stretches of gravel and small stones. It averages 25-35 feet wide, with summer depths of one to three feet. Terrain is lowland forests and marshlands. Trout are planted annually, and flies-only fishing regulations are in effect from Proud Lake outlet to Wixom Road. Access and parking are

❷ good at **Wixom Road Bridge**, where a motor-vehicle permit is required and parking is prohibited from 10:00 p.m. to 8:00 a.m. Paddlers planning to park overnight should contact the Metropoli-

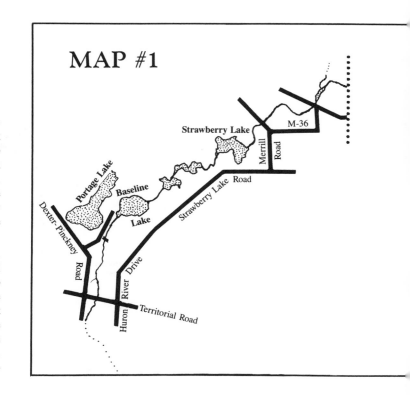

MAP #1

tan Parks Authority to make arrangements. (See Appendix V, page 132, "Further Information, Huron River.")

Access is fair at Burns Road Bridge, and roadside parking is very limited.

3 In Milford, there is a community park next to the **bridge on Main Street** (Milford Road). The river is accessible, but parking is allowed only during daylight hours. The river widens here to enter the backwaters of Milford Dam. Portage the dam on the right.

Below Milford, the river continues much as it did above but, just below Dawson Road, widens again and enters Kent Lake. Just downstream from General Motors Road (no access) is a **Kensington Metropark canoe campground**.

4

Dawson Road Bridge has good access and parking for half a dozen vehicles and is a good take-out for paddlers who want to avoid large Kent Lake.

There are numerous well-marked parks, picnic areas and access sites on Kent Lake, which is large enough to support a marina and sailboats and is capable of producing high winds and large waves. Just past the I-96 Bridge, portage **Kent Dam** on the left, where there is also parking and access. To reach the dam by road, enter Island Lake Recreation Area off Kensington Road.

5

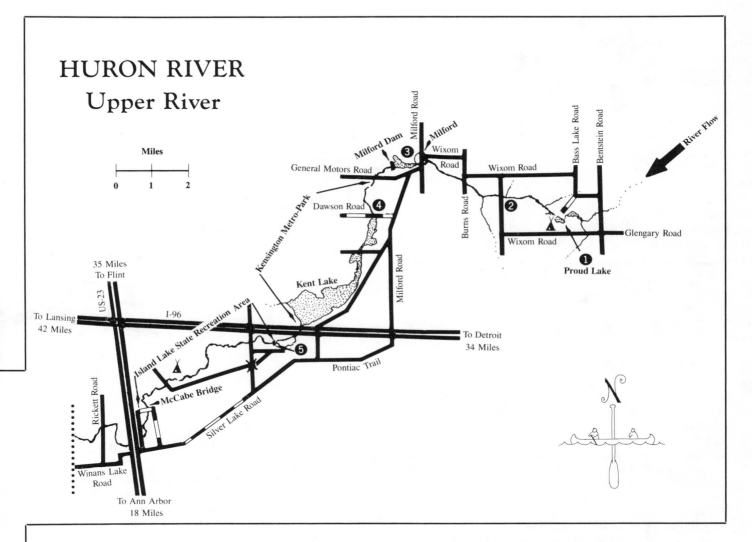

HURON RIVER
Upper River

Kent Lake Dam to Baseline Lake Dam
19.5 Miles
5 1/2 - 7 1/2 Hours

Below Kent Lake, through Island Lake Recreation Area, the river is 40-60 feet wide and slowly meanders through lowland forests. It is subject to fallen trees that seem to be regularly cleared.

There is no access at Kensington Road Bridge, but there is access and parking at several picnic areas and launch sites as well as at a canoe campground in the park downstream.

McCabe Road Bridge has fair access and parking.

Ricket Road has poor access and parking.

Neither the bridge at Winans Lake Road nor at M-36 has access to the river.

We bypassed the series of lakes beginning with Strawberry Lake and have only incomplete information about them. Strawberry Lake, especially, is heavily developed, but there are uninhabited marshlands surrounding the channels between the lakes and the shorelines of several of them.

Portage the control dam below Baseline Lake on the left and the rock barrier immediately downstream on the right. (Note: There is a public access site on Portage Lake connected by a channel to the Huron River below Baseline Lake.)

MAP #2
HURON RIVER

Miles

0   1   2

MAP #2: HUDSON MILLS METROPARK to FLAT ROCK — 54.5 MILES

Hudson Mills Metropark to Ann Arbor Parks
16.5 Miles
5 - 6 1/2 Hours

6 Put in at **Hudson Mills Metropark**, where there is good access and parking just below Territorial Road. Upstream, there is fair access and parking at Bell Road. The river here is 60-90 feet wide and alternates sections of slow water one to four feet deep with sections of very shallow riffles. Low water in summer will produce some bottom-bumping. Hudson Mills has been the site of a sawmill, gristmill, cidermill and plastermill, the earliest dating back to 1827. Today, only the ruins of foundations and a short stretch of light rapids mark the spot just below Territorial Road Bridge where the mills were located. The rapids can be run down the chute at left center. Pumpkin- to bushel-size rocks create standing waves that could become fairly high during high water. If in doubt, portage on the left just beyond the bridge.

Light riffles extend well into Hudson Mills Metropark, where there are several access sites and two overnight canoe campgrounds. This is one of the finest sections of the Huron River. The current alternates from quick to slow, and water is clean and clear as it flows over sand, gravel and rocks up to bushel size. The river passes through low hills of upland forests. There are occasional houses, especially near Dexter, but generally this is a quiet, relatively remote section that supports a variety of wildlife. A runnable drop over a rock barrier just upstream from Dexter should be scouted during high water. Run it through the chute at right center.

Access and parking are poor at the bridge in Dexter; supplies are a short walk from the bridge.

A mile downstream, there is good access and parking at **Dexter-Huron Metropark** picnic grounds. Riffles near the park **7** give way to slow water two to five feet deep. Just above Zeeb Road is another rock barrier, which can be run on the right.

Zeeb Road Bridge has fair access and good parking for five or six vehicles. From here to Delhi is a one- to 1-1/2-hour float through wide river with slow to moderate current.

At **Delhi** is a locally famous rapids that should be scouted, **8** especially by beginning or intermediate paddlers. Islands divide the river into two main channels, both of which can be run except during low water when exposed rocks prohibit passage. Spring's high water attracts kayakers to this stretch of rare southern-Michigan whitewater. Paddlers with any whitewater experience will negotiate these short, straightforward rapids without difficulty. Descent over jumbled rocks is quick for about 200 feet; jammed logs and other debris may create obstacles. To avoid the rapids, take out at a good access site on the right or portage either right or left. There is also good access and parking at Delhi Road Bridge, immediately below the rapids.

From Delhi to Barton Pond, riffles extend about one-half mile, then slow water precedes the reservoir. There is no access at Huron River Drive or at Maple Road Bridge. Good access and parking for several vehicles can be found beside Huron River Drive next to the railroad trestle. These trestles are low and may require portaging during high water.

⑨ Portage **Barton Dam** at the marker on the right. From here to Argo Pond the river is wide and deep. Take the left channel at Argo Dam, then portage. Island Park, one-half mile below the dam, has good access and parking, as do several parks in Ann Arbor.

Ann Arbor to Lower Huron Metropark
22.5 Miles
7-9 Hours

This section contains an almost continuous series of backwaters with four dams to portage. Its virtue is that it provides a pleasant and unusual means of viewing Ann Arbor and Ypsilanti. Because the cities are anxious to promote the recreational uses of the river, there are several large parks with access sites, parking, picnic areas, drinking water and restrooms. Portages are well-marked and obvious, except at Belleville Lake Dam (also known as French Landing), where, on the right side, the portage through an industrial area is long and difficult. High winds can be a nuisance in the open waters of Ford Lake and Belleville Lake.

Lower Huron Metropark to Flat Rock Dam
15.5 Miles
5-6 Hours

There is no access at French Landing; put in one mile downstream at **Lower Huron Metropark**. The river from here to Flat **⑩** Rock passes almost entirely through metropark property and is managed for recreational uses. Current is slow to moderate, similar to much of the river upstream, although the water is not as clear. The river is 75-90 feet wide and two to four feet deep; bottom is sand and gravel with occasional larger stones. Most of the terrain is lowland forests of hardwoods.

There is a canoe campground — as well as several picnic areas that provide access to the river — in Lower Huron Metropark.

There are numerous access sites in **Willow Metropark**, 10 **⑪** miles below Lower Huron. There is also fair — and free — access, with parking for several vehicles, at the bridge on Willow Road.

Oakwoods Metropark has parking, access, and other facili- **⑫** ties and is the last good access before Flat Rock Pond.

There is a problem at Flat Rock Dam: Portaging is simply not permitted, and fences and locked gates put an effective end to a trip. Because there is no suitable access at the east end of the reservoir, the best procedure for those who wish to continue downstream is to take out at Oakwoods Metropark before the river enters Flat Rock Pond and arrange a shuttle to the park in Flat Rock below the dam.

Flat Rock to Pointe Mouillee (Lake Erie)
(Not on map)
9.5 Miles
3 1/2 - 4 1/2 Hours

This final section of the Huron is wide, slow, and discolored and does not equal the quality of the river upstream. The access in Flat Rock at the community park is good but uncertain due to signs directing use by Flat Rock residents only. There are several bridges before the end of the river, but only River Road has access (poor) with roadside parking. At Pointe Mouillee State Game Area, just upstream from the mouth of the river, there is good access, parking, water and restrooms.

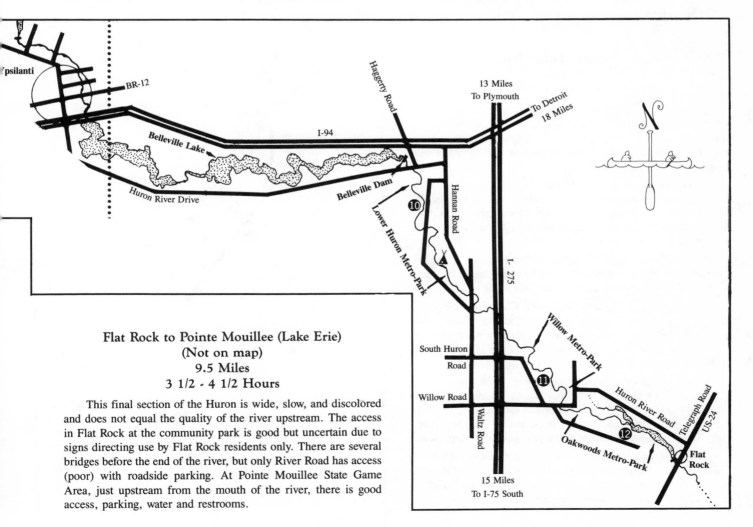

JORDAN RIVER

Counties:	**Antrim, Charlevoix**
Start/End:	**Graves Crossing to Lake Charlevoix**
Miles:	**10.5**
Gradient:	**6.2 ft/mile**
Portages:	**None**
Rapids/Falls:	**None**
Campgrounds:	**Few**
Canoe Liveries:	**Several**
Skill:	**I-II**
Topo. Maps:	**Boyne City (15 min.)**

This small, lovely Wild-Scenic designated river has long been considered one of Michigan's finest trout streams. Perhaps because of its size, it has not attracted a great deal of statewide attention among canoeists, although it is popular enough with locals to draw good numbers during summer weekends. The Jordan's most striking feature is the clarity of its water; in fact, it is regarded as having possibly the purest water of any Lower Peninsula river. Water levels do not fluctuate greatly and will not be excessively low even in dry summers. Generally quick current in the upper section combined with tight bends make having basic paddling skills advisable.

Fishing is for resident brook, brown and rainbow trout, as well as lake-run rainbows and browns. Currently, an extended fishing season from April 1 to December 31 is in effect up to Webster Bridge.

Camping is mostly limited to the state-forest campground near Graves Crossing. Although parts of the river flow through state land, most of the shoreline is thickly overgrown with cedars and tag alders, and good riverside campsites are not common.

Graves Crossing to Lake Charlevoix
10.5 Miles
3-4 Hours

❶ The river upstream from **Graves Crossing** is generally considered to be too small and too choked with fallen trees to be negotiated. About a mile upstream is the junction of a major tributary, the Green River; above that, fallen trees and logjams make the river virtually uncanoeable.

At Graves Crossing — where access is good and there is adequate parking for a dozen or more vehicles — the river is 30-50 feet wide and two to five feet deep. Moderately fast current flows over gravel and stones up to fist size. Water is clear and very cold.

A short distance from the bridge on Graves Crossing Road is a state-forest campground that offers the best camping in the area. Primitive facilities include water, toilets and picnic tables.

Between Graves Crossing and Lake Charlevoix are three evenly spaced bridges. Access is fair at Old State Road, with
❷ parking limited to the roadside; **Webster Road** has a public access site with good access and parking; and there is a public site
❸ at **Rogers Road** with good access and parking.

Expect the river to remain moderately quick, narrow and winding most of the way to Rogers Road. Frequent limestone ledges and sudden dropoffs make fishing in waders tricky for such a small river. Fallen trees may be an occasional problem, especially in early spring, but most of the year passage is kept clear.

The final mile of river between Rogers Road and Lake Charlevoix is a flat and still float through marshlands. Continue into the lake beyond the bridge at M-32 and take out on the left at
❹ the **public boat ramp**, where access and parking are good.

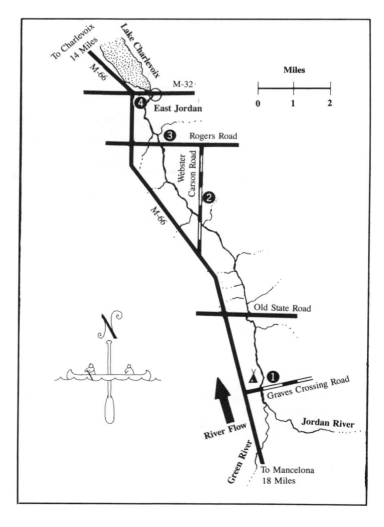

KALAMAZOO RIVER

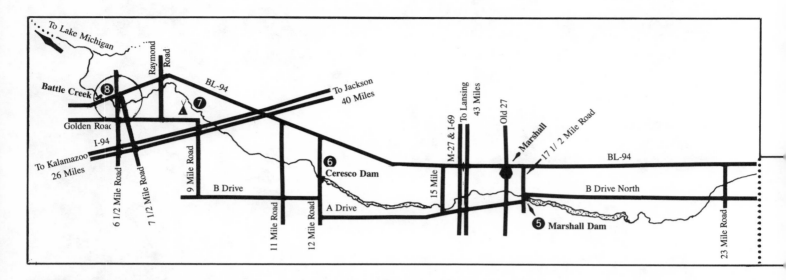

Counties:	Jackson, Calhoun
Start/End:	Goose Lake Road Bridge (above Homer) to Battle Creek
Miles:	46.5
Gradient:	2.8 ft/mile
Portages:	One dam, easy; three dams, difficult; occasional fallen trees on South Branch
Rapids/ Falls:	None
Campgrounds:	Few
Canoe Liveries:	Several
Skill Required:	I

This major southern Michigan river has much to offer canoeists — in spite of certain handicaps — and is zealously supported by local paddlers. In many ways it is a fine river. Much of it flows through forested, uninhabited countryside; current is strong enough to make an enjoyable float, yet is gentle enough for beginners; and water quality, especially in the upper reaches, appears to be good.

There are, however, problems. Access and parking are so difficult in places that we gave up on entire stretches in frustration. There are difficult portages at Marshall, Ceresco, and especially in Battle Creek, where there seems to be little attempt made to promote the recreational potential of the river. In the heart of Battle Creek the river has been diverted down a nearly mile-long concrete sluice, where storm fences and city ordinances prevent further progress and force paddlers to arrange shuttles around this barrier or face the unpleasant prospect of a mile portage through busy city streets. Partly because access and passage are deterred at Battle Creek and partly because the river quickly loses velocity and quality below that city, we ended our trip there.

South Branch:
Goose Lake Road Bridge to Homer
9 Miles
3 1/2 - 5 1/2 Hours

❶ The river as far upstream as **Goose Lake Road Bridge** is navigable, although it is very small (10-15 feet wide, one to three feet deep) and is subject to obstruction from fallen trees. Expect to find a few fallen trees most of the way to Homer, although there are fewer below 29 Mile Road Bridge than in the upper stretches.

❷ Better put-ins are at **Folks Road Bridge** or at the private campground just downstream, where there is access, parking and supplies. The river at Folks Road is slow, winding and generally shallow. Water is clear over mostly sand bottom. Fishing is for warm-water species, including smallmouth bass and northern pike. The river averages 25-35 feet wide and six inches to two feet deep. Expect to drag bottom in places during the summer. Terrain is lowland marshes and low hills of mixed hardwoods, much of it state-owned. Signs of human habitation are infrequent even though the river is usually within a half-mile of roads.

At Van Wert Road Bridge, access and parking are poor. Twenty-nine Mile Road Bridge offers better access and is often used to start a short one- to two-hour trip to Homer that avoids many of the obstacles that slow progress upstream.

In Homer, there is good access and parking at the **old grist-mill.** The low dam just before the mill can be run on the right if there is enough water; otherwise expect to scrape on concrete and on the rocks at the bottom. If in doubt, portage on the right. **❸**

Homer to Albion
9 Miles
3-5 Hours

Below Homer the river varies from 25-60 feet wide, with some sections very shallow in summer. Expect an occasional fallen tree, although canoe liveries succeed in keeping passage clear most of the year. There is fair access and limited roadside parking at most of the half-dozen bridges in this section. Current speed varies from slow to moderate, and bottom is sand or silt with occasional stretches of gravel. Before Albion, there is a long stretch of slow water that meanders through marshland before entering the backwaters of Albion Dam.

4 Access is good off M-99 at **Albion Pond**, or continue to the dam at Haven Road and portage on the right, through a community park. The river is diverted into several channels here, making the portage two to three hundred yards long. Access and parking are good.

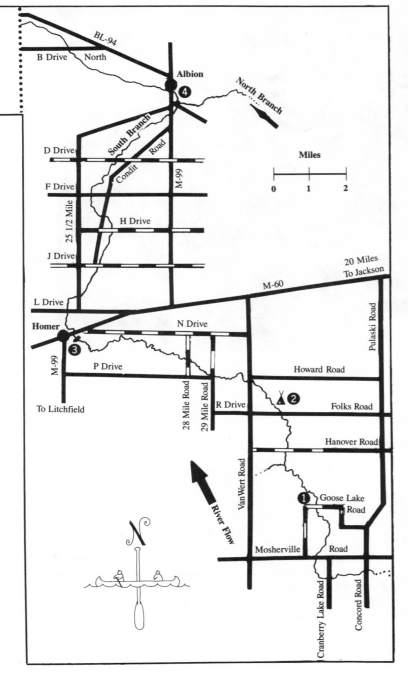

Mainstream: Albion to Ceresco Dam
19.5 Miles
6-8 Hours

In Albion the South Branch is joined by the North Branch to form the Kalamazoo Mainstream. The North Branch is said to be canoeable as far upstream as the town of Concord, but with many obstructions. We found it to be distressingly small and shallow and did not attempt to canoe it.

In Albion, put in either at the dam at Haven Road or downstream at East Cass Street. The river through town is slow to moderate in speed and shallow over gravel, rocks and the usual urban deposits of tires and bottles. Be prepared for the novelty of following the river beneath the sidewalks and floorboards of the downtown district.

Below town the river is 40-75 feet wide and one to three feet deep. Water quality — with silt and sand bottom and water that tends to be clouded — is not as good as in the two branches above Albion. Farmlands of rolling hills alternate with patches of hardwoods, where fallen trees may occasionally reach across the river. There are bridges at B Drive North, where access and parking are fair; at 23 Mile Road, where there is no access; and for a second time at B Drive North, where access is good and there is limited roadside parking.

Near Marshall, a long backwater can be a problem during low water when mud flats make passage difficult. Portage the **dam** on the right and follow the signs for a 250-yard portage **5** across 17 1/2 Mile Road, then through the gates of an industrial complex to the river.

Below the Marshall Dam, there is a stretch of fairly fast riffles over rocks and gravel, but most of the river continues slow to moderate over sand and gravel bottom. West of Marshall the river passes beneath I-69 (M-27) and beneath the bridge at 15 Mile Road, where access is poor and there is no parking. From here the river is wide and slow coming into Ceresco Pond. As in the backwaters at Marshall, mud flats may hinder passage during low water. There is no clear portage at **Ceresco Dam**. The best **6** chance is to the left, but because you must cross over private property, permission may have to be granted to pass through, as well as to put in below the dam.

Ceresco Dam to Battle Creek
9 Miles
2 1/2 - 3 1/2 Hours

This short stretch is a popular trip, although even on summer weekends it will probably not be excessively crowded. There is a canoe livery and campground midway through it, and access is relatively good in several places. Putting in at Ceresco Dam can be difficult due to private property, and permission should be sought at the small office building on the left side of the dam.

The river at Ceresco is 60-90 feet wide and one to four feet deep over gravel and rock. Current ranges from slow to moderately fast, with numerous riffles that are very shallow in summer. Most of the section passes through lowland forests of mixed hardwoods — including oak, maple, sycamore and basswood — with heavy streamside brush. There are occasional houses, but they are widely scattered.

Eleven Mile Road Bridge has fair access and roadside parking and is an alternative to putting in at the dam upstream. Beneath the bridge, there is a short stretch of relatively fast water with scattered bushel-size rocks to avoid.

(Continued on following page)

Kalamazoo River (continued)

(7) Just below the I-94 and Nine Mile Road bridges is a **picnic area and public access site**. Immediately across the river is a private campground and canoe rental. From here until Battle Creek the river continues to alternate slow water with light riffles. There is access on the outskirts of the city at Raymond Road, but the access road has been blocked, making it necessary to park at the roadside and carry a short distance to the river.

(8) Below Raymond Road the river slows to enter the backwaters of a **water-control dam** in Battle Creek. Near the corner of 6 1/2 Mile Road and 7 1/2 Mile Road there is fair access to the backwaters. This is the last decent access to the river before the dam, and a nearly mile-long concrete sluice below it make further progress difficult. We were told that hardy paddlers sometimes make the long portage through busy Battle Creek streets, but we found the

logistics too complicated and ended our trip at Raymond Road.

Paddlers wishing to explore the Kalamazoo downstream from Battle Creek will find it to be a large, generally slow river, winding through a variety of woods and farmlands. There are major dams and reservoirs at Comstock (Morrow Lake), Otsego, Trowbridge and Allegan (Lake Allegan). It is worth investigating the Allegan State Game Area, west of Allegan and about 10 miles east of Lake Michigan. In this large area of marshlands, the river passes beneath bluffs of pine and oak and branches into many bayous. Waterfowl and other wildlife are abundant, and fishing is said to be excellent. This section of the river and down to the mouth in Saugatuck is a Michigan Natural River and is designated Wild-Scenic.

LITTLE MANISTEE RIVER

Counties:	Lake, Mason, Manistee
Start/End:	Indian Bridge (Irons Rd.) to Stronach Road Bridge
Miles:	30.5
Gradient:	Indian Bridge to Nine Mile Bridge — 6 ft/mile
	Nine Mile Bridge to Six Mile Bridge — 14 ft/mile
	Six Mile Bridge to Stronach Road Bridge — 4 ft/mile
Portages:	DNR weir below Six Mile Bridge, easy; occasional fallen trees
Rapids/Falls:	Unnamed rapids between Nine Mile Bridge and Six Mile Bridge — Class I-II
Campgrounds:	Several
Canoe Liveries:	Few
Skill Required:	I-II
Topo. Maps:	Wellston, Freesoil, Manistee (15 min.)

Although the Little Manistee is well known for its trout and salmon fishery, canoeists have often overlooked it in favor of the nearby Pere Marquette, Pine and Big Manistee rivers. Yet those who have canoed the Little Manistee are quick to list it among their favorite rivers. Small, quick-spirited, clean and relatively stable, it flows through long stretches of largely undeveloped national forest land with several USFS campgrounds on its banks. Current is moderate to fairly quick along much of the river and suited to paddlers with basic skills. The section between Nine Mile and Six Mile bridges, however, is one of the fastest and most challenging stretches in the Lower Peninsula and requires more advanced ability. Fallen trees can slow progress, especially in the upper reaches, but they appear to be cleared fairly regularly.

Brook, brown and rainbow trout are abundant, as are spring and fall runs of steelhead. Special fishing regulations include an extended season (currently April 1 to December 31) up to Johnson's Bridge and flies-only from Spencer Bridge to Johnson's Bridge.

Indian Bridge (Irons Road)
to Driftwood Valley Campground
10 Miles
4 1/2 - 5 1/2 Hours

There are campgrounds on or near the river at M-37, at Spencer Bridge (Peacock Road) and at Indian Bridge. The M-37 and Spencer Bridge campgrounds are along stretches of river too small and choked by fallen trees to be easily navigated. The **campground at Indian Bridge** has fair access down a steep bank to the river; access is somewhat better at Indian Bridge itself. The river here is small (15-20 feet) and shallow and has its share of logjams and fallen trees. Be prepared to go over and around several obstructions. The current is moderate and steady over sand and gravel bottom. Terrain is hilly with upland hardwood and pine forests; cedars and tag alders line the banks.

The river opens up somewhat after Johnson's Bridge at Johnson Road, where access and parking are poor. Passage is through a continuous series of tight bends with few places to really dig a paddle in for speed. During the early season, there might be enough water volume to make a few tight spots tricky for beginners. Basic paddling and maneuvering skills are sufficient during normal flow.

There is fair access at Dewitts Bridge, with parking along the road. It is easy to be confused at Dewitts, Fox and Pole bridges because of their close proximity and lack of markings.

Fox Bridge (Bass Lake Road) has a designated public access site with good parking. It is marked at the site as "10 Mile NE Bridge" and as "Fox Bridge" on most maps.

Pole Bridge (Mitchell Road) is unmarked but can be identified by a gravel road and by the wooden bridge, which looks from the river like it could be a low railroad trestle. Access and parking are poor. Immediately downstream the road closely parallels the riverbank. **Driftwood Valley Campground** is just downstream on the left. It is not marked on the river and could easily be missed — look across the river for stones piled into a partial dam with a narrow, quick passage through the center. On the left, there are wooden stairs and handrails leading up the bank. From here the river is large enough and open enough for easy passage. Current remains generally moderate, though there are both some slow and some fairly quick stretches; a few tricky bends require good maneuvering skills.

Driftwood Valley Campground to Nine Mile Bridge
9.5 Miles
3 - 4 1/2 Hours

This makes a short trip for overnighters not wanting to run

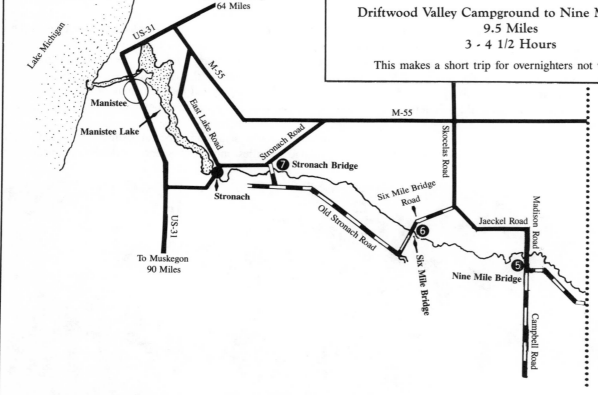

LITTLE MANISTEE RIVER

the fast water below Nine Mile Bridge. Those who want to continue can go the additional two to three hours to Six Mile Bridge and the access there. The stretch to Nine Mile Bridge is typical of northern Lower Peninsula rivers, with its sand and gravel bottom, moderate to moderately fast current, and cedar-lined banks backing up to high ground of hardwoods and occasional pines and hemlocks.

Eighteen Mile Road Bridge has poor access and parking. A short distance below it, there is good access and parking at **Beartracks Campground (USFS)**. Like Driftwood Valley Campground, it is unmarked from the river but can be recognized by brown painted handrails on the ridge above the left bank and steps leading down to the river.

There is good access and parking at **Nine Mile Bridge** (Campbell Road).

Nine Mile Bridge to Stronach Road Bridge
11 Miles
4 1/2 - 6 1/2 Hours

After Nine Mile Bridge is a locally famous stretch of fast water. The river speeds noticeably near the bridge; within a mile it drops quickly over bottom of gravel and rocks to pumpkin size. Expect about four miles of very quick, tricky water. The challenge does not come from whitewater, of which there is little, but from extremely tight bends with logjams and leaning trees. The

fast, strong current is naturally funneled into the obstructions on the outside of the bends. There is also thick brush of tag alders and willows that narrows passage in places to as little as five feet. Precise maneuvering is necessary, with backstrokes and especially drawstrokes indispensible. This is a delightful and challenging stretch for experienced paddlers and those seeking more experience but is not recommended for beginners or families with small children. The water is not generally deep, but fast-water dredging beneath logjams and fallen trees always creates the potential for hazards.

Near **Six Mile Bridge** the river slows and widens somewhat. From here downstream, current is slow and predictable, and there are few obstructions that cannot be easily avoided. Frequent sandbars make excellent picnic and swimming sites. Access is fair at Six Mile Bridge, with parking limited to the designated lot 100 yards up the hill to the north on the right side of the river.

One to 1 1/2 hours below Six Mile Bridge is a DNR weir; portage on the right. From here on is slow water and sandy bottom, with stretches of very deep water alternating with stretches of very shallow water. This is a leisurely float through mostly lowland with few houses or other development.

Access and parking are good at **Stronach Road Bridge**. This is the recommended take-out. From here to the final bridge in the village of Stronach (in sight of Manistee Lake) are two miles of slow water through marshlands. Parking and access at the bridge in Stronach are poor compared to Stronach Road Bridge above.

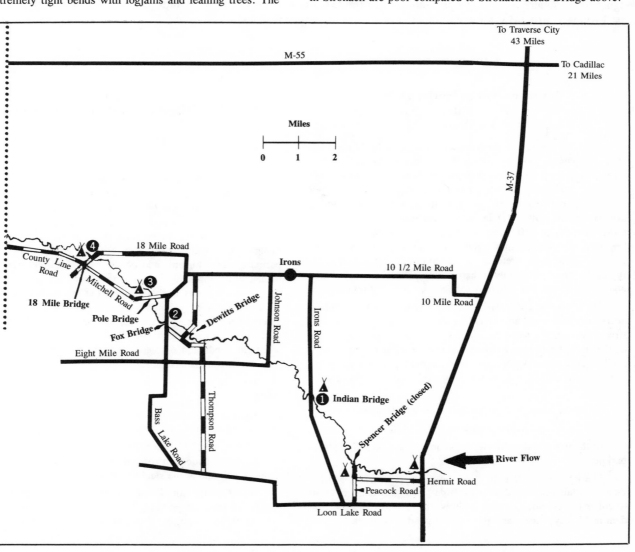

LITTLE MUSKEGON RIVER

Counties:	Mecosta, Montcalm, Newaygo
Start/End:	Altona Dam to Croton Pond (junction with the Muskegon River)
Miles:	33.75
Gradient:	Altona to Morley — 3.6 ft/mile
	Morley to Croton Pond — 6.2 ft/mile
Portages:	Two dams, easy; occasional fallen trees
Rapids/Falls:	Several unnamed rapids below County Line Road Bridge — Class I
Campgrounds:	Few
Canoe Liveries:	Several
Skill Required:	I-II

The Little Muskegon is often overlooked by paddlers traveling north to more famous rivers, yet its clear water, quick current and relatively remote surroundings make it one of the most attractive rivers in central Michigan. Rising out of headwaters in northeastern Mecosta County, the Little Muskegon is not large enough to be easily navigated until it reaches the village of Altona, 20 miles downstream. From there to the Muskegon River at Croton Pond is a two-day trip through a variety of terrain, including woodlands and farms. Current velocity varies from moderate to quick, with some stretches, especially in the section below Morley, fast enough to be challenging to beginners. Camping opportunities are limited, unfortunately, due to private property and a lack of established camp-grounds. Fishing is primarily for smallmouth bass and, in the upper reaches, some trout.

Altona Dam to Morley Dam
11 Miles
4-5 Hours

1 In Altona, there is a **community park**, with fairly good ac-cess and parking, just below the small dam at the east end of town. The river is 25-30 feet wide, varies from six inches to three feet deep, and flows over a bottom of mostly gravel and small stones. Current is moderate to fairly quick, with basic paddling skills more than sufficient in the shallow water and meandering turns. Some light riffles are too shallow for free passage during low-water periods and may require walking through. The terrain is fairly open, with stretches of meadows and tag alders inter-rupted by small woodlots of hardwoods. There are occasional houses and farms, but generally expect a quiet, fairly remote trip.

2 At the end of Three Mile Road is a state-maintained **public access site** with good access and parking. A short distance down-stream is a narrow, short backwaters and a small dam to portage on the right. From here to Morley is water similar to above, with shallow riffles and occasional rocks alternating with slow water and sand bottom. Passage is generally clear, but fallen trees are a possibility.

Access at 130th Avenue Bridge is fair with roadside parking.

Fair access and roadside parking are at 155th Avenue Bridge.

At the upper end of Morley Pond are fair access and roadside parking.

The bridge at Jefferson Road, at the upper end of Morley Pond, has fair access and poor roadside parking. It is better to go to either the community park midway on the north shore or the dam in Morley; access and parking are good at both sites.

Morley Dam to
Croton Dam (Junction with the Muskegon River)
22.75 Miles
6 1/2 - 8 1/2 Hours

3 In Morley, put in at the **Old US-31 Bridge** below the dam, where there is good access and parking. The river from here is 25-40 feet wide and one to three feet deep. The bottom is sand, gravel and rock. Water added from Big Creek and other tributar-ies helps keep levels higher than in the river above Morley, al-though a few shallow riffles may still be bottom-draggers in dry periods. Minor logjams and occasional fallen trees may require maneuvering through or portaging. There are a few scattered houses and cottages in this section, but it mostly flows through quite remote hills of hardwoods and pines with patches of tag alders at the banks. The current can be surprisingly fast, espe-cially in the final stretch after West County Line Road Bridge, and tight bends and occasional obstructions make having basic maneuvering skills advisable.

There is poor access and roadside parking at 190th Avenue Bridge.

There is no access at either the bridge at Washington Road or the new US-131 Bridge. Stretches of fast riffles in this area alter-nate with stretches of low, deeper water over sand bottom.

Access is poor with roadside parking at Amy School Bridge (Long Road) and at the steel and wood bridge at Dagget Road.

4 **West County Line Road Bridge** (Newcosta Avenue) has fair access and roadside parking. There are quite a few houses in the vicinity of the bridge, but they dwindle quickly. Current is slower than above, and the river meanders through low woods, where windblown trees — some of which may require going over or around — are common.

West County Line Road Bridge is the last access before the landing at Croton Pond. This final section is a three- to 3-1/2-hour trip through the most remote — and the fastest — portion of the river. The course twists through high sand and clay banks wooded with maple, oak, birch and pine. Long stretches of riffles and light rapids make a quick descent over gravel, stone and scattered bushel-size and larger rocks. Tamarack Creek increases water volume by half and frequently clouds the water of the mainstream. Riffles and tight bends continue until shortly before Little Muskegon Pond, where current slows, bottom becomes sand, and lowlands and marshes appear. At the pond, head for the bridge — visible at the west end — and enter Croton Pond. There ❺ is a **public landing** on the west shore, just north of the power station. Parking and access are good, and there are several private and township campgrounds in the vicinity of the dam and along Croton Drive to Newaygo.

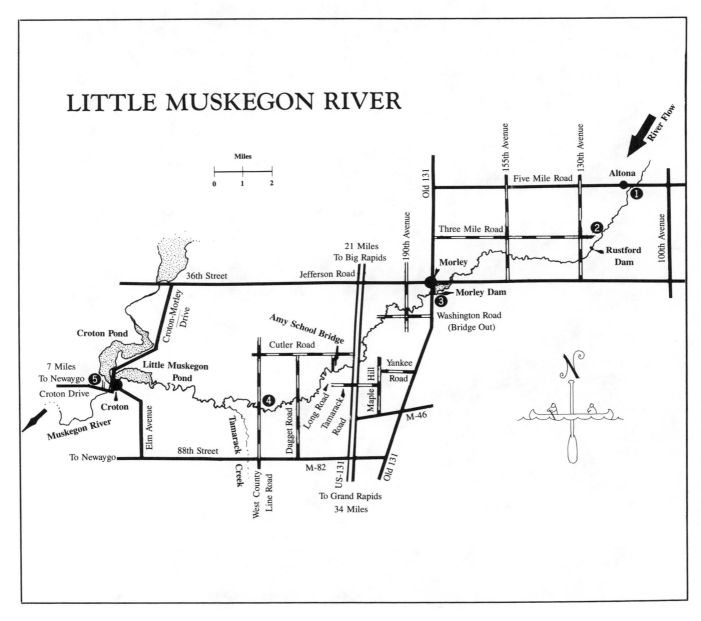

LITTLE MUSKEGON RIVER

MANISTEE RIVER

Counties:	**Crawford, Kalkaska, Missaukee, Wexford, Manistee**
Start/End:	**Deward to Manistee Lake**
Miles:	**151.5**
Gradient:	**4 ft/mile or less**
Portages:	**Two dams, moderately difficult**
Rapids/Falls:	**None**
Campgrounds:	**Numerous**
Canoe Liveries:	**Numerous**
Skill Required:	**I**

Rising from headwaters in Antrim and Otsego Counties, the Manistee River does not gain significance for canoeists until it enters the northwest corner of Crawford County near the ghost town of Deward. Named after 19th-century lumber-baron David Ward, Deward was built in the heart of the last big stand of virgin white pine in the Lower Peninsula. Around the turn of the century it boasted a population of 800 and a daily output of up to a quarter of a million board feet of lumber. Thousands of weathered stumps still dot the surrounding hills and meadows as a reminder of the forests that once made the Manistee one of the most important log-driving rivers in the state.

Canoeists will find the Manistee one of the finest rivers in the Lower Peninsula for expedition canoeing and camping. Numerous campgrounds and access sites are found the entire length of the river. Long stretches of undeveloped and uninhabited countryside and clear, clean water have caused the Manistee to be considered (along with the Au Sable and Lake County's Pine River) for inclusion in the National Wild and Scenic Rivers System. Current is slow to moderate, with occasional light riffles that should not challenge paddlers with basic skills. Water levels, like those on the nearby Au Sable, are very stable.

Fishing is for brook and brown trout in the upper reaches and brown trout down as far as the Baxter Bridge area above Hodenpyle Backwaters. Walleyes, smallmouth bass and northern pike predominate in the lower reaches, and steelhead and salmon run in large numbers up to Tippy Dam. Special fishing regulations include flies-only and extended season (currently April 30 - October 31) in a 7.5-mile stretch above the CCC Bridge, and an extended year-round season for the entire river below US-131.

Deward to M-72
14.5 Miles
5 1/2 - 7 Hours

Although the river near Deward is large enough and open enough for canoeing, access is uncertain because of private property and poorly marked dirt roads. Access is better either four miles downstream at **Cameron Bridge** or two miles farther at Red Bridge (Co. Rd. 612). Parking at both bridges is at the roadside and limited to two or three vehicles.

The river in the upper section is small, meandering and beautiful. Width averages 30-50 feet and depth one to three feet with deeper holes. The bottom is alternating gravel and sand, with sand predominating, and is occasionally congested with stumps and sunken logs. Cottages and houses are interspersed with parcels of public land.

Upper Manistee River State Forest Campground is a short distance below Red Bridge and is reached off Goose Creek Road. It has primitive facilities in two camping areas — one for car campers, the other for canoeists.

Manistee River Bridge State Forest Campground is on the west side of the river just before the bridge at M-72 and has good access and parking.

Supplies and canoe rental are available at the **M-72 Bridge**. There is a good access site on the downstream side of the bridge. However, it belongs to the canoe livery across the highway, and a modest fee is asked for launching and for overnight parking.

M-72 Bridge to CCC Bridge
14 Miles
4-5 Hours

Expect a nice float through this section but with lots of company on summer weekends. The river averages 40-80 feet wide and one to four feet deep with deeper holes. Bottom is predominantly sand with scattered patches of gravel. The current is generally steady, with some stretches that can be tedious in a head wind. Much of the way is lined with cottages or is posted no-trespassing, making it difficult to find suitable resting places. Plan to camp or picnic at **CCC Bridge**, where there are two campgrounds — one just before the bridge on the right, the other immediately below the bridge on the left. There is good access at the bridge and a fair amount of parking.

CCC Bridge to
Lower Sharon Bridge (West Sharon Road)
9.5 Miles
2 1/2 - 3 1/2 Hours

Below CCC there are fewer cottages and, generally, also fewer canoeists and fishermen than in the upper section. Riffles over shallow gravel alternate with stretches of very deep, shaded

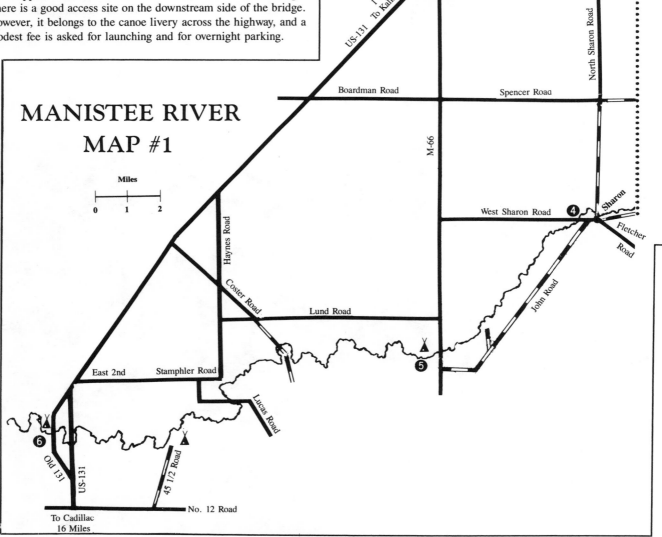

MANISTEE RIVER
MAP #1

pools. The terrain varies from hardwoods and high banks to low-lands of cedar and tag alders. Some stretches through steep valleys of maples and aspen provide outstanding scenery in autumn.

Near Sharon the current increases to moderately fast in places with occasional pumpkin- to bushel-size rocks to avoid. There is plenty of water volume from here downstream, and many locals seem to prefer outboard-powered boats to canoes. Property owners with good humor have erected signs that need not be taken seriously: "Sharon Falls 5 Minutes."

Upper Sharon Bridge (North Sharon Road) has fair access and parking.

4 **Lower Sharon Bridge** is 1.5 miles downstream and has good access and parking.

Lower Sharon Bridge to M-66 Bridge
9.5 Miles
2 1/2 - 3 1/2 Hours

Below Sharon the river slows and widens somewhat, averaging 60-90 feet wide and three to four feet deep with many pools up to 10 feet deep. Largely sand-bottomed, it passes through lowlands of cedars, tag alders and dead elm. There is a public access

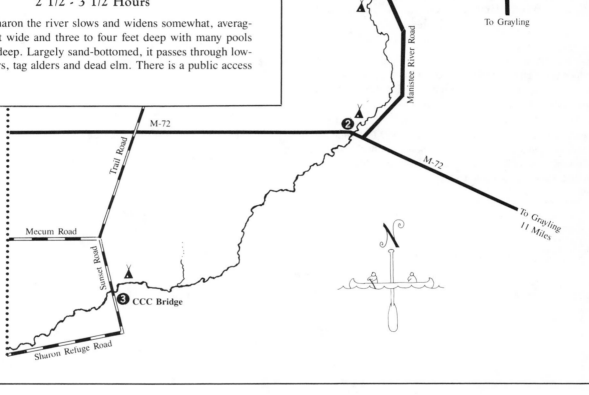

site 1 1/2 to two hours below Sharon at John Road. With restrooms and picnic area, it is one of the few suitable rest stops on this section.

Just above Smithville Landing at M-66 are private campgrounds restricted to canoe-rental customers. Other campers should continue five minutes beyond the bridge to **Smithville Forest Campground and public access site** on the right. Supplies are available at the M-66 Bridge.

5

M-66 Bridge to Old US-131 Campground
25 Miles
6-8 Hours

Immediately below M-66 begins a long series of moderately fast riffles over gravel bottom and some fairly large rocks. High banks of maple, birch, and red and white pine alternate with grass banks and meadows. There are very few cottages through this stretch and — at least compared to the popular water upstream — also few canoeists.

Shortly before Coster Road Bridge, cottages appear. The river deepens and slows somewhat, the bottom becomes predominantly sand, and the current is slow and heavy —characteristics typical of the Manistee the remainder of its length. Access and parking are good at Coster Road Bridge.

From Coster Road to Lucas Road Bridge is a four-mile, one- to two-hour trip. There are a few more stretches of light riffles with gravel and stone bottom, but they become less and less frequent. Again, there are few cottages and much solitude.

Chase Creek Campground is on the left side of the river and has good primitive facilities as well as good access and parking. Take out at the second access site — the first is a steep climb up stairs.

One and a half to 2 1/2 hours below Chase Creek is the US-131 Bridge with good access and parking.

Old US-131 State Forest Campground is one-half mile below US-131 and has primitive facilities and good access and parking.

MAP #2: OLD US-131 CAMPGROUND to TIPPY DAM — 51.5 MILES

Old US-131 Campground to Baxter Bridge (29 1/2 Road)
10 Miles
3-4 Hours

Generally expect much the same water and terrain below US-131 and Old US-131 as immediately above them — moderate current and stretches of gravel bottom alternating with long stretches of slow, deep water over sand bottom.

There is a state-forest campground (in cooperation with Consumers Power Company) at **Baxter Bridge**, where access and parking are good, but attend to the map carefully to find it by road.

Baxter Bridge to Glengary Bridge
17.5 Miles
5-6 Hours

From Baxter Bridge to Glengary Bridge and the backwaters of Hodenpyle Dam, the water is often murky with sediment; bottom is of sand and silt. The current remains steady and moderate most of the way.

Harvey Bridge (No. 19 Road) has good access and parking at a public site. Here, the river averages 60-100 feet wide and three to four feet deep with very deep holes at the bends. Hills of hardwoods overlook the river valley, with tag alders, cedars, aspen and dead elm near the banks. Houses and cottages are infrequent.

Access at the M-37 Bridge is poor, but a canoe livery on the left below the bridge offers access and supplies.

Just below M-37 the river slows and widens as it enters the Hodenpyle Backwaters. Long, shallow sandbars make it necessary to seek deeper channels during low water. Parking and access are fair at **Glengary Bridge**, or continue 1.5 miles downstream to the M-115 Bridge, where there is better access and parking and a large picnic area, though much more traffic noise.

Hodenpyle is a 6.5-mile crossing. Watch for drowned stumps, especially when it is windy and they are obscured by waves. There is a private campground at the northwest end of the pond.

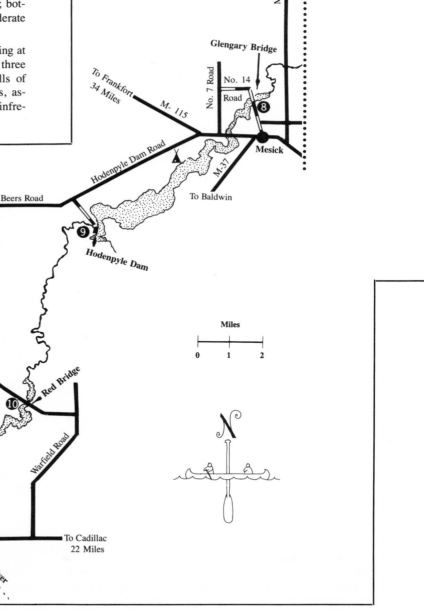

MANISTEE RIVER
MAP #2

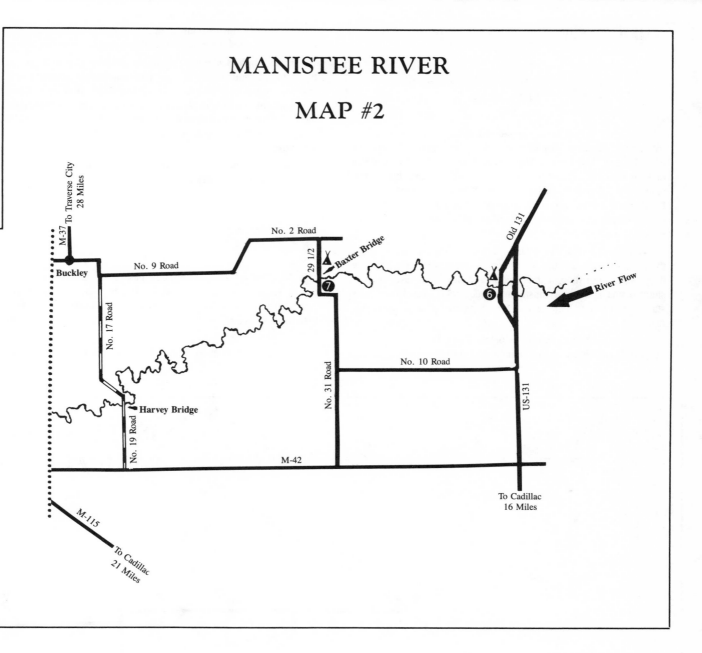

9 At **Hodenpyle Dam**, the portage trail is to the right (north) of the dam face. It is not a marked portage but is visible as a sand scar above the concrete retaining wall at the end of the power-company fence. There is a parking area over the bank reached via Hodenpyle Dam Road. Portage beyond the parking lot down a marked trail but use caution on the steep bank and loose rocks.

Hodenpyle Dam to Red Bridge (Coates Highway)
10 Miles
3-4 Hours

This may be the most interesting and unpredictable section of the Manistee. Water level is determined by flowage from a Consumers Power Company hydroelectric dam and can change from very low to very high within a short time. During low water, expect a leisurely four-hour float over easy glides and calm pools and past gravel and sand bars. During high flow, expect a three-hour trip, with current moderately fast, heavy, and tricky enough in places to be difficult for beginning paddlers. Discharges often occur in the early morning, although there is no set schedule and they can occur at any time.

The river is 80-100 feet wide with depths of two to eight feet. Surrounding land is almost entirely undeveloped. High clay cliffs with seeping springs line the way, and tributaries with waterfalls up to eight feet high are frequent. Hardwoods predominate on the high banks, and wildlife is abundant and varied. Numerous low banks are high enough to be potentially good campsites.

A few miles above Red Bridge, the current slows, and the river channel widens as it enters lowlands before the backwaters of Tippy Dam. Several large bays and channels lead into bayous before the bridge.

Access and parking are good at **Red Bridge**. **10**

Tippy Pond begins immediately downstream and is a six-mile crossing. Shorelines are remote and undeveloped, and wildlife is abundant. Follow the right (north) shore to avoid the possibility of inadvertently bearing south into the lower Pine River. Portage **Tippy Dam** on the right and follow the road down to the public access site below the dam.

MAP #3: TIPPY DAM to MANISTEE LAKE —

27.5 MILES
Tippy Dam To Bear Creek Access Site
14.25 Miles
4-6 Hours

Plenty of parking and clear access below Tippy Dam accommodate the crowds of salmon fishermen who congregate here during fall runs. The river is large enough (up to 200 feet wide) to make it possible to float through during peak fishing, but be prepared to run a gauntlet of hurled lures. The campground on Tippy Pond, north of the dam on Dilling Road, is a good choice except during spring and fall, when it is likely to be overrun with fishermen.

The river below Tippy Dam, as below Hodenpyle, is subject to sudden flow rises due to discharges from the dam. It is big, deep water, and though it is wider and does not have as many sharp bends as the river upstream, large rocks, gravel bars, logs, stumps and minor logjams call for occasional precise maneuvering.

One and a half to two hours below Tippy Dam is the original site of High Bridge, a well-named and now-dismantled railroad trestle. Shortly downstream is the new, not-so-well-named High Bridge, with good access, parking and supplies near the bridge.

From High Bridge to the mouth of Bear Creek is an easy three- to four-hour trip. The river has slowed and widened to 100-200 feet and is generally three to 10 feet deep. Houses and other development are rare in this marshy stretch. During high water, there are many backwaters and side channels into broad marshlands to explore; watch especially for waterfowl. Good campsites are infrequent.

At the mouth of Bear Creek is a **public access site** with restrooms and good parking.

Bear Creek to M-55 and Manistee Lake
13.25 Miles
4-5 Hours

Wide, slow water continues past Bear Creek. The river passes entirely through lowland forests, bayous, and marshlands and is largely undeveloped. It is water better suited to powerboats than canoes, but abundant wildlife and solitude make it a pleasant trip.

Access is good at **M-55** just before Manistee Lake.

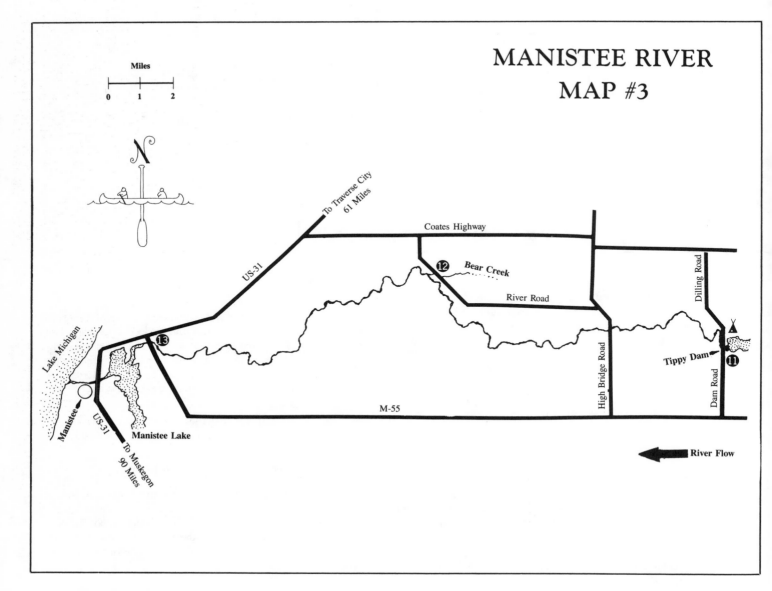

Rapids on the Upper Peninsula's Black River.
—Photo by Gail Dennis—

MUSKEGON RIVER

Counties:	**Missaukee, Roscommon, Clare, Osceola, Mecosta, Newaygo, Muskegon**
Start/End:	**Reedsburg Dam to Bridgeton**
Miles:	**170**
Gradient:	**Entire river — 4 ft/mile or less**
Portages:	**3 dams, easy to moderately difficult; one dam, very difficult**
Rapids/Falls:	**Big Rapids — Class I-II**
Campgrounds:	**Numerous**
Canoe Liveries:	**Numerous**
Skill Required:	**I**

This longest of Michigan rivers is navigable almost from its headwaters, north of Houghton Lake, to its mouth, in Lake Michigan at the city of Muskegon. And, except for fast water at Big Rapids, the entire Muskegon is well-suited for beginners and families. The dams at Rogers, Hardy and Croton ponds are the only major obstacles, and only the portage at Hardy Dam is forbidding enough to be a deterrent to passage. Like the Au Sable and Manistee, the Muskegon offers interesting opportunities for extended camping and canoeing trips. Yet, in spite of the great variety of water and terrain, good access, lots of state land and many developed campgrounds, much of the river — except for a few popular stretches — is not frequently paddled.

Fishing is good in places — rainbow and brown trout near Evart; bass, walleyes, pike and muskies elsewhere; and runs of salmon and steelhead up to Croton Dam that are exceptionally heavy and attract large numbers of fishermen.

MAP #1: REEDSBURG DAM to M-66 BRIDGE — 72.5 MILES

Reedsburg Dam to Cadillac Road Bridge
15 Miles
6-8 Hours

1 Put in either at **Reedsburg Dam** — below Houghton Lake, where there is a state-forest campground — or four miles downstream at the roadside park near M-55 Bridge. From here downstream the river is slow and meanders through lowland forests, where frequent fallen trees make progress slow.

Access at Kelly Road Bridge (Hi-Lo Bridge) is fair with limited parking.

2 Just before **Cadillac Road Bridge**, where access is fair with roadside parking, is a private campground with all facilities.

Cadillac Road Bridge to Leota Bridge
20.5 Miles
8-10 Hours

Most of the river in this section is 30-60 feet wide and one to six feet deep, with much deeper pools, and flows with slow to moderate current over sand and very occasional gravel and stone bottom. Terrain is low, though generally dry, with oaks and pines as well as lowland varieties of trees common. Most fallen trees have been cleared, but expect to go around a few. Much of the bordering land is state forest dotted with infrequent cottages.

Low Bridge on Dolph Road has fair access and parking. Within three or four miles is Camp 1, a former state-forest campground, now closed, that has been overrun by dirt bikes and other off-road vehicles. Camping is prohibited, but there are good sites on high ground and state land just downstream.

Below Camp 1 at regular intervals are Camp 2 and Camp 3. These were the sites of "beat camps" established during log drives in the mid and late 19th century. Each camp based 30 rivermen whose duties were to relay logs through the slow water and break up jams in their assigned stretch of river. Many sunken logs and stumps — further evidence of past logging activities — create minor obstacles for paddlers during low water.

Not far above the Jonesville Bridge is a stretch of gravel bottom with occasional large rocks to avoid. Moderate to moderately fast current is still far from challenging, even to beginners, although winding around obstacles will be less eventful with basic paddling skills. Take out at Jonesville Bridge, where access and parking are fair, or continue two miles to **Leota**, where access **3** and parking are good and supplies are available one-half mile west of the bridge.

Leota Bridge to M-61
23 Miles
7-9 Hours

Below Leota the river remains generally slow with sand bottom. Fed by frequent springs and small streams, it is fairly clear and cold. Width is 40-75 feet; depth is one to five feet. The terrain remains low, with maple, basswood and ash common. There are few suitable campsites, although much of the section is quiet and secluded with only a few scattered cottages.

Several tributaries join the Muskegon below Leota. Most significant is the Clam River, a fairly fast, cold trout stream that is small but that can be canoed from as far upstream as the town of Falmouth.

Access and parking are good at **Church Bridge**, on Pine **4** Road. From here to M-115 is a four- to five-hour trip that is quite popular and may be relatively crowded on summer weekends. Below the bridge the river widens to 100 feet or more, with very shallow water in summer. During low water, careless navigating will run a loaded canoe aground on sand bars and flats. At one point, the main flow of water is diverted through a narrow channel that is blocked by fallen trees. This impassable diversion creates an ox-bow of depleted riverbed, and in summer expect a quarter-mile walk through ankle-deep water that barely floats an empty canoe.

5   Access and parking are good at **M-61**. There is a state-forest campground one-half hour below the bridge. Also, high ground on state land below the campground has many good sites.

M-61 Bridge to M-66 Bridge
15.5 Miles
4-6 Hours

The river remains up to 200 feet wide and, in places, is very shallow from M-61 to M-115. Numerous houses and cottages near the bridge dwindle as you move downstream.

At M-115 Bridge, there is a private campground and canoe livery. Access is good, but private with a small fee required for use.

Between M-115 and M-66 the river is slow enough that head winds can halt progress. Most of the bordering land is private, and cottages are scattered much of the way.

6   Access and parking are good at the **M-66 Bridge**.

MUSKEGON RIVER
MAP #1

M-66 Bridge to Evart
10 Miles
3-4 Hours

The river in this section alters slightly, with perhaps more light riffles than above. Brown and rainbow trout are regularly planted and are caught along with smallmouth bass and occasional northern pike.

Between Sears Road (50th Avenue) and Evart is a private campground with supplies and good access. In Evart, there is good access and parking at the **municipal park and campground** between the first and second bridges in town.

7

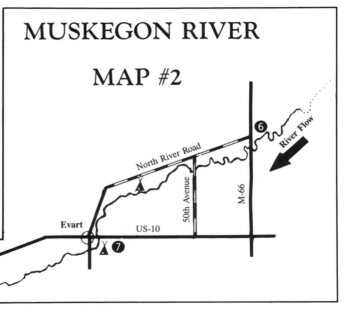

MUSKEGON RIVER
MAP #2

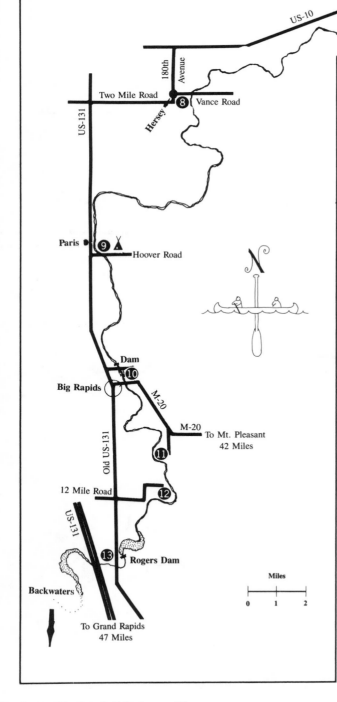

Evart to Big Rapids
28 Miles
8 1/2 - 10 1/2 Hours

Below Evart the river slows and deepens and flows through mostly uninhabited lowlands of thick underbrush and hardwoods. Slow sections alternate with light riffles. Water levels are usually sufficient for enjoyable floating.

In Hersey, there is fair access and poor parking at the **bridge on Vance Road** (Fourth Street). Supplies are available one-half mile west. **8**

In Paris, there is camping, supplies, access and parking at the **county park** just before the bridge at Hoover Road. There is a small fee for use of the access at the park. Hoover Road has no access or parking. The river to Big Rapids continues to alternate slow pools with long, gentle riffles. Width averages 150-200 feet and depth two to eight feet. **9**

In Big Rapids, there is good access and parking at several sites. At **Baldwin Street**, there is a public access on the left before the bridge. This access is immediately below a potentially dangerous low-head dam that looks runnable but must be portaged. Dangerous undertows and the added hazard of exposed reinforcing rod and broken concrete make this a poor spot to exhibit bravado. Running it is not recommended; portage on either the right or the left. From here the river quickens into riffles beneath Baldwin Street Bridge. The canoe livery and landing on the left has supplies. **10**

About 1,000 yards below the low-head dam is a stretch of Class I-II rapids. An island splits the river into two channels. The left is the smaller and is too shallow for passage except in very high water. In the right channel the bulk of the flow slides close to the right bank, creating several hundred feet of standing waves. Descent is quite steep but there are few obstructions. During high water, waves can be substantial enough to swamp an open canoe, and good judgment should be used.

Another access is at **Highbanks Park**, just south of Big Rapids. Access is good, though the climb is fairly long; parking is also good. Picnic grounds, water and toilets are available. **11**

River Bend Bluffs is a public access site about five miles below Big Rapids. It is a small site nestled between rows of cottages that line the wide, shallow river near Rogers Pond. Take out here or at the access site off US-131 just west of **Rogers Dam**. **13**

MAP #3: ROGERS DAM
to BRIDGETON — 49.5 MILES
Rogers Dam to Croton Dam
22.5 Miles
7-9 Hours

We chose not to paddle this section of virtually continuous backwaters. The portage at Rogers Dam is on the left — opposite the public access site — and is not particularly long or difficult. Several miles of slow, winding river lead to Hardy Pond. Just before the pond, off Polk Road, is Browers Park County Campground.

Hardy Pond is the largest and most formidable of the Muskegon River reservoirs. The approximatley seven-mile crossing can be difficult or dangerous due to large waves. There are several county parks and campgrounds, in addition to Newaygo County State Park, on the pond.

The portage at Hardy Dam is very long and very difficult. The left side of the dam is fenced and apparently closed to public access. On the right, across 36th Avenue, is a long, tortuous, steep and discouraging descent of at least a mile to the river. All semblance of a trail ends where the thick woods meet the thick swamp, half a mile from the river. Progress from here is determined by willpower alone.

Croton Pond is almost immediately downstream. This small pond is not a difficult crossing. Take out at the public access site

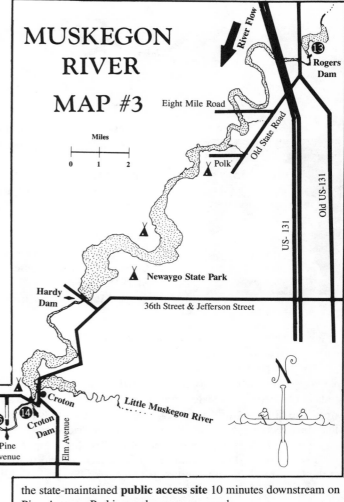

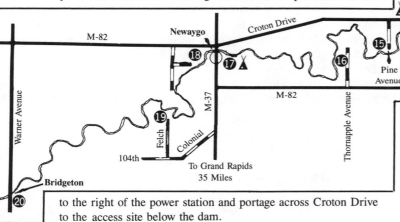

to the right of the power station and portage across Croton Drive to the access site below the dam.

Croton Dam to Newaygo
13 Miles
3-5 Hours

Access and parking are good at the county-run site below **⑭ Croton Dam**. Day-use stickers must be purchased for parking. A canoe livery and private campground with toilets, water and other facilities is located just west of the dam above the access site.

Below Croton, the Muskegon is wide and, at least until Newaygo, moderately fast. The confluence with the Little Muskegon River in Croton Pond adds significantly to water flow. It flows over a bottom of gravel and stone or sand and averages 150-200 feet wide and two to six feet deep with much deeper pools. Water levels fluctuate quite rapidly due to discharges from Croton Dam. Most discharges — announced by a warning horn — occur during early morning.

The river passes through a valley with high banks wooded with oak, maple and pine. Sections of fairly quick riffles alternate with pools of still, deep water. Houses and cottages — dense concentrations in several places — are scattered throughout much of the section.

As an alternative to the county park below Croton Dam, use

the state-maintained **public access site** 10 minutes downstream on Pine Avenue. Parking and access are good. **⑮**

One to two hours below Croton on the left, reached off Thornapple Road, is a public access known as **High Rollaway** or **⑯ Carmichal**.

On the right, shortly before the M-37 Bridge in Newaygo is a **county park** with good access and parking for a fee. There is also **⑰** fairly good access and parking on the right bank just before the bridge. Underneath the bridge is a short stretch of broken water that can be tricky for inexperienced paddlers, especially in high water. Moderately quick water continues for a mile or so, then slows and deepens. Take out at the public access site on the right, off **North River Drive** below Newaygo. **⑱**

The **public access site** on the left, off Felch Road, has good **⑲** access and parking.

Newaygo to Bridgeton
14 Miles
2 1/2 - 3 1/2 Hours

From Newaygo to Bridgeton the river remains wide and slow, with much of the bordering land uninhabited and alternating between lowland forests and high, wooded banks. Access and parking are good at the public site in **Bridgeton**. **⑳**

Below Bridgeton are 19 miles of river, then the city of Muskegon and Lake Michigan. Maple Island Bridge is approximately five hours below Newaygo. Access and parking are good at the public site before the bridge, just after the junction with the Maple River. This is the last reliable access site before the river passes into expansive marshes and enters Muskegon and Muskegon Lake.

Lower Peninsula/Muskegon River   53

OCQUEOC RIVER

County:	**Presque Isle**
Start/End:	**Sportsmen Dam Reservoir to US-23 Bridge**
Miles:	**30**
Gradient:	**Co. Rd. 638 Bridge to Ocqueoc Falls — 14.8 ft/mile**
	Ocqueoc Falls to US-23 Bridge — 4.7 ft/mile
Portages:	**Two Dams, easy; Ocqueoc Falls, fairly difficult; DNR weir, easy; occasional fallen trees and minor logjams**
Rapids/Falls:	**Numerous unnamed rapids below Co. Rd. 638 — Class I-II; Ocqueoc Falls**
Campgrounds:	**Few**
Canoe Liveries:	**One**
Skill Required:	**I-II**
Topo. Maps:	**Hawks (7.5 min.), Onaway (15 min.)**

The Ocqueoc is one of the most interesting and frequently overlooked rivers in the Lower Peninsula. It is best known for Ocqueoc Falls, a series of two- to six-foot drops and ledges that are considered the only Lower Peninsula falls of any consequence.

For our purposes, the river divides conveniently into three sections. The upper section includes a series of lakes connected by narrow, slow channels and is well-suited to beginning paddlers or those looking for remote, expedition-like trips. The middle section ends at Ocqueoc Falls State Forest Campground, just before a fairly strenuous half-mile portage around the essentially unnavigable falls area. The difficulty of that portage and numerous rapids below Co. Rd. 638 make this section a poor choice for inexperienced paddlers. The final section, from the falls to the US-23 Bridge near the mouth of the river, is a better choice. However, occasional deadfalls and logjams and lack of good access could be a problem for beginners.

Fishing is good in the entire river, with bass and northern pike predominating in the upper and lower sections and brook trout found in the Ocqueoc Falls area and most tributaries. Spring and fall runs of steelhead and salmon are said to be good.

Sportsmen Dam Reservoir to Co. Rd. 638 Bridge (Millersburg Road)
10.5 Miles
4-5 Hours

The Ocqueoc is often considered to begin in Lake Emma, but we put in farther upstream at Sportsmen Dam Reservoir. This is beautiful, uncivilized country — if you can find it. Take Co. Rd. 638 out of Millersburg to Lake May Road. Just past Lake May (visible on the right), turn right, on gravel 634 Highway and follow it south 1.25 miles. A half-mile after the road bends west past an area of open marshes, watch for a **two-track road** almost immediately after the marsh gives way to high ground and hardwoods. There is good access and parking at the end of this short two-track trail. The reservoir is undeveloped, bordered by forests of pine and hardwoods, and rimmed with lily pads. Water is remarkably clear, and fishing is excellent for largemouth bass and northern pike. Much of the shoreline is privately owned, which strictly limits camping.

Portage the small dam at the north end of the pond and put into the river — hardly more than a creek — below. With depths of two to six feet, the river is nearly as deep as it is wide, but passage is easier than it looks. Tight bends might seem to bring the bow-man back to meet the stern-man, but we made it through without much difficulty in our 17-foot-nine-inch Sawyer. There is good fishing in the deeper holes. The current is almost imperceptible — just strong enough to point aquatic weeds downstream. Pass through a long stretch of marshes as the river gradually widens and gains depth. Signs of civilization begin to appear near Lake Nettie, and the shoreline of the lake is spotted with cottages.

Once in the lake, bear right — around the first point to the **public access site** on the southeast shore — or continue across the remainder of Lake Nettie and portage the small water-control dam. Beyond, there are several smaller lakes plus a stretch of slow, fairly shallow river before Millersburg.

At Millersburg, there is a **community park and public access site** just south of the village at the Co. Rd. 638 Bridge.

Co. Rd. 638 Bridge to Ocqueoc Falls Forest Campground
6.75 Miles
2 1/2 - 3 1/2 Hours

From Millersburg to Ocqueoc Falls expect a lively trip through a great variety of water. Average descent through this section is the fastest of any Lower Peninsula river. At the Co. Rd. 638 Bridge, the river is narrow (15-25 feet) and fairly slow until past the first bends, where stretches of quite-fast water begin. Riffles and light rapids alternate with slow pools the remainder of the distance to Ocqueoc Falls, with some narrow chutes requiring precise maneuvering and occasional fallen trees needing to be negotiated. This section is best run in spring or early summer during high water; low water exposes shallow riffles and rock gardens, some of which will have to be walked through. Rocks on the Ocqueoc are irregular, sharp and hard on canoe hulls. An abrupt four-foot falls, locally known as Chipmunk Falls, follows a stretch of slow water. It can be run, we found, but only at the price of a battered boat. The terrain is largely upland forest of mixed hardwoods and conifers with cedars and aspens near the

OCQUEOC RIVER

Miles

0   1   2

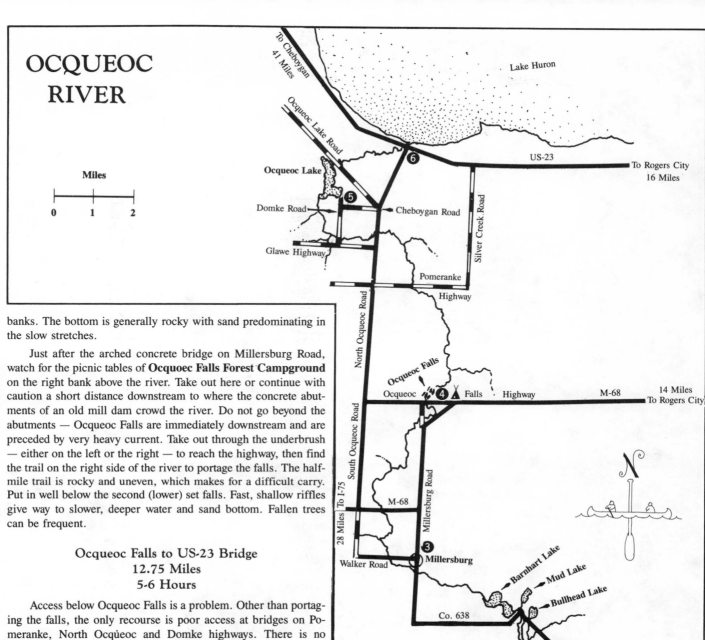

banks. The bottom is generally rocky with sand predominating in the slow stretches.

4   Just after the arched concrete bridge on Millersburg Road, watch for the picnic tables of **Ocquoec Falls Forest Campground** on the right bank above the river. Take out here or continue with caution a short distance downstream to where the concrete abutments of an old mill dam crowd the river. Do not go beyond the abutments — Ocqueoc Falls are immediately downstream and are preceded by very heavy current. Take out through the underbrush — either on the left or the right — to reach the highway, then find the trail on the right side of the river to portage the falls. The half-mile trail is rocky and uneven, which makes for a difficult carry. Put in well below the second (lower) set falls. Fast, shallow riffles give way to slower, deeper water and sand bottom. Fallen trees can be frequent.

Ocqueoc Falls to US-23 Bridge
12.75 Miles
5-6 Hours

Access below Ocqueoc Falls is a problem. Other than portaging the falls, the only recourse is poor access at bridges on Pomeranke, North Ocqueoc and Domke highways. There is no parking at Pomeranke and only limited roadside parking at the other bridges. The river is steady, with moderate but heavy current. The water is dark — stained by passage through swamps — and water depths vary from three to eight feet. The bottom is generally sand. Meadows, farmlands and cedar swamps alternate, and there are occasional short stretches of rock bottom and light riffles. Be alert for farmers' low wires stretched across the river.

From North Ocqueoc Highway is a one-hour float through thick cedars and tag alders to Ocqueoc Lake. The current is stronger than it looks, and a few tricky eddies at bends, as well as at least one logjam, require attention. Just before Ocqueoc Lake the river divides into channels. During low water, portage the sandbars that form. Follow the right shoreline of the lake to the

5   **public access site**.

Just below the lake, portage the DNR lamprey control station at Ocqueoc Lake Road Bridge — get out on the left side and take the trail around the fence. The river here is 35-50 feet wide with strong current and deep holes. It widens and slows the final mile or two before US-23 and the mouth.

6   At **US-23 Bridge**, there are supplies and a private launching site, where access, for a small fee, is good.

PERE MARQUETTE RIVER

Counties:	Lake, Mason
Start/End:	M-37 Bridge to M-31 Bridge at Ludington
Miles:	56
Gradient:	M-37 to Sulak Landing — 5 ft/mile
	Sulak Landing to Ludington — 2 ft/mile
Portages:	Occasional fallen trees in upper sections
Rapids/Falls:	Rainbow Rapids below Rainbow Rapids Landing — Class I
Campgrounds:	Numerous
Canoe Liveries:	Numerous
Skill Required:	I

The Pere Marquette is one of Michigan's finest and best-known rivers. It is a very popular river, both with fishermen and canoeists, and on summer weekends it can be difficult to have very sizable stretches to yourself. Canoe traffic, like that on the Au Sable, Pine and a few other rivers, is heavy enough to create problems on occasion. In an effort to monitor canoeing on the Pere Marquette, in 1983 the U.S. Forest Service implemented a permit system similar to the one in use on the Pine River. There is no fee for the permits — which are required from May 10 to September 20 — and they can be picked up at the ranger station on M-37 at the south end of Baldwin or at canoe liveries in the area. (See Appendix IV, "Permits and Special Regulations", page 130.)

The Pere Marquette, at the time of this writing, is the only Michigan river — and one of only about two dozen in the country — to be included in the National Wild and Scenic Rivers Program. Although it is, for the most part, a fairly gentle river, water fluctuations are quite extreme, with high levels common in early spring. Low water will seldom be a problem. The opposite is more likely to be true, with heavy rains sometimes raising water levels and current speed to a degree that beginning paddlers might find challenges their abilities.

In 1884 the Pere Marquette was the site of the first planting of brown trout in North America, and it has been first-class trout water ever since. Spring and fall runs of steelhead and salmon are some of the heaviest in the state. Special regulations include an extended season (currently April 1 - December 31) up to M-37 Bridge and flies-only from Gleason's Landing up to M-37 Bridge.

Much of the river passes through national forest land, where good campsites and developed campgrounds are plentiful.

M-37 Bridge to Bowman Bridge (Carr's Road)
11 Miles
3 1/2 - 5 Hours

1 Put in at the **M-37 Bridge** south of Baldwin or go upstream one-half mile to Forks Landing. Both are fine, well-maintained access sites with restrooms and plenty of parking.

This first section is quite representative of the entire upper river. The current is steady, moderately fast and not difficult during normal water levels for paddlers with basic skills. The river follows a winding course of switchbacks and sharp bends that makes for many more river miles than expected. Terrain is largely wooded and hilly, with white and red oak predominating and tag alders and cedars near the water. High banks on the bends were often used as high rollaways during the logging era. There are occasional fallen trees, stumps and minor logjams to avoid. The river averages 40-60 feet wide and one to three feet deep with very deep holes at the bends. Bottom is sand and gravel. The water is generally clear and clean but it tends to cloud quicky after rain. There are not many houses and cottages in this section, especially after the first few miles below the bridge.

2 There is a USFS campground, with primitive facilities and no fee, at **Gleason's Landing**. Access and parking are good. From here downstream the river slows and deepens somewhat as it flows through mostly uninhabited upland forests.

3 There is access off **Bowman Bridge** (Carr's Road), but parking is limited to the roadside. Ten minutes downstream, there is a public access site with good access and parking. Camping is permitted (all facilities) at Bowman Bridge Recreation Area.

Bowman Bridge to Sulak Landing
10.5 Miles
3-4 Hours

Below Bowman Bridge the current remains moderate with many stretches of slow, deep water. Shortly before Rainbow Rapids Landing the current quickens until it runs fairly fast over gravel and stone riffles. Terrain remains similar to above — high hills of hardwoods predominate and a few meadows and open banks appear. There are few houses, but much of the bordering land is private, including a very large private holding in the middle of the section, where access to the banks is prohibited.

4 Rainbow Rapids are a short distance below the access and parking site at **Rainbow Rapids Landing**. They are a short, fast Class I run over gravel and rock, with two or three easy bends to negotiate. Although not recommended for absolute beginners, they should present no real challenge for anyone with moderate paddling experience. From here to Sulak the river remains relatively fast with numerous riffles over gravel bars and occasional pumpkin-size rocks. Terrain is high banks and hardwoods. There are a few scattered cottages and occasional secluded campsites on national forest land.

5 Access and parking are good at the public site at **Sulak Landing**.

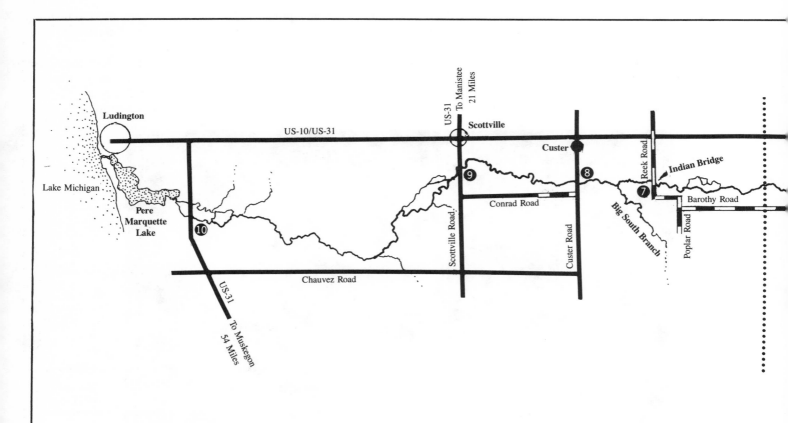

PERE MARQUETTE RIVER

Sulak Landing to Custer Bridge
16.5 Miles
5-7 Hours

Below Sulak the river slows and widens into the large water typical of the lower Pere Marquette. Current is slow to moderate, bottom is consistently sand, and water is deep and often clouded.

6 Good access and parking are found at **Upper Branch Bridge** (South Branch Road) and at Lower Branch Bridge (Landon Road).

Access and parking are good at the public site at Walhalla Road Bridge. Below here the river is 60-75 feet wide and is slow and deep. Terrain is largely lowlands of hardwoods and tag alders down to swamps of drowned timber. Shortly below Walhalla Bridge is the "spreads," an area of marshlands where the river divides into channels and subchannels that meander around sandbars and islands of cattails and tag alders. There seems to be no single best way through; some channels, however, are more congested than others. Be prepared to walk through some shallows in summer. The river gathers itself together again for a time, enters lowland forests, then — a half-mile or so before Indian Bridge — divides again through a swamp of cedar, tag alder and drowned timber. Here the channels are narrow and deep; all seem negotiable and lead to the bridge.

7 Access and parking are good at **Indian Bridge** (Reek Road).

From Indian Bridge to Custer Road Bridge is a 2.5-mile stretch of wide, slow water. The Big South Branch of the Pere Marquette joins here and swells the mainstream by half again. This major tributary can be canoed from as far upstream as Huntley Bridge (Dickerson Road) in Newaygo County. From there to the junction with the mainstream is a 10- to 12-hour trip through a variety of lowlands and wooded hills. Current is generally slow with a few stretches of moderately fast water over gravel and stone bottom. Fallen trees create frequent obstructions.

About a mile below the junction with the Big South Branch is **Custer Bridge** with good access and parking. **8**

Custer Bridge to M-31 Bridge (Ludington)
18 Miles
4-5 Hours

This final section remains wide and slow and passes mostly through lowland forests. It is more often navigated in powerboats than in canoes.

There is camping at **Scottville Park** (all facilities), before the **9** bridge in Scottville. Access and parking are available downstream from the bridge as well as at the Scottville Park.

Access and parking are good and supplies are available at the **M-31 Bridge** south of Ludington. Here, the river is slow, wide **10** and often split into channels that pass through extensive marshlands. Pere Marquette Lake is immediately downstream.

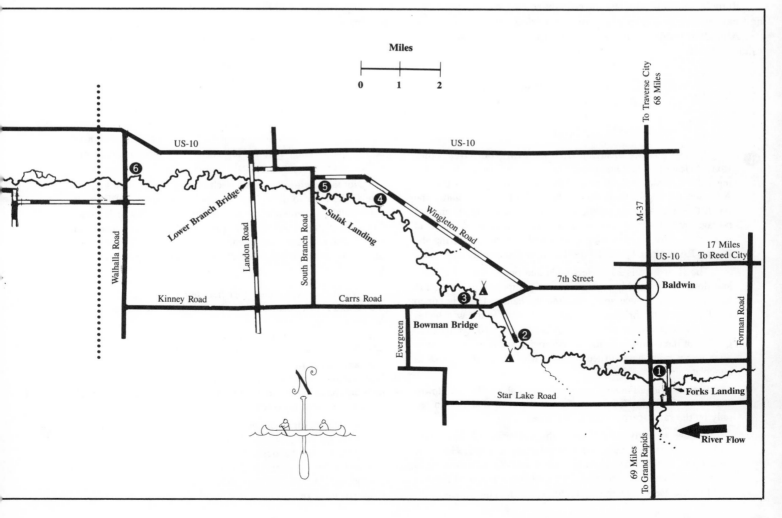

PIGEON RIVER

Counties:	Otsego, Cheboygan
Start/End:	Sturgeon River Valley Road Bridge to Mullet Lake
Miles:	28.5
Gradient:	Pigeon River Road to below M-68 — 14.3 ft/mile
	All other sections average — 9.3 ft/mile
Portages:	Numerous fallen trees, logjams and beaver dams — easy to difficult
Rapids/Falls:	Numerous unnamed rapids from Pigeon River Road to below M-68 — Class I-II
Campgrounds:	Several
Canoe Liveries:	Few
Skill Required:	I-II
Topo. Maps:	Heatherton, Tower, Wolverine (15 min.)

Flowing through the heart of the Pigeon River Country State Forest, the Pigeon is one of the Lower Peninsula's most beautiful and remote rivers. In recent years, controversy surrounding oil and natural-gas drilling in the Pigeon River State Forest has focused much attention on the river, resulting in an increase in the numbers of canoeists, fishermen and campers. Purist wilderness paddlers will be pleased to note, however, that the Pigeon has remained unspoiled and continues to maintain large numbers of fallen trees, logjams, beaver dams and other challenges. One of Michigan's Wild-Scenic Rivers, the Pigeon is well within the range of the only elk herd in the state.

Remote sections and fast current make this river a poor choice for inexperienced paddlers. The swift current and extremely sharp and narrow bends — especially during periods of high water — will test maneuvering skills of even experienced paddlers.

Abundant public land and several developed campgrounds make camping opportunities excellent. Fishing is for brook, brown and rainbow trout.

Sturgeon River Valley Road Bridge
to Red Bridge (Webb Road)
12 Miles
5-7 Hours

1 A short distance upstream from the **Sturgeon River Valley Road Bridge** is a dam and private pond at the Song of the Morning Ranch. (Many county maps label it "Lansing Club Pond.") Although the Pigeon is navigable for a short distance above the pond, the river there is small, fallen trees are common, and the portage around the dam is a nuisance. Sturgeon River Valley Road is a more convenient starting point, with the river entering the Pigeon River Country State Forest a short distance downstream.

The river here is 25-40 feet wide and one to three feet deep and flows fairly quickly over gravel and pumpkin-size rocks. Tag alders, poplars, spruce and pines line the banks. There is fair to good access at the bridge, with parking limited to a few vehicles at the roadside; better parking is found in a lot 100 yards east. Quality of the clear to slightly tea-colored water is excellent, even after heavy rains have turned other nearby rivers and creeks to chocolate.

Pigeon Bridge Forest Campground is a short distance downstream on the right. It is unmarked at the river and recognized only by the sand-scarred trail to the water.

Passage is fairly easy through the beginning of the section with only a few sweepers and downed trees to avoid. However, tight turns in the quick current make basic maneuvering skills necessary. Even competent paddlers, especially in loaded canoes, will find themselves being swept into the brush at the river's edge.

The terrain continues to be wooded low hills but alternates occasionally with small open meadows and marshes.

About seven miles downstream from Sturgeon River Valley Road is **Pigeon River Forest Campground** with primitive facilities. Just downstream at an unmarked road is a bridge with fair access and parking. Take the left culvert and stay left to negotiate a short drop over jumbled rocks and boulders. **2**

Not far downstream is a stretch of very old logjams that have caused the river to divide into channels. Passage is difficult. We got through by combining portaging, lining, paddling and cussing. Chest waders are a definite advantage. Fast current in places compounds the difficulty, and some channels that can be negotiated require advanced techniques such as draw strokes, pry strokes and back strokes.

When the river comes together into a single channel again, the respite is brief thanks to beavers that have, at least at the time of this writing, placed a large dam across the entire width of the river. Portage is difficult but possible through the thick and partially flooded woods on the right. We found a partial break in the dam and ran it like any whitewater chute, with tree trunks and face-slapping branches adding an air of novelty. The river from here alternates tight bends and fast, boulder-studded riffles with stretches of slow, deep water.

By **Tin Bridge**, the current, though moderately strong in **3** places, is generally slower than above. Access and parking are fair. The terrain becomes mostly lowlands which edge many drowned trees. Between Tin Bridge and Pine Grove Forest Campground, we encountered one narrow chute through a logjam that required lining or portaging.

4   **Pine Grove Forest Campground** is recognized by a trail down a short, steep bank on the right. A bend or two later is a wooden footbridge across the river that gives sure identification.

5   **Red Bridge** is on Webb Road about an hour downstream from the campground. Shortly before the bridge the current increases, with riffles over gravel and rock bottom. Low hills and upland forests predominate. At the bridge, access is good and parking is limited.

Red Bridge to Clement Road Bridge at Mullett Lake
16.5 Miles
6-8 Hours

From Red Bridge to M-68 the river is serviced by at least one canoe livery, and passage is cleared and better-suited to beginning canoeists than in the section above. Although there is mostly private property in the vicinity of Red Bridge, a quarter-mile downstream the river again enters state forest, where camping potential is good. An often-used clearing and campsite with access to Montgomery Road is known as McIntosh Landing. Beyond here is a long stretch of lowlands and thick brush with very few possible campsites. Plan to end a day-long trip no farther than McIntosh Landing unless there is time to make the two- to three-hour trip to Pigeon River Bridge (Pigeon River Road). The river through this stretch is slow, sand-bottomed and lined with thickets of tag alders. The current is slow to moderate.

6   **Pigeon River Road Bridge** has good access and fair roadside parking. From here the current increases dramatically; expect five to six miles of nearly continuous riffles and light rapids. The bottom is composed of bedrock, gravel and rocks to bushel-size. Descent is steep enough that high water in the spring and after heavy rains makes this one of the longest and most interesting fast-water stretches in the Lower Peninsula. Summer levels are apt to be low enough that some bottom-scraping will occur. Paddlers with basic maneuvering skills should not have difficulty except in the stretch below M-68 or during very high water.

Afton Road Bridge, one-half hour below Pigeon River Road, has good access and good, though limited, parking.

7   Another 15 minutes downstream is the **M-68 Bridge**, with good parking and access downstream on the right. The fast water to here contains few serious obstructions — other than scattered boulders — through rock gardens and shallow riffles. It is an easy, relaxing run that can easily lull a paddler into overconfidence. Below M-68 the current continues fast, but the riverbed changes character: Bends suddenly become very sharp, and fallen trees and sweepers create unexpected hazards. Inexperienced paddlers will find this water frustrating and dangerous, especially during high-water periods, and should avoid it. Except for houses and cottages near M-68, there is no access — in case of emergency — for seven miles until Mullett Lake. Much of this section is within state forest, but lowlands make good campsites infrequent.

About three miles below M-68 the current slows, and an inactive beaver dam has created a major logjam. This is another difficult portage with no clear or marked trail. We portaged left and walked our canoe down a small side channel 100 yards until we found the main river. Another small jam just downstream may require portaging.

In the final miles before Mullett Lake, the river divides into spreads, with some channels blocked by logjams and some too shallow to float through. The bottom is sand, and the current is steady to slow until the final stretch of reeds and cattails, when it slows to enter Mullett Lake.

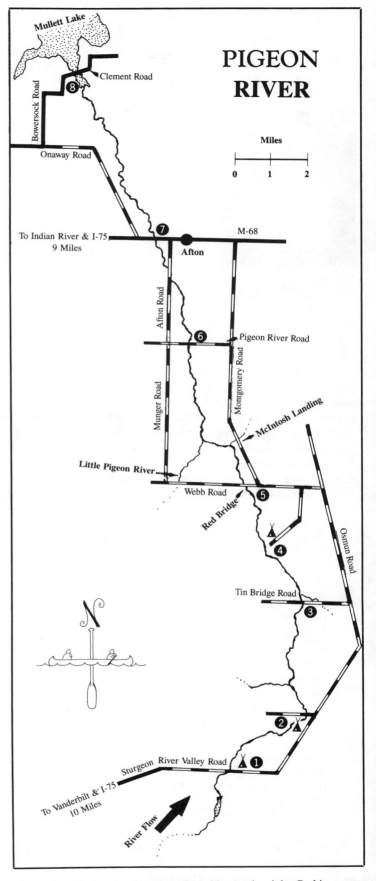

Access at Clement Road is at the bridge on the right. Parking is limited to the roadside off the bridge approach. Supplies are available one-eighth mile east.   **8**

PINE RIVER

Counties:	**Lake, Wexford, Manistee**
Start/End:	**Edgetts Bridge (Raymond Road) to Low Bridge (Tower Line Road)**
Miles:	**38.5**
Gradient:	**9.9 ft/mile**
Portages:	**One dam, easy; occasional fallen trees and minor logjams**
Rapids/Falls:	**Numerous unnamed rapids above and below Peterson Bridge — Class I-II**
Campgrounds:	**Several**
Canoe Liveries:	**Numerous**
Skill Required:	**I-II**

Besides being a beautiful and largely unspoiled river —and one being considered as a National Wild and Scenic River — the Pine also has one of the fastest average flows of any Lower Peninsula river. The major problem on the Pine today is simply that it is sometimes too popular. Summer weekends demonstrate the irony implicit in a such a river: The virtues that make it appealing in the first place can sometimes lead to its misuse. According to U.S. Forest Service data, more than 2,000 canoes a week — most of them on the weekends — were counted between Lincoln Bridge and Low Bridge in July and August 1978.

In an effort to prevent the river from suffering from such heavy use, the U.S. Forest Service implemented an experimental permit system on the Pine, the first of its kind in Michigan. The system requires permits on any craft that enters or leaves the river using national forest land (which is virtually every public access site) in the Pine River "corridor" between May 1 and October 1. The corridor is defined as the land one-quarter mile on each side of the river in the last 26 miles of river, roughly from Lincoln Bridge to the mouth at Tippy Pond. Camping is prohibited in the corridor, except at Peterson Bridge Campground, and the number of watercraft allowed on the river is limited. For more information about regulations and advance permit reservations, see Appendix IV, page 130, "Permits and Special Regulations."

Aside from crowded summer weekends and the mild inconvenience of permits, the Pine remains one of Michigan's favorite rivers. For canoeists and kayakers, much of the appeal is undoubtedly the fast water and light rapids in the Peterson Bridge area. For fishermen, the appeal is healthy populations of brook, brown and rainbow trout.

Edgetts Bridge (Raymond Road) to Elm Flats
18 Miles
5 - 6 1/2 Hours

① Although we begin our description at **Edgetts Bridge**, access and parking there are only fair. Much better access is found at the two public sites below Skookum Bridge.

This upper section passes through mostly wooded hills of hardwoods and pines with cedars and tag alders near the river. It averages 25-40 feet wide and one to four feet deep with pools to six feet. Fallen trees and minor logjams occasionally block the river, especially in the spring. Current is moderate to fairly quick over sand and gravel. There are occasional houses and cottages.

Meadowbrook Bridge is out.

② Private property prevents access or parking at **Skookum Bridge**. However, there are two public sites with good access and parking within one-half mile downstream. Within one-quarter mile of the lower access site begins an eight- mile stretch of private property belonging to the Ne-bo-shone Club, where access to the banks is prohibited. The area is clearly posted.

③ There is no access at Walker Bridge (State Road), but **Silver Creek Forest Campground** is just downstream and has good access and parking.

④ **Lincoln Bridge** (10 Mile Road) is out, but there is a public site at Lincoln Bridge Forest Campground with good access and parking. From here downstream, special Pine River corridor regulations are in effect.

Elm Flats (off 11 1/4 Road) has good access and parking at a public site. **⑤**

Elm Flats to Peterson Bridge (M-37)
12.5 Miles
3 1/2 - 5 Hours

Below Elm Flats, there is some quick water, but generally the current remains steady and moderately strong with many tight bends and switchbacks. High banks at the bends are often eroded and should not be disturbed.

Dobson Bridge (50 Road) has a designated launch site with **⑥** good parking, toilets and water. From here the current speed increases slightly, and light riffles become more frequent. Some tight bends are tricky for beginners and will pull unwary paddlers into trees and logs.

High School Road Bridge has no access. From here to beyond Peterson Bridge, fast water and light rapids predominate. While the rapids don't amount to much by most whitewater standards, scattered bushel-size and larger rocks and bedrock ledges create small standing waves and require a fair amount of maneuvering. Usually rated Class I or Class II in high water, these moderately challenging rapids create their share of mischief. Although we do not recommend the Pine for anyone without basic maneuvering skills, beginners often float it and often come away telling stories that serve to enhance the Pine's reputation for being a difficult river. We have heard of no drownings or serious injuries, but the potential for them certainly exists for careless or inexperienced paddlers. Generally, stay to the inside of bends and avoid the larger rocks. No rapids require scouting, but beginners should go slowly and wear floatation devices. In spring, standing waves will occasionally reach two feet but will not be dangerous except, perhaps, in unusually high flood stages.

7 Access and parking are good at **Peterson Bridge** at M-37. There are restrooms and water there, as well as a USFS campground.

Peterson Bridge to Low Bridge (Tower Line Road)
8 Miles
2 1/2 - 3 1/2 Hours

Fast water extends much of the way between Peterson Bridge and Stronach Dam. Many narrow chutes formed by underwater rock ledges can simply be ruddered through. Some tight bends require more strenuous paddling techniques, especially draw strokes. Nowhere, however, are there hazards that paddlers with basic skills can't handle.

There is little streamside development in this section. High banks, up to 100 feet, line the river, and hardwoods and pines predominate, with scattered thickets of willows, cedars and tag alders near the water.

The river gradually slows and widens as it approaches Stronach Dam. Portage on the left. There is access to the dam via a two-track from the south, but it is a poor, badly marked road and is not recommended.

Low Bridge is 10-15 minutes below the dam on Tower Line **8** Road and has good access and somewhat limited parking on Consumers Power Company land. Just downstream is M-55, with poor access, and Tippy Pond, on the Manistee River, beyond it.

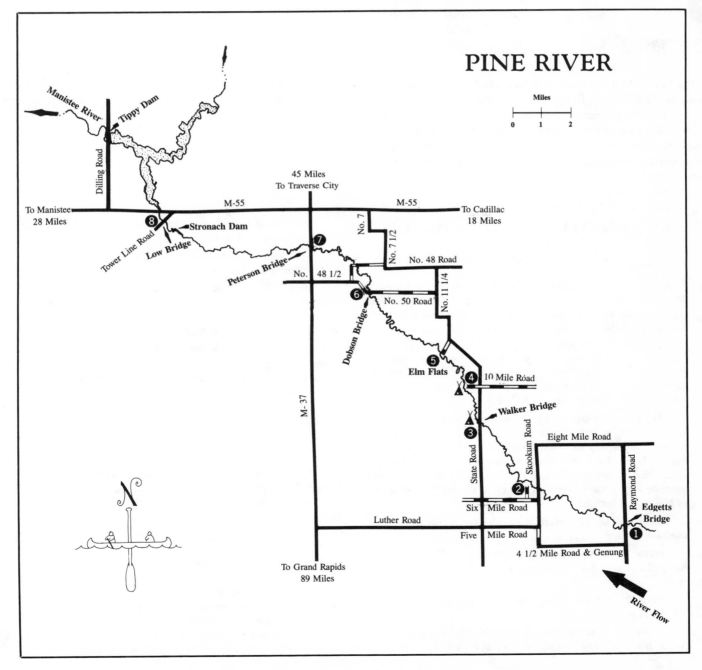

PLATTE RIVER

County:	**Benzie**
Start/End:	**US-31 Bridge to Lake Michigan**
Miles:	**16**
Gradient:	**US-31 Bridge to Platte Lake — 12.9 ft/mile**
	Platte Lake to mouth — 2.7 ft/mile
Portages:	**DNR weir, easy; occasional fallen trees and logjams**
Rapids/Falls:	**None**
Campgrounds:	**Several**
Canoe Liveries:	**Several**
Skill Required:	**I**

The Platte has a reputation that far exceeds its small size. Known for years as a fine trout stream, it has, since the late 1960s, become famous as the site of the first plantings of Pacific salmon in Michigan. Salmon runs are so heavy today that paddlers attempting autumn trips will literally be bumping the backs of cohos and Chinooks.

Platte Lake divides the river into upper and lower sections, with the upper tending to be shallow and quick and the lower being slow and serene. Summer canoeing is popular in the section from M-22 to the mouth of the river; the upper section will rarely be crowded. State-forest campgrounds are found along both the upper and lower reaches.

US-31 Bridge to M-22 Bridge Below Platte Lake
12 Miles
4-5 Hours

❶ Access and parking are good at the **US-31 Bridge** at Veteran's Memorial State Forest Campground, which has toilets, water and a picnic area. The river here is small — 30-40 feet wide and one to 2-1/2 feet deep — and flows quickly over gravel and small stones. Water is clear and clean. Shallow riffles will not float a loaded canoe during low-water periods. Logs and fallen trees often obstruct the upper reaches of this section, causing it to be generally not recommended. Passage is much clearer and the river is wider below Pioneer Road Bridge

The terrain through the upper reaches to the village of Honor consists of rolling hills of upland forests, with cedars common on the valley floor near the river. Banks are consistently wooded, as high as 100-150 feet and quite steep in places. Much of the bordering land is state-owned, although there are intervals of private property with scattered cottages as well as several concentrations of houses and cottages.

Just below US-31 is Haze Road, with fair access and limited roadside parking.

❷ **Platte River State Forest Campground**, off Goose Road, has parking, primitive camping facilities and good access to the river.

North Pioneer Road Bridge has fair access and limited roadside parking.

In Honor, there are bridges at South Street and at Henry Street, but access and parking are poor at both sites.

Just west of Honor the river is accessible off US-31, but parking is prohibited on the roadside.

A few hundred yards downstream at Indian Hill Road Bridge, there is fair access but no parking.

Below Indian Hill Road the river slows and deepens as it enters swamps before Platte Lake. The lake is three miles long and not a difficult crossing, although prevailing west winds can be tedious and can raise high waves.

A short distance below Platte Lake is the M-22 Bridge; good access, parking, camping and other facilities are available at the **Platte River State Forest Campground**, below the bridge on the right. Stores at the bridge have canoe rentals and supplies. **❸**

M-22 Bridge to Rivermouth at Lake Michigan
4 Miles
1 1/2 - 2 1/2 Hours

This short trip through the Sleeping Bear Dunes National Lakeshore is a popular summer float and ideal for beginners and families with small children. The river is 50-70 feet wide and two to five feet deep, with consistently slow to moderate current over mostly sand bottom. The river valley is shallow and wooded with assorted pines and hardwoods. Cedars are common close to the water. Much of the bordering land is publicly owned, but there are frequent, though widely spaced, houses and cottages.

The remainder of the section is through low hills and an increasing number of open sand dunes. Junipers and other flora are abundant. Take out at the launch ramp one mile from the end of the river or go to the **public access site at the mouth**, where **❹** there is good access and parking as well as toilets and water.

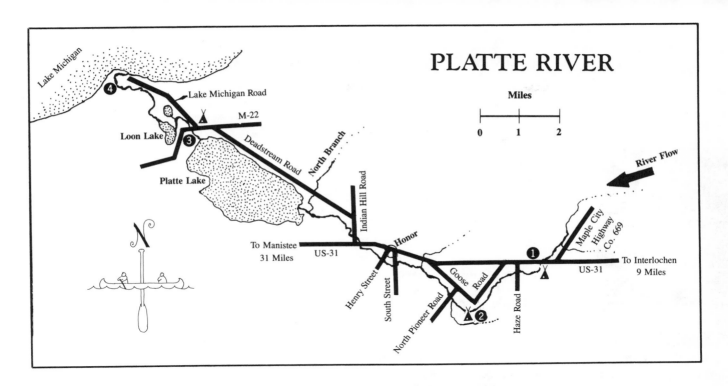

PLATTE RIVER

Miles

0 1 2

River Flow

Lake Michigan

④

Lake Michigan Road

M-22

Loon Lake

③

Platte Lake

Deadstream Road

North Branch

Indian Hill Road

Honor

①

Maple City Highway Co. 669

N

To Manistee 31 Miles

US-31

Henry Street

South Street

Goose Road

North Pioneer Road

②

Haze Road

To Interlochen 9 Miles

US-31

RIFLE RIVER

Counties:	**Ogemaw, Arenac**
Start/End:	**Sage Lake Road Bridge to Stover Road Bridge**
Miles:	**47**
Gradient:	**Sage Lake Road to Maple Ridge Road — 5.7 ft/mile**
	Other sections — 3 ft/mile or less
Portages:	**Occasional fallen trees**
Rapids/Falls:	**Overhead Pipeline Rapids, below M-55 — Class I-II**
	Unnamed rapids below Greenwood Road — Class I
Campgrounds:	**Several**
Canoe Liveries:	**Numerous**
Skill Required:	**I**

Emerging from a cluster of lakes and small streams in the Rifle River Recreation Area, near the town of Lupton in northeast Ogemaw County, the Rifle begins as a small, clear sand- and gravel-bottom trout stream. Attractive surroundings, generally clear water flowing through pools and riffles, and two locally acclaimed rapids are reasons the Rifle ranks with the Au Sable, Manistee and other high-quality Michigan rivers. A designated Michigan Wild-Scenic Natural River, it is popular and well-suited to either short trips or expeditions of several days. Summer weekends can be crowded.

Water levels seem to fluctuate greatly — spring flooding is common; summer levels are sometimes so low that canoes must be walked through some shallow riffles and rock gardens. Paddlers with basic skills should have no problem negotiating both sets of Rifle River rapids during normal water levels.

Campgrounds and public land in the upper section are abundant. Fishing is good for both resident trout and anadromous salmon and steelhead, with an extended season, currently from April 1 to October 1, up to Sage Lake Road.

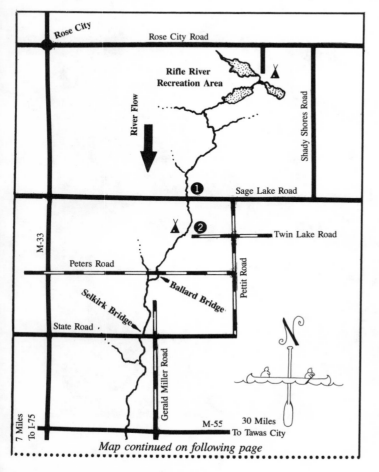

Map continued on following page

Sage Lake Road Bridge (White Ash Bridge) to Maple Ridge Road Bridge (Moffatt Bridge)
24 Miles
8 - 9 1/2 Hours

It is possible to put in above Sage Lake Road in the Rifle River Recreation Area and work down the small river to **Sage Lake Road**, where parking and access are good. At the bridge the river is small — 25-40 feet wide and one to two feet deep — with rock-strewn bottom and moderate current. Terrain is lowland forests with thickets of poplars and tag alders at the banks.

About one-half hour below Sage Lake Road is a **state-forest campground** with good access and parking and primitive facilities. Except for several campgrounds in the Recreation Area above Sage Lake Road, this is the only public campground on the river.

Ballard Bridge on Peters Road has fair access and limited parking.

Selkirk Bridge on State Road has poor access due to private property. The river here is clear and quick, with stretches of riffles over gravel and rock alternating with smooth glides and pools. Water volume has increased as a result of tributaries and springs, and width has increased to 30-50 feet. Low hills of hardwoods, with some pines and cedars, border the river, and there are occasional low areas and open banks. Much of the bordering land from here downstream is private property with scattered houses and cottages. Some shallow riffles are bottom-bumpers in low water. Also, pick your way around rocks in boulder gardens and over the artificial reefs of stones and boulders that property owners have erected.

Access — with a steep trail to the river — is poor at M-55, and parking is very limited. Below here, pools and riffles continue to alternate, the water is generally deeper, and there are several long stretches of nearly still water. Some tight bends may be tricky in high water.

About four miles below M-55 are Overhead Pipeline Rapids,

gets increasingly slower and is fairly deep with sand bottom. Terrain remains similar to above, with pines abundant and streamside houses and cottages infrequent.

Greenwood Road Bridge has limited parking and fair access down a steep, slippery bank. There is better access and parking (for a fee) at the canoe livery and private campground just upstream from the bridge.

Shortly after Greenwood is another short set of rapids similar to the ones at Overhead Pipeline. Again, solid rock shelves and small ledges create standing waves and minor chutes during high water. In summer we walked through in our tennis shoes. From here to Moffatt Bridge, on Maple Ridge Road, the river is wide and shallow with frequent, shallow riffles, and there are many rocks to avoid. The current is slow to moderate; the water tends toward murkiness. Cottages are scattered much of the way.

Access and parking are good both above and below **Moffatt Bridge**.

Moffatt Bridge (Maple Ridge Road)
to Stover Road Bridge
22.5 Miles
6 1/2 - 8 1/2 Hours

From Moffatt Bridge to Old M-70 (Melita Road) the river remains wide (to 100 feet) and alternates slow pools with shallow riffles. Pick your way around stones and through the deeper channels in summer.

At Old M-70 (Melita Road), there is a **public site**, with good access and parking 200 yards downstream from the bridge and a private campground with supplies near the bridge. From here to Omer, riffles over gravel and stone bottom alternate with sand bottom and slow water.

At Pinnacle Bridge, on Grove Road, there is a private campground, but access at the bridge is private.

Near Omer the best access is at a **public site** on River Road downstream from the city. A few light riffles here give way finally to slow, discolored water over sand and clay bottom.

There is poor access and parking at Hickory Island Bridge.

Stover Road Bridge has fair access and roadside parking. This is the last access before the Rifle opens into marshlands, then empties into Saginaw Bay.

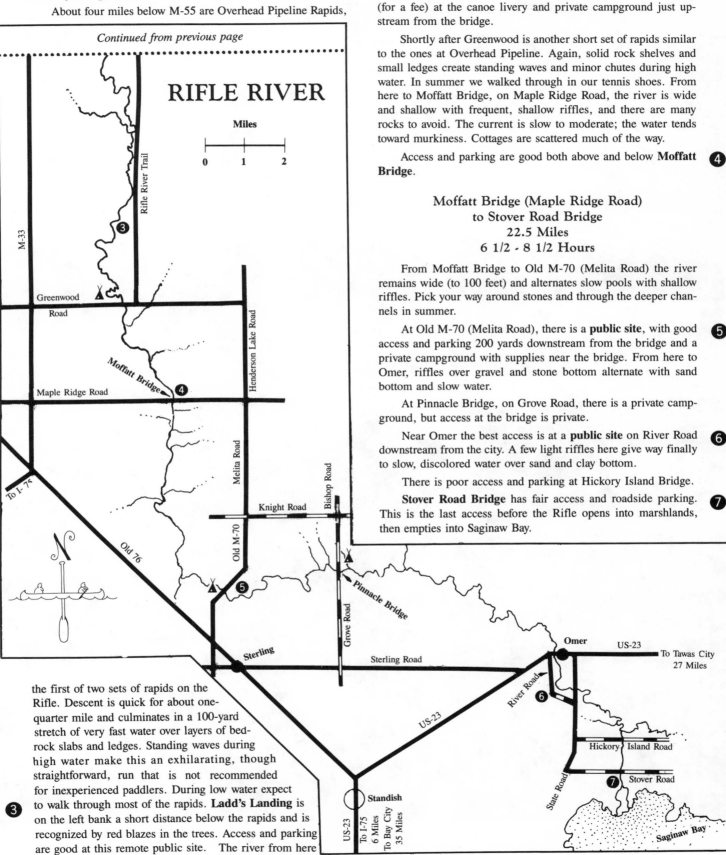

the first of two sets of rapids on the Rifle. Descent is quick for about one-quarter mile and culminates in a 100-yard stretch of very fast water over layers of bedrock slabs and ledges. Standing waves during high water make this an exhilarating, though straightforward, run that is not recommended for inexperienced paddlers. During low water expect to walk through most of the rapids. **Ladd's Landing** is on the left bank a short distance below the rapids and is recognized by red blazes in the trees. Access and parking are good at this remote public site. The river from here

—*Photo by Gail Dennis*—

SHIAWASSEE RIVER

Counties:	Shiawassee, Saginaw
Start/End:	Byron to Fergus Road Bridge
Miles	65.5
Gradient:	Byron to Owosso — 2.9 ft/mile
	Owosso to Fergus Road — 3.8 ft/mile
Portages:	Two Dams, easy
Rapids/Falls:	Short rapids at old dam sites near Martin Road and Ditch Road — Class I-II
	Two runnable dams in the city of Owosso — Class I-II
Campgrounds:	Few
Canoe Liveries:	Several
Skill Required:	I

A generally quiet, moderately paced river, the Shiawassee rambles through farmlands and woodlots while draining the southern Saginaw Valley. Occasional riffles, especially in the Owosso area, add variety to a river that is slow to moderate most of its length. Except for several dams and old mill-sites that may need portaging, the entire river is well-suited to beginning paddlers. Water fluctuations are quite extreme — early spring levels are too high for safe paddling some years; some riffles will be quite low during dry summers.

Streamside camping is limited to one private campground, making extended trips difficult but possible. Fishing is for bass, pike and other warm-water species.

Byron to Geeck Road Park
13 Miles
4-5 Hours

During high water, there is canoeable river as far upstream as Holly, in Oakland County. Fish Lake Road Bridge in Holly has fair access, but the river is small — 15-25 feet wide — and even after a wet September, we found it too shallow and choked with fallen trees to be easily navigated. Likewise, at the mill dam in Linden — where the river is slightly larger — shallow water and the lowland woodlots it passes through below town convinced us to begin our trip in Byron, where the junction of the South Branch makes the mainstream consistently large enough to navigate.

From Byron, the Shiawassee is 45-60 feet wide and one to four feet deep with water that tends to be slightly clouded. Current is slow to moderate and flows over sand and gravel bottom. Terrain is lowland forests in a narrow valley which is surrounded by pastures and fields.

 Access is difficult in **Byron**. The areas both above and below the small dam in town are private, and access at the bridges on both Byron Road and Bath Road is only fair with parking along the streets. East of town, access is, again, only fair at New Lothrop Road Bridge, but parking along the county road is better than in town.

At Lehring Road, there is no access from the bridge, but there is a canoe livery and private campground with a landing, a picnic area and supplies.

Cole Road Bridge has fair access and limited roadside parking.

At Geeck Road, the best **access and parking** are at a town-ship park and picnic area just downstream from the bridge.

Geeck Road to Corunna Park
16 Miles
5 - 6 1/2 Hours

From Geeck Road the river continues through terrain much like that above, although the banks are somewhat higher in many places. Current is mostly slow to moderate, with depths of one to four feet over sand and gravel and occasional rocks up to bushel-size. Some light riffles may be bottom-bumpers during low-water periods.

Access is fair with roadside parking at both Business 69 Bridge and downstream at Newburg Road Bridge.

Before the dam at the village of Shiawassee is a long, narrow and marshy backwaters. Portage the **dam** on the right. There is good access and parking at the county park and picnic area at the dam.

Access at M-71 is fair with very limited roadside parking. The river from here is noticeably larger and more clouded due to the addition of the Maple River and other tributaries.

Goodal Road below Vernon has no access.

At Martin Road, where access is poor, there is a light rapids at the site of a washed-out mill dam. It should create no difficulty except during very high water, when standing waves might develop.

Lytle Road Bridge has good access but limited parking.

In Corunna, there is good **access and parking** at the city park beyond the downtown district.

Corunna to Henderson Road Park
13 Miles
4-5 Hours

About two miles below Corunna, there is access and parking at an empty lot beside the M-21 Bridge in Owosso. Immediately below the bridge is a low dam that may require portaging on right or left. A chute through the center is runnable, but standing waves make it fairly challenging, especially during high water. There is another similar dam a short distance downstream just before the Oliver Street Bridge; the same conditions apply.

Below Owosso, expect slightly faster water than upstream. Light riffles (some will be shallow in summer) with scattered large rocks are frequent. The river valley is quite deep in places and is wooded with oaks, maples and other hardwoods.

❺ There is good **access and parking** at the picnic area 2.5 miles below Owosso off M-52.

There is no access at Juddville Road Bridge.

❻ **Henderson Road Bridge** has poor access and parking, but the county park just downstream has good access. Note that the park is open only during the summer.

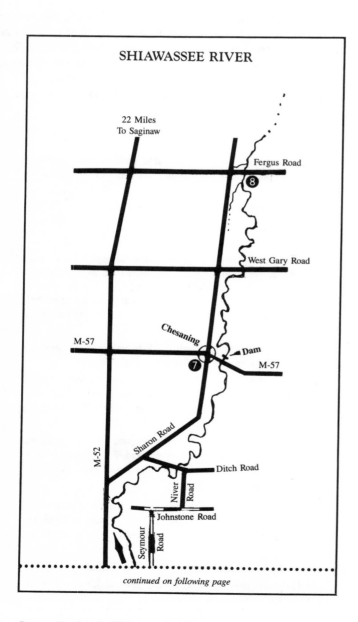

continued on following page

Henderson Park to Fergus Road
23.5 Miles
6 1/2 - 7 1/2 Hours

Below Henderson Park the river averages 80-100 feet wide as it flows through a fairly steep-sided valley. Deep water and strong, moderately fast current alternate with shallow riffles. During high water, some riffles will create standing waves and become light rapids.

M-52 Bridge has no access.

Access and parking are fair at Six Mile Creek Road Bridge.

Johnstone Road Bridge is out and has no access or parking.

Ditch Road Bridge has fair access and parking. There is a washed-out dam just upstream, with fast water spilling through several channels. Take the left channel but watch for concrete slabs and reinforcing rod. Also, high standing waves develop during high water.

In **Chesaning**, there is good access and parking at two city parks, one above the bridge at M-57, the other below it. Just below M-57 is a six-foot dam that must be portaged on the right. Use caution near the spillway, where there is no barrier. ❼

Below Chesaning at West Gary Road Bridge, access is fair with roadside parking. The river is slow to moderate, is deeply discolored, and passes through continuous lowlands until the junction with the Flint River. From Chesaning to the state game area at Fergus Road, the river valley is quite shallow, and the narrow border of silver maples and willows backs up mostly to pastures and cultivated fields.

Fergus Road Bridge has good access and limited roadside parking. ❽

Fergus Road Bridge to
South Miller Road or the Flint River
9 Miles
3-4 Hours
(Not on Map)

We have not paddled through the Shiawassee State Game Area below Fergus Road and have not included it on the map. It is an area of lowlands, bayous and flooded woods and is popular enough with duck hunters to be crowded during that season. Camping possibilities are limited due to wet ground, and mosquitos can be overwhelming in summer. Access at the lower end of the game area is not easy. About 3.5 miles below Fergus Road is the junction with the wide, slow-moving and discolored Bad River. There is good access and parking at a public site on Hulein Road one mile upstream on the Bad. Take out here or continue downstream to the South Miller Road Bridge on the Shiawassee. At the time of this writing, South Miller Road is closed at the Marsh Creek Bridge, one mile short of the river. Marsh Creek is large enough to be navigated to its junction with the Shiawassee, and there is good access and parking at a public site at the bridge. Use caution in this area — expansive marshlands and slow currents on the Shiawassee and Flint rivers and Marsh Creek make it difficult to tell upstream from down and even to discern one watercourse from another.

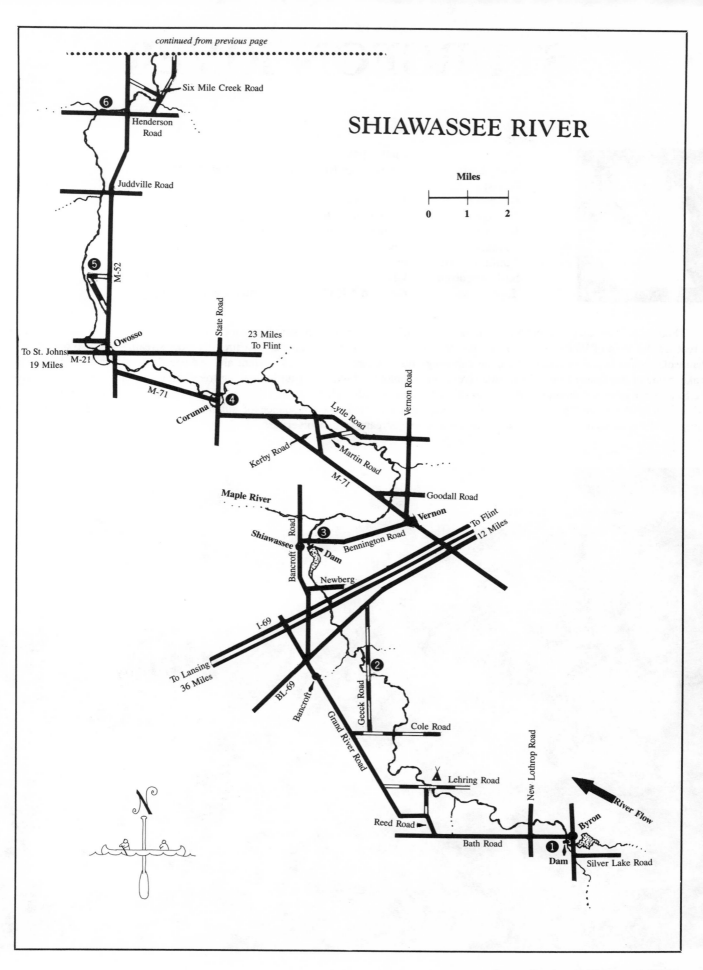

continued from previous page

SHIAWASSEE RIVER

Miles

0   1   2

Six Mile Creek Road

⑥

Henderson Road

Juddville Road

⑤

M-52

Owosso

To St. Johns
19 Miles

M-21

M-71

Corunna

④

State Road

23 Miles
To Flint

Lytle Road

Vernon Road

Kerby Road

Martin Road

M-71

Goodall Road

Maple River

Shiawassee

Bancroft Road

③

Dam

Bennington Road

Vernon

To Flint
12 Miles

Newberg

I-69

To Lansing
36 Miles

BL-69

Bancroft

②

Gecck Road

Cole Road

Grand River Road

Lehring Road

New Lothrop Road

River Flow

Reed Road

Byron

Bath Road

①

Dam

Silver Lake Road

STURGEON RIVER

County:	**Cheboygan**
Start/End:	**Trowbridge Road Bridge to Indian River**
Miles:	**16**
Gradient:	**13.8 ft/mile**
Portages:	**Occasional fallen trees**
Rapids/Falls:	**Numerous unnamed rapids**
Camgrounds:	**Few**
Canoe Liveries:	**Few**
Skill Required:	**I-II**
Topo. Maps:	**Gaylord NE (7.5 min.), Wolverine (15 min.)**

Though its headwaters are in Otsego County near Gaylord, the Sturgeon is neither wide nor open enough for enjoyable canoeing until it reaches the town of Wolverine, 20 miles downstream. The Sturgeon — considered a premier trout stream — is also one of the Lower Peninsula's most beautiful and challenging canoeing rivers. Consistently quick current and average descent of almost 14 feet per mile make it one of the fastest Lower Peninsula rivers. That, combined with tight turns, leaning trees and occasional obstructions, also make the Sturgeon a river not recommended for absolute beginners, although paddlers with basic maneuvering skills should have little trouble.

Much of the river flows through state forest, where there is an abundance of suitable campsites. In addition, a state-forest campground is located on the river about two miles downstream from Wolverine.

Trowbridge Road Bridge to
M-68 Bridge or Burt Lake
16 Miles
5-7 Hours

(1) Most paddlers put in at Wolverine, near the junction of the West Branch and the mainstream of the Sturgeon, but it is possible to begin a trip on the mainstream four miles upstream at the Trowbridge Road bridges. There is a haphazardly maintained **public access site** above the upper Trowbridge Road Bridge, or put in at either of the two bridges. Parking is along the road. The river in this section, near I-75, is 15-30 feet wide and varies from quick-flowing and very shallow over gravel to slow and one to three feet deep over sand and rocks. Tight bends, frequent fallen trees and minor logjams make slow going in places; several short portages or lift-overs are usually necessary. Thickets of poplar and tag alders alternate with stretches of open meadows. Expect a one- to two-hour trip from the upper Trowbridge Road Bridge to the park in Wolverine.

(2) Access and parking are good at **Wolverine Park**, where there are toilets, picnic tables and water. The river below the junction with the West Branch widens to 30-50 feet, and the current is moderately quick over gravel and cobble-size rocks. Giant poplars and willows line the river below the park. One or two chutes create light rapids and standing waves within the first half mile, then the current slows, the water deepens, and the river winds through an area of open meadows and cedar clumps. There are no houses or cottages immediately below Wolverine and few along the entire river until near Indian River.

(3) A **public access site** with good access and parking is on the right, about a mile below Wolverine. From here the current increases in speed and remains relatively fast through numerous tight bends that require basic maneuvering skills.

(4) **Haakwood State Forest Campground** is identified by a sand trail visible on the left bank just below a railroad trestle with a U.S.G.S. water-gauging station beside it. Other sandy trails downstream on the left also lead to the campground.

(5) Rondo Road Bridge has poor access, but there is good access and parking one-half mile downstream at a **public site** at the railroad trestle reached off Trowbridge Road.

From Haakwood Campground to the first White Road Bridge, locally known as Midway, the river remains fast, with riffles and pools alternating with light Class I-II rapids over fist- to bushel-size rocks. Descent is quick — sometimes through long, straight lanes between cedars and other times through series of bends. Occasional chutes between large rocks and ledges require fairly precise maneuvering, especially during high water when standing waves develop. Water levels, even during dry seasons, should be sufficient for clear passage. Fallen trees, stumps and logs are present but seem to be regularly cleared by canoe liveries and paddlers.

Access and parking are fair at the first White Road Bridge. The second bridge is about two miles downstream and has fair access with roadside parking. By the second bridge the current has slowed gradually and continues at moderate speed over gravel and sand. Topography changes to lowland forests, with cedars near the water, and occasional small meadows.

(6) From the **access site** at the end of Fisher Woods Road, where access and parking are good, the river continues moderately fast, but houses appear and traffic from M-68 becomes audible.

Before the M-68 Bridge in Indian River, there are supplies, a restaurant and a canoe livery. Take out here (with permission) or

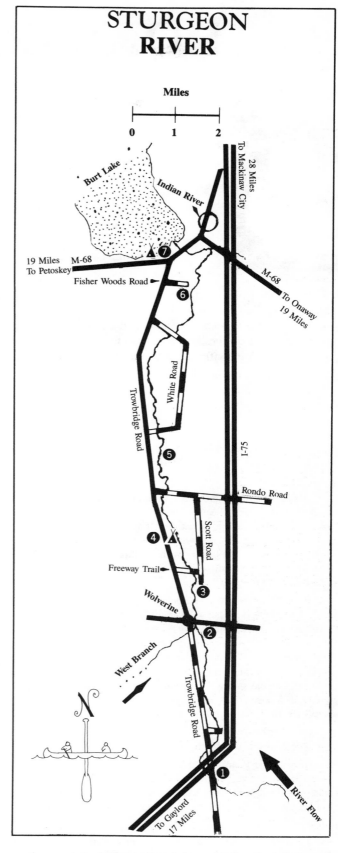

continue past the bridge to Burt Lake and follow the left shore a short distance to a boat-launching site that is within **Burt Lake State Park**. Camping and all facilities are available at the park; a vehicle permit is required to camp and to use the access site. **(7)**

THORNAPPLE RIVER

County:	**Barry**
Start/End:	**Nashville Dam to Irving Dam**
Miles:	**25.5**
Gradient:	**2 ft/mile**
Portages:	**Occasional fallen trees**
Rapids/Falls:	**Ruehs Rapids in Alaska (not on map) — Class I**
Campgrounds:	**Few**
Canoe Liveries:	**Few**
Skill Required:	**I**

The Thornapple, like most tributaries in the Grand River system, is a gentle river with moderate current flowing over sand and gravel bottom. It passes primarily through lowlands and low hills of hardwoods and in the upper half is not heavily developed. Camping is severely limited due to private property and a lack of developed campgrounds. Fishing is primarily for warm-water species, especially bass, but in the upper reaches, trout are also found. The lower end of the river, below the village of Irving, consists of a series of dams and impoundments. We confined our trip to the upper reaches.

Nashville Dam to Thornapple Lake
7 Miles
3 1/2 - 4 1/2 Hours

This is essentially the upper limit of canoeable river. Above Nashville the river is heavily choked with aquatic weeds and is too small and shallow to be easily canoed. There is good access and parking below the **Nashville Dam** on the left. The river here is 30-50 feet wide and is slow with a bottom of sand and gravel. The water is discolored, with visibility to two to three feet. Current is slow to moderate.

Below Nashville, the Thornapple enters a low valley of farmlands and lowland forests. Silver maples predominate and often form an overhead canopy. Some open meadows come to the bank, but the dominant feature is hardwoods above tangles of underbrush and vines. Fallen trees can be a problem. The livery in Hastings clears them annually, but there are always new ones, especially in the spring. We made the trip in April and encountered half a dozen trees and logjams that had to be portaged. The banks are firm, and portaging is not difficult.

An hour below Nashville is a small bridge at Gregg's Crossing. The bridge is closed and access is poor.

Thornapple Road Bridge is two to three hours below Nashville and has fair access from the little bay on the right upstream side of the bridge. Parking is limited to the roadside. From here to Thornapple Lake is water similar to above, with slow current and frequent fallen trees.

Barger Road Bridge is about 1.5 miles below Thornapple Road and has good access and roadside parking.

Just below Barger Road is Thornapple Lake. This is a natural lake, not a reservoir, and is quite popular as a resort and recreation area. The outlet is a wide channel beneath the bridge at the west end of the lake.

Charlton County Park — with supplies, a museum, picnic grounds, good access and parking — is on the right, before the bridge. Supplies are also available one-half mile south on Charlton Park Road at the corner of M-79. There is camping for a fee at the commercial campground across the channel from the county park.

Charlton Park to Hastings City Park
6.5 Miles
2-3 1/2 Hours

The lake outlet beneath Charlton Park Road is a wide, deep channel that remains slow and wide, with depths of two to eight feet, for a mile or more. Banks are quite heavily developed with cottages.

McKeown Road Bridge has poor access and parking. By here the river has increased in velocity, with the water shallow over gravel and small rocks and the current moderate to fairly quick. From here to Hastings, light riffles alternate with slower water. Some of the riffles are shallow and will be bottom-draggers during low water. Cottages diminish in frequency. Terrain is low hills of hardwoods and large sycamores. Generally, the river below Thornapple Lake is wide enough, at 40-65 feet, that fallen trees do not obstruct the entire river.

There is fair access and roadside parking at River Road Bridge and at Center Road Bridge. The remainder of the trip to **Hastings City Park** (Tyden Park) is through the backyards of the city.

Access and parking are good at the park, where there are restrooms, water and picnic grounds.

Hastings City Park to Irving Dam
12 Miles
3-4 1/2 Hours

The river from Hastings to Irving is similar to the section above Hastings — mild riffles with gravel and rock bottom alternate with stretches of slower water. There are only a few streamside cottages and houses, and most of the bordering land is low hills of hardwoods. Expect one or two fallen trees to partially obstruct the river.

4 **Airport Road Bridge** is two to three hours below Hastings. A couple of hundred yards downstream on the left is a public access site with good access and parking. From here to the backwaters of Irving Dam, there are more riffles — some fairly fast — and a few houses and cottages.

5 Well before Irving the river slows and widens, then enters the narrow backwaters of **Irving Dam**. Stay to the left and portage the left dam. There is another dam down the shore to the right, but water levels below it are often extremely low, and there are likely to be obstructions downstream. Below the dam on the left is a slow channel leading to yet another dam (a power generator), that is best portaged on the left, though it is not an easy or well-marked take-out. Use caution climbing down the steep bank below the dam.

We ended our trip at Irving Pond. Much of the remainder of the distance to the junction with the Grand River consists of backwaters and wide, slow sections of river between them. Most of the impoundments seem to be heavily developed and used for recreational purposes.

One stretch worth noting is at Ruehs Park, in the town of Alaska. There is a 75-foot-long run of fast water just before the 68th Street Bridge. It is a basic, straightforward rapids that, though not challenging by most whitewater standards, could be tricky during high water when standing waves develop. If in doubt, portage on the left, through the park.

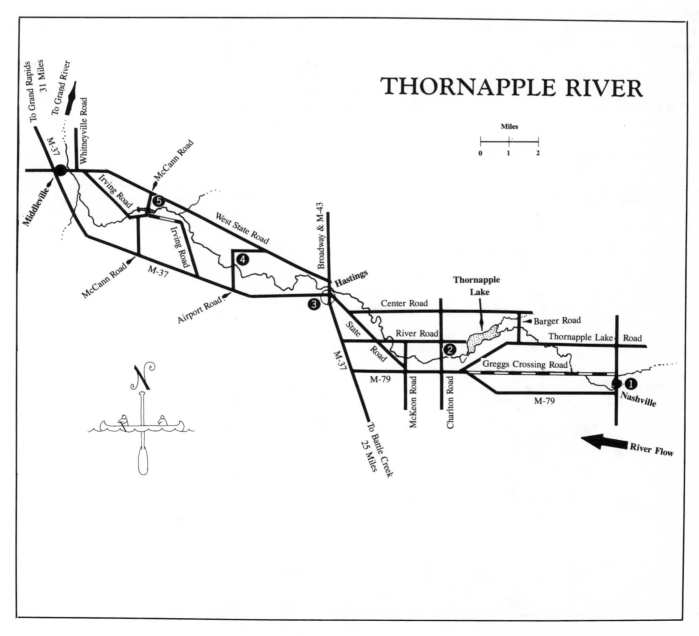

THUNDER BAY RIVER

Counties:	**Montmorency, Alpena**
Start/End:	**Atlanta Dam to Alpena**
Miles:	**57.25**
Gradient:	**Atlanta to Hillman — 6.4 ft/mile**
	Hillman to Seven Mile Pond — 4.2 ft/mile
Portages:	**Four dams, moderately difficult;**
	occasional fallen trees
Rapids/Falls:	**Speehley Rapids, below M-65 Bridge — Class I**
Campgrounds:	**Few**
Canoe Liveries:	**Few**
Skill Required:	**I**

From its headwaters, southwest of Atlanta, to its mouth, in Lake Huron at Alpena, the Thunder Bay is a moderately paced river that is well-suited to paddlers of all abilities. Though shallow and fairly quick in the upper reaches, most of it winds slowly through a variety of woodlands. The final 10 miles is composed of a series of dams and reservoirs. Water level fluctuations are quite extreme, making early season trips inadvisable, especially at Speehley Rapids, below Long Rapids Park on M-65. Low water is seldom a problem except in the section from Atlanta to Hunt Creek Bridge (Hall Road), where some shallow riffles will slow progress.

Much of the river passes through the Thunder Bay State Forest, but good campsites are not common. Developed campgrounds are found at the municipal park in Hillman and at a state-forest campground above Atlanta at Lake Fifteen. Fishing is primarily for warm-water species, including smalllmouth bass and northern pike.

MAP #1: ATLANTA DAM to SALINA ROAD BRIDGE — 32 MILES

Atlanta Dam to Hunt Creek Bridge (Hall Road)
11.5 Miles
3 1/2 - 5 Hours

❶ Access and parking are good at the **Atlanta Dam**. The river here is small — 15-25 feet wide and one to two feet deep — and flows slowly over sand bottom. Water is remarkably clear. Thickets of tag alders and other underbrush line the banks, and devel-

opment is light, with only occasional cottages.

Airport Road Bridge has fair access and poor parking. Not far downstream, slow water gives way to riffles over gravel bottom and scattered larger rocks. Some stretches are fairly quick and moderately challenging during high water. Occasional rock

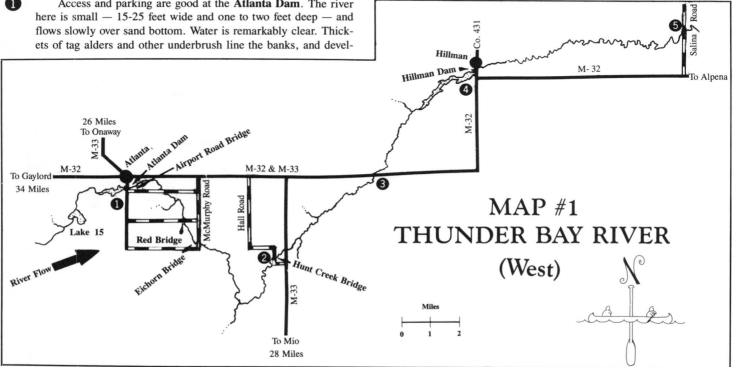

MAP #1
THUNDER BAY RIVER
(West)

reefs usually have a clear chute near the center. During low-water periods expect to drag bottom.

Access is good at Eichorn Bridge (McMurphy Road), but parking is limited and on the roadside. From here, current slows and the river deepens and widens. Average width is 30-50 feet and depth, two to five feet. Bottom becomes predominantly sand. Terrain is lowland forests. Fallen trees are common but seem to be regularly cleared.

2   **Hunt Creek Bridge** (Hall Road) has fair access and parking.

Hunt Creek Bridge to Hillman Dam
10.5 Miles
4-5 Hours

Shortly below Hunt Creek Bridge is M-33 Bridge, with poor access and parking. From here, current remains steady and moderate, and water is usually murky. Lowland forests alternate with hills of hardwoods; cedars and tag alders commonly border the river.

3   **M-32 Bridge** has good access but limited parking in a small lot beside the bridge. Slow, deep and discolored water is typical of most of the remainder of the river. Bottom is sand, and banks are thickly overgrown.

4   The backwaters of **Hillman Dam** are long and narrow and lined with stumps. Hillman Park is a municipal park and campground on the right shore of the reservoir within sight of the dam. There are both primitive and modern campsites, and supplies are within walking distance.

Portage Hillman Dam on the right.

Hillman Dam to Salina Road Bridge
10 Miles
4-5 Hours

Much of the bordering land in this section is within the Thunder Bay State Forest. Good campsites are not abundant but can be found. Current is slow to moderate through constant tight bends and switchbacks.

5   **Salina Road Bridge** has fair access and parking.

MAP #2: SALINA ROAD BRIDGE TO ALPENA — 25.5 MILES

Salina Road Bridge to Seven Mile Pond
15.25 Miles
6-8 Hours

Five miles below Salina Road, at **Long Rapids County Park** at the M-65 Bridge, are good access and parking. The 7.75-mile section from here to Orchard Bridge, on Herron Road, includes the Thunder Bay's only rapids, called Long or Speehley rapids. Beginning 1.5 miles below the bridge, they are a series of cascading riffles that will not challenge paddlers with whitewater experience, although they are an exhilarating run after the miles of slow water upstream. Rapids extend for about 1,200 feet over fist- to pumpkin-size rocks. Descent is not very steep, passage is straightforward, and only during high water will there be substantial standing waves and other hazards. Streamside banks are 10-20 feet high and slope gradually away from the river. **6**

Orchard Bridge (Herron Road) has fair access and parking.

Shortly below Herron Road, the backwaters of Seven Mile Dam begin. It is a four-mile crossing to the dam, or take out at a **public access site** on the north shore of the pond at the end of Dietz Road, one-half mile after the junction with the North Branch. The Lower South Branch also joins the mainstream in Seven Mile Pond. **7**

Seven Mile Pond to Alpena
10 Miles
4-5 Hours

We bypassed this section of almost continuous backwaters. There are portages at Seven Mile Dam, one mile downstream at Four Mile Dam, and five miles downstream at the Ninth Street Dam in Alpena. Shorelines of the impoundments are heavily developed with cottages and houses.

Take out at the municipal park in **Alpena**, where parking and access are good. **8**

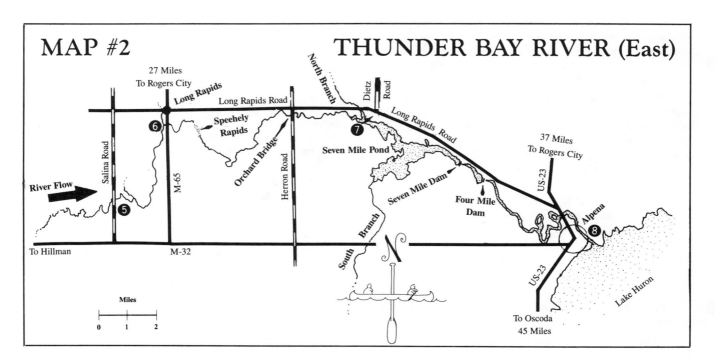

WHITE RIVER

Counties:	**Oceana, Muskegon**
Start/End:	**Hesperia to BR-31 Bridge in Whitehall**
Miles:	**32.5**
Gradient:	**Hesperia to Pines Point Campground — 11.7 ft/mile**
	Other sections — 2.5 ft/mile
Portages:	**None**
Rapids/Falls:	**None**
Campgrounds:	**Several**
Canoe Liveries:	**Several**
Skill Required:	**I**

Because it is between two well-known and popular rivers — the Muskegon, to the south, and the Pere Marquette, to the north — the White River tends to be overlooked by canoeists and fishermen alike. A definite lack of accessibility makes it less appealing than its famous neighbors, but, on the other hand, quiet and solitude on this Wild-Scenic designated Natural River may make it more appealing.

A relatively small river, it divides conveniently into upper and lower sections, each with a distinct personality. The upper reaches, from Hesperia to Pines Point Campground, are generally shallow and rocky with many riffles, while the lower section tends to be slower and deeper and have sand bottom. Except during spring and other periods of high water (when the upper river, especially, may be rather challenging), the entire river is suitable for beginning paddlers and families with small children. Although much of the river passes through state-forest land, access can be a problem, with many of the better sites privately owned or restricted to canoe-livery customers. It may be necessary to acquire permission to obtain access in certain sections. Several public and private campgrounds make overnight trips possible.

Fishing is primarily for smallmouth bass in the upper river; bass and northern pike are found in the lower section. Spring and fall runs of steelhead and salmon are reported to be heavy, though fishing pressure is light. An extended season from April 1 to December 31 is currently in effect for the entire river to Hesperia Dam.

Hesperia Dam to Pines Point U.S.F.S. Campground
8.5 Miles
3-4 Hours

Above Hesperia the river is too shallow and choked with obstacles for enjoyable paddling. Below the dam, low water is common in summer, and some shallow riffles may require walking through. Parking and access are good at **Hesperia Dam** and at Vida Weaver Park, a short distance downstream.

The river throughout the upper section averages 40-60 feet wide and six inches to three feet deep. Gravel and rock bottom, with many shallow riffles, predominates. Current is moderate to fairly quick. Frequent sharp bends, some quite tricky, require basic maneuvering skills. Terrain is low hills and upland hardwood and pine forests. Most bordering land is private with cabins frequent.

Taylor Road Bridge access is controlled by a canoe livery and should not be used without permission. A small store at the bridge has supplies. Fairly quick descent and rock and gravel bottom make the river to here a challenging spring trip and is not recommended for beginners at that time.

Podunk Road access is controlled by a canoe livery and is not for public use.

Pines Point Campground is a U.S. Forest Service Campground with good access and parking, picnic grounds and primitive camping facilities.

Pines Point Campground to County Line Bridge
14 Miles
5-7 Hours

Below Pines Point the river tends to widen and deepen, although not far below the campground, there is a one-mile stretch that can be very low in summer. Bottom changes to predominantly sand. Most of this section flows through the Manistee National Forest, but much of the bordering land is low and swampy, making good campsites infrequent. Abundant wildlife and a sense of seclusion are the main appeal of the lower White. Three to four hours below Pines Point, there is a private campground with supplies and secluded primitive sites.

There are access sites used by canoe liveries at Cisco Rollaway and, one hour further, at Twin Rollaway. However, the roads to them are obscure and difficult to find, and low, steep banks make access difficult.

The North Branch of the White joins the mainstream in this section, adding significant amounts of water. Several minor tributaries are often discolored, and the White from here downstream tends to be murkier than above.

Access at **County Line Bridge** (Skeels Road) is fair with limited roadside parking. Take out on the left.

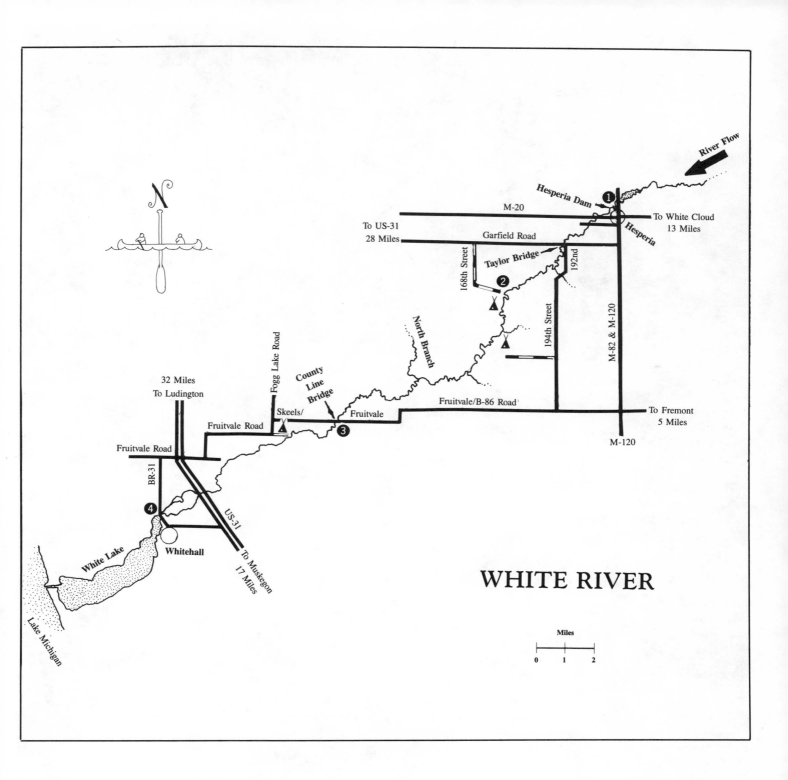

WHITE RIVER

Miles

0   1   2

**County Line Bridge (Skeels Road)
to BR-31 in Whitehall
10 Miles
5-6 Hours**

From County Line Bridge the river remains slow and deep. Width is 60-70 feet, and depth is three to six feet with deeper holes. There is mostly private land with occasional scattered cabins in this area of lowland forests and marshes

One-half hour below County Line Bridge, the river spreads through extensive marshlands, with channels branching in many directions. Stay to the right and follow the widest, deepest route.

One hour below County Line Bridge is a private campground with all facilities and some supplies. Most of the remaining river is slow and murky and passes through marshlands. About two hours below County Line Bridge is a private canoe landing that should be used only with permission. Shortly below the landing, the river enters a delta area of wide marshes.

There is no access at the US-31 Bridge, but **BR-31 Bridge** in Whitehall just before White Lake has a public access site with good access and parking and nearby supplies.

Chippewa Falls on the Black River.
—Photo by Jerry Dennis—

UPPER PENINSULA

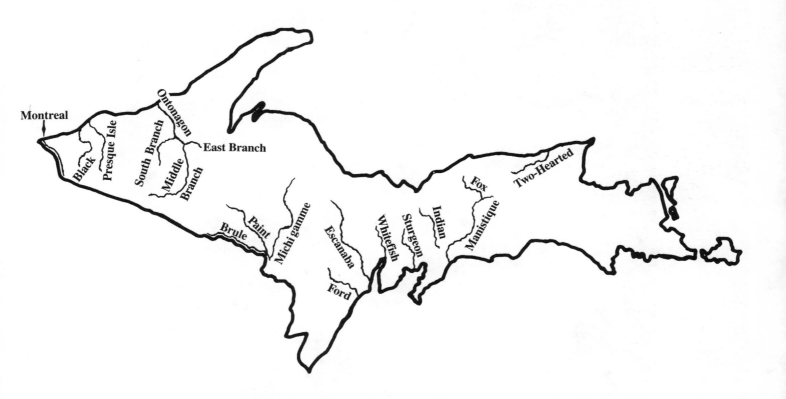

Potawatomi Falls, Black River

BLACK RIVER

County:	Gogebic
Start/End:	Co. Rd. 513 Bridge to Black River County Park at Lake Superior
Miles:	28.5
Gradient:	Co. Rd. 513 to US-2 — 17.5 ft/mile
	Covered Bridge to Narrows Park — 8.4 ft/mile
	Narrows Park to unnamed road — 25 ft/mile
	Unnamed road to Lake Superior — 48.6 ft/mile
Portages:	Numerous falls
Rapids/Falls:	Granite Rapids below Co. Rd. 513 — Class II
	Numerous unnamed rapids above and below Ramsay — Class I-II
	Several unnamed rapids below Covered Bridge — Class I-II
	Numerous unnamed rapids below Narrows Park —Class II-III
	Eight major falls — essentially unrunnable

Campgrounds:	Few
Canoe Liveries:	None
Skill Required:	II-III
Topo. Maps:	Ironwood, Wakefield, North Ironwood (15 min.)

One of Michigan's finest whitewater rivers, the Black is also one of the state's most difficult rivers and is not recommended for paddlers without whitewater experience. At least eight impassable falls limit passage and make extended expeditions extremely difficult.

Like most western Upper Peninsula rivers, the Black is subject to extreme flow fluctuations, with levels varying perhaps more than on the neighboring Montreal and Presque Isle rivers. Levels are somewhat dependent on discharges from Black River Dam, five miles above the Co. Rd. 513 put-in, but late summer and fall often find this river a virtual trickle. We paddled it in late May — usually an ideal time — but spring rain had been light, and we found many sections quite low. Most of the major rapids and drops that have given the Black the reputation of being one of the best Class II-III rivers in the Upper Peninsula were lowered a full degree by low water. On the other hand, a day and night of solid rain brought the river up to blood-pressure-raising levels, and some of the same rapids we had traipsed through with impunity became challenging runs capable of swamping open canoes.

Generally, consider the month of May for the best chance of finding ideal levels; go in April if you're equipped for cold water and can handle very heavy, very fast water and technical maneuvering around numerous rock and log obstructions. At all times, phone calls to various agencies and businesses in Ironwood, Bessemer, Ramsay and Wakefield can give up-to-the-minute reports. (See Appendix V, page 131, "Further Information.")

Co. Rd. 513 Bridge to US-2 Bridge
8 Miles
3-5 Hours

This upper section of the Black is small — with current varying from very slow to very fast — and is suitable for paddlers with basic skills and experience. In addition to numerous Class I rapids, there is one short Class II drop at Granite Rapids

❶ **Access** is good from the bridge at Co. Rd. 513, with parking limited to the roadside. The river is 15-30 feet wide — as it is through most of the section to US-2 — with depths of one to six feet during early summer. Current is slow over rock and sand bottom and beds of aquatic vegetation. The water is dark enough to make the river's name seem apt.

Just downstream is a private bridge with no access. From here the river winds through lowlands of spruce and tamarack with tag alders at the banks. Occasional short, light riffles punctuate stretches of slow water.

❷ **Granite Rapids** can be heard before they are seen. Their approach is also marked by a house on the bluff to the left. Take out on the left to scout or portage. The rapids are a run of about 50 feet over a series of low ledges and a three-foot drop. At the drop, take the main chute at right-center. The primary hazards are large standing waves during high water and exposed rock during low water. There is access and room to park at the dead-end road beside the rapids.

From Granite Rapids to the town of Ramsay, Class I rapids — through rock gardens and over minor chutes and ledge drops — alternate with stretches of slower, deeper water. Several pine-covered knolls make good campsites. Just before Ramsay, a USGS water gauge is on the right, next to a gauge station.

In Ramsay, there is good **access and parking** at a community **❸** park between the first and second bridges. The sluice dam here can be run through either the left or right spillways, if open, but use caution during high water. From the dam to the US-2 Bridge is three-quarters of a mile of continuous Class II rapids. This is a difficult run for inexperienced paddlers. The river's small size — 25-35 feet wide — makes it susceptible to blockage by fallen trees and debris. Infrequent eddies and continuous, very fast water make it difficult to stop for obstructions or to scout, and high,

steep, heavily overgrown banks make it difficult to get out. Quick, precise maneuvering is demanded to avoid obstructions and reach clear chutes and channels.

Do not proceed beyond the US-2 Bridge. Neepikon Falls and Gabro Falls are a short distance downstream and are impassable and extremely dangerous. Portage trails are indistinct and difficult. We recommend shuttling the two miles of river from US-2 to the covered bridge at Blackjack Ski Area.

 Access at US-2 is difficult, with a long, steep climb up an embankment and no clear trail through the underbrush. Parking is on the wide shoulder of the highway.

Covered Bridge to the Narrows Roadside Park
9.5 Miles
3-4 Hours

This meandering, relatively peaceful section is suitable for most paddlers. However, the risk of missing the access at the Narrows Park and being swept into the rapids below causes us to not recommend it to beginners. Inexperienced paddlers should plan to take out at either Bessemer Road Bridge or the unnamed bridge below it. Float times for this abbreviated trip are 1 1/2 to three hours.

There is good access and abundant parking at the **covered bridge** at the entrance to Blackjack Ski Area. The addition of the Little Black River, Jackson Creek and other tributaries swells the mainstream to 40-80 feet wide. Rapids in this section are light and alternate with long stretches of slow and nearly still water. Some slow pools culminate in short drops over light, boulder-strewn rapids that require only basic maneuvering skills. Watch for unseen rocks in slow water. Terrain is low woodlands of underbrush and hardwoods including silver maples. Most bordering land is in the Ottawa National Forest, and there are no houses or cabins.

At **Bessemer Road Bridge**, access is good and roadside parking is adequate. Class I rapids at the bridge can produce large waves during high water. From here, rapids intensify somewhat but continue to alternate with slow water.

The bridge at the unnamed road just off Black River Road has fair access and limited roadside parking. Through the next four to five miles, pools and light rapids continue as above, although descent continues to increase. Terrain changes gradually to upland forests of hardwoods and hemlocks.

After four miles, watch for a gravel-road ford across a shallow riffle. About three-quarters of a mile past the ford is the take-out at the **Narrows Roadside Park**. Access is up a high, steep, slippery bank on the left. There is a trail, but it is poor and nearly invisible from the river. Also, watch for the island that splits the river immediately below the Narrows. One way or another, stop before the island and get out on the left (west) to Black River Road (Co. Rd. 513). Narrows Roadside Park has toilets, picnic tables, limited parking and several very basic campsites.

Narrows Park to
Black River County Park at Lake Superior
11 Miles
7-10 Hours (est.)

Below the Narrows are four miles of nearly continuous Class II-III rapids to an alternate take-out at an unnamed two-track road. Unfortunately, the road is private, with a gate and no-trespassing sign at Black River Road. This creates a very difficult situation for advanced paddlers wanting to run this challenging and interesting section. There are two choices: End at the unnamed road and risk arrest for trespassing or continue downstream and risk the loss of equipment or worse at a series of six major falls before Lake Superior.

From the Narrows to the take-out at the unnamed road, plan to take 2 1/2 - 3 1/2 hours. This leaves ample time to scout several two- to four-foot drops, including Chippewa Falls, the major rapids in this section. The rapids through most of the section are nearly continuous and are composed of bedrock slabs studded with pumpkin- to Volkswagen-size boulders. Descent is approximately 25 feet per mile. Expect standing waves and back-rollers substantial enough to swamp open canoes during high water. During low water, hazards still exist, but finding the deepest and clearest channels and avoiding rocks are the primary challenges. Terrain in this section is upland forests of hardwoods, pines, and hemlocks on high and very steep hills. Banks along the river range from 20-120 feet high and are extremely steep. Copper Peak Ski Jump is visible on Chippewa Hill, to the west of the river.

Chippewa Falls — a short series of steep drops among boulders and ledges leading to a sharp bend to the right — are one-half mile before the take-out at the unnamed road. The falls are preceded by a long, boulder-strewn rapids. During high water they rate a solid Class III and are runnable but should not be attempted by anyone other than very advanced whitewater paddlers with covered boats. We ran them successfully in low water by keeping to the main chutes at the center. If in doubt, portage on the right. Scouting is most effective on the left.

Below Chippewa Falls is one-half mile of straightforward Class I-II rapids and riffles. Toward the end of the long straight stretch that runs northeast, watch for a shallow ford and narrow **two-track road** on the left. It is very easy to miss. There are no certain distinguishing marks except for a slight gap in the hemlocks that opens into the road away from the river. If you miss it, look forward to six major falls and portages.

We have not attempted the vigorous seven-mile trip from the unmarked road to Lake Superior, and, in fact, have heard of no one who has. Our information, therefore, is incomplete. Algonquin Falls, for instance, are a mystery. Steep 120-foot-high banks line both sides of the river, but the size of the falls and possibilities for portage are uncertain.

Portage Conglomerate, Potawatomi and Gorge falls on the left. Boardwalks and stairs simplify the three-quarter-mile portage.

We have not seen Sandstone Falls and do not know whether they can be run or easily portaged.

Rainbow Falls can be portaged on the left. Trails are clear but tortuous. Put in below the falls and paddle one-half mile of slow water to **Black River County Park**, near the rivermouth. Parking and access are good, and there are toilets and picnic facilities. A U.S. Forest Service Campground with most facilities is located one-quarter mile south of the county park on Black River Road.

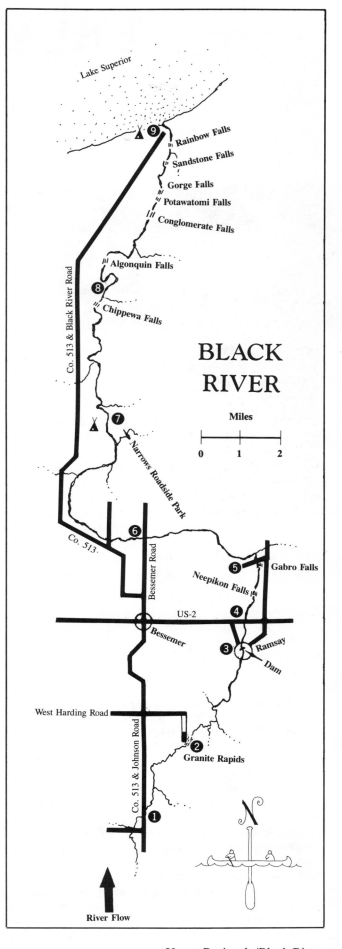

BLACK RIVER

Miles

0   1   2

River Flow

BRULE RIVER

County:	Iron
Start/End:	M-73 Bridge to Menominee River (with Menominee rapids)
Miles:	43
Gradient:	M-73 to Pentoga — 6.4 ft/mile
	Pentoga to US-2 — 10.4 ft/ mile
	US-2 to Brule River Flowage — 8.9 ft/mile
Portages:	One dam, moderately difficult
Rapids/Falls:	Several unnamed rapids above Pentoga — Class I-II
	Unnamed rapids below Pentoga — Class II
	La Chapelle Rapids, above Washburn Bridge — Class I-II

Campgrounds:	Few
Canoe Liveries:	None
Skill Required:	I-II

Both Wisconsin and Michigan paddlers claim title to this river that forms about 45 miles of border between the two states. Beginning at Brule Lake, just inside the Michigan border, it winds southeast until it joins the Paint and Michigamme rivers and becomes the Menominee.

Although numerous Class I rapids occur at intervals along most of its length, it is generally a mild-tempered river that will not prove difficult for most paddlers in normal water conditions. There are rapids both above and below the town of Pentoga that usually rate Class I or II, as do La Chapelle Rapids, before the Washburn Bridge near the end of the river. Inexperienced paddlers should approach these stretches with caution and should, perhaps, portage. Low water does not seem to be the perennial concern it is on other area rivers. Midsummer trips can be accomplished with only a minimum of bumping and scraping, and most of that will be in the upper section above M-189.

Much of the land bordering the river in both states is public, with good campsites abundant. Fishing is for brook and brown trout in the upper reaches and in many tributaries, and for smallmouth bass and northern pike in the lower sections.

M-73 Bridge to M-189 Bridge
13 Miles
3-4 1/2 Hours

This uppermost section of navigable river is a little more than two miles below the source at Brule Lake. There is no access or parking at the M-73 Bridge, but just inside the Wisconsin border, a **U.S. Forest Service Campground** has campsites a short carry to the river. As an alternative, continue south on M-73 (Wisconsin-55) about five miles into Wisconsin to FS-2457, then take five miles of good dirt road to FS-2172 landing. There is good access and limited parking at this site, on the Wisconsin side of the river.

The Brule through this section is 30-50 feet wide and one to two feet deep over sand, gravel and small-stone bottom. Water is clean but stained dark. Shallow, light rapids and riffles alternate with slower, deeper water here and throughout much of the river's length. In the upper section during periods of low water, expect to scrape frequently. Terrain is low hills of mixed hardwoods and conifers with tag alders at the banks.

There is a possible access site at the washed-out Ford Bridge, reached by Brule River Road, but the road is narrow and brushy, and parking is limited and remote. The river immediately below the bridge is narrow and fairly tricky at tight bends and at a short rapids that sometimes rates Class I.

At **M-189 Bridge** (Wisconsin-139) take out on the right upstream side. Access is fair, but the only parking is 100 yards away at a small lot beside the highway on the Wisconsin side of the bridge.

M-189 Bridge to Pentoga Bridge
12 Miles
4-6 Hours

In this section the river becomes noticeably deeper and faster after being joined by several tributaries, especially the Iron River. From here downstream, there should be enough water even during dry seasons for pleasurable canoeing. Unfortunately, the Iron

River contributes not only increased flow to the Brule but also a deep red color and the faint but unmistakable odor of fuel oil — byproducts of the mining region it drains.

Don't look for a bridge at Scott's Landing; it washed out years ago. There is good access and limited parking on the Michigan side. Most of the Scott Lake area is farmlands, with pastures and meadows to the river in several stretches. Otherwise, occasional hardwood stands and patches of tag alder, cedar and dead elm border the river.

Below Scott's Landing are several stretches of fairly easy Class I rapids with medium-sized boulders to avoid. This water should not be difficult for moderately experienced paddlers except during high water, when more caution should be used. Steep, overgrown banks — mostly wooded with hardwoods and tag alders in this stretch — make access to shore difficult. An abandoned railroad bed that follows the left shore the entire distance to Pentoga can be utilized in emergencies.

At **Pentoga**, the bridge is below several channels and islands as well as a large eddy at the site of an old dam. Take out on the right (Wisconsin) side, upstream from the bridge. Use caution if you choose to continue beneath the bridge — low clearance and quick water can be tricky. Access at the bridge is good on the Wisconsin side, but parking is very limited.

Pentoga Bridge to US-2 Bridge
13.5 Miles
4-6 Hours

Below Pentoga the character of the river and terrain alters little. About an hour downstream, watch for a two-foot ledge that can be tricky and is usually rated Class II. It can be run on the right-center at the most prominent chute. However, during heavy flow, high waves develop that are capable of swamping an open canoe. If in doubt, portage on the right. Light rapids and riffles continue downstream.

Rainbow Trail (FS-2150) has fair access and parking on both the Michigan and Wisconsin sides of the river. The bridge is out. Current is generally fairly quick in this area, with some shallow riffles requiring careful navigating in low water.

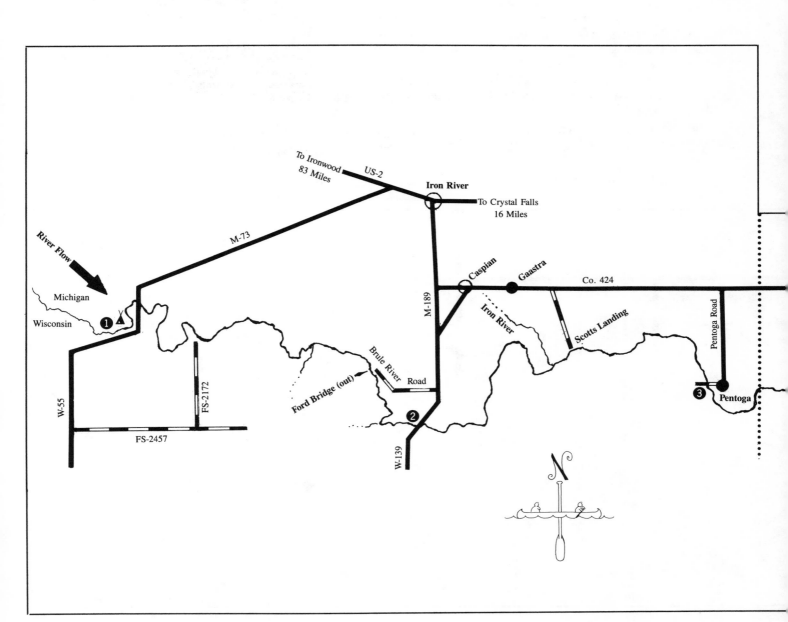

④ **Carney Dam Public Access Site** has good access and parking on the Michigan side. There is no existing dam. Below here the river tends to slow, but there are still intervals of quick rocky runs and small riffles. Width averages 75-100 feet, and depths vary from one to six feet. There are very few acceptable campsites in this section.

⑤ **Access** at US-2 is on the left downstream side of the bridge. Parking is good but limited.

US-2 Bridge to Brule River Flowage
4.5 Miles
1 1/2 - 3 Hours

Below US-2, riffles and stretches of consistent, steady current continue two miles to La Chapelle Rapids. This rocky rapids extends for several hundred feet and generally rates Class I-II. In high water, inexperienced paddlers may wish to avoid standing waves. Scout or portage on the right. Light rapids and riffles extend to Washburn Bridge.

Access and parking are poor at Washburn Bridge. This is apparently a private bridge, reached only from the Wisconsin side, and is the final access before the backwaters of Brule River Flowage. A USGS water gauge has been reported to be located here, but we could find no trace of it.

⑥ One mile below Washburn Bridge is a **public landing** with good access and parking on the Wisconsin shore of the upper Brule River Flowage.

To continue to the dam, follow the right shore two miles. The broad inlet to the north is the Paint River. At the dam, portage on the right.

Brule Island Dam to Menominee River Rapids
(not on map)

Although the Menominee River does not actually begin until about two miles below the Brule Dam where the Michigamme River joins the Brule, this entire section of river is big water and deserves to be treated with caution. Inexperienced paddlers should end their trip at the Brule River Flowage or at the dam.

We have chosen not to include the Menominee River proper — which is generally extremely wide, slow water better suited to powerboats than canoes — but there are two major sets of rapids that deserve to be mentioned. The first of these are Big Bull Rapids, one mile below the junction with the Michigamme River. These rapids are rated Class III, but in the Menominee's large water volume, they are much more difficult and dangerous than Class III rapids on smaller rivers. Use caution and sound judgment. There is a landing on the Wisconsin side about one mile below the rapids.

The second notable rapids is at Piers Gorge, located south of the town of Norway, in Dickinson County 28 miles below the junction of the Brule and the Michigamme rivers. This half-mile rapids is one of Michigan's fiercest stretches of river and rates Class III-IV. It follows a Class II-III rapids called Sand Portage Falls, a few miles below Little Quinnesac Falls Dam. There is good access to the Piers Gorge area at a public site reached off US-8 before it crosses the river into Wisconsin. The rapids are a series of drops and chutes — beginning with eight-foot-high Misicot Falls — with backrollers, souse holes and other hazards present in large numbers, even in low water. This entire stretch should definitely be carefully scouted from the left bank and should only be run by advanced whitewater paddlers. All others will probably be content to view the rapids from the safety of trails and observation points on the Michigan side of the river.

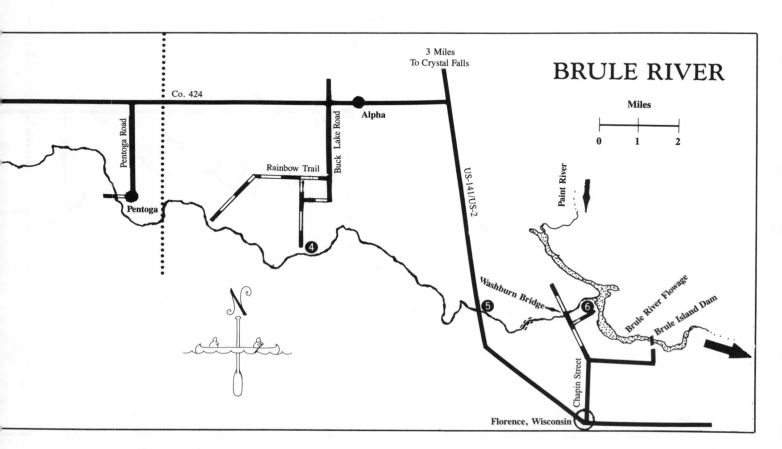

ESCANABA RIVER

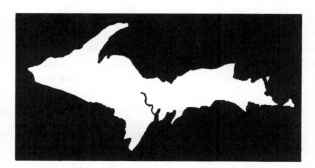

Counties:	Marquette, Delta
Start/End:	Gwinn Community Park to Co. Rd. 420 Bridge
Miles:	46
Gradient:	Gwinn to Boney Falls — 5.9 ft/ mile
	Boney Falls to Co. Rd 420 — 10.6 ft/mile
Rapids/Falls:	Unnamed rapids below Gwinn —Class I-II
	Unnamed rapids before the junction with the West Branch — Class I-II
	Unnamed rapids before Boney Falls Basin — Class I-II
	Unnamed rapids below Boney Falls Dam — Class II-III

Campgrounds:	Few
Canoe Liveries:	None
Skill Required:	II

One of the Upper Peninsula's longest river systems, the Escanaba has for many years also been one of the most important for both recreation and power production. Much of the reason is due to location: It flows between Marquette and Escanaba, the two largest Upper Peninsula cities, and is paralleled much of its length by M-35.

The mainstream of the river — the Middle Branch —begins in lakes north of the town of Champion, about 20 miles west of Marquette. Although we have heard that the many miles of river between Champion and Gwinn are navigable by canoe, we chose to bypass that section because of long stretches of shallow rock ledges, falls, and extremely narrow gorges that appear impassable, and also because of reports of extensive logjams and fallen trees. Below Gwinn, the Middle Branch is a relatively large river and flows through a variety of terrain before ending at a series of dams and reservoirs in Escanaba. The river is prone to low water, and there are many shallow riffles that will often need to be walked through in summer. Remote country and several rapids make it a poor choice for inexperienced paddlers, and during high water, rapids — especially below Boney Falls Dam —will prove difficult even for those with much experience.

Campgrounds and abundant public land make long expeditions possible. Fishing is for brook and brown trout in most of the mainstream and its tributaries, and smallmouth bass and pike in the lower river and impoundments. Special regulations apply from Boney Falls Dam to Dam Three, where there is no closed season.

Gwinn Community Park (East Branch) to Escanaba River Forest Campground
19 Miles
6-8 Hours

❶ In **Gwinn**, there is good access and parking on the East Branch of the Escanaba at the community park adjacent to downtown. Access might be possible a few miles upstream of Gwinn on the Middle Branch at Cataract Basin Dam, except that the Upper Peninsula Power Company road at that site is gated and chained a long carry from the river. The dam, incidentally, has no discernible portage for paddlers coming down from upper sections; the only way around it is probably on the right, and it is a long, steep and difficult carry through heavy underbrush. We chose to avoid the Cataract Basin area and put in at Gwinn, on the East Branch. It is a short distance down this small rock and gravel trout stream to the Middle Branch. A mile or so upstream, there is camping at the Gwinn Tourist Park, on Iron Street.

Brown- and brook-trout fishing in the Middle Branch is quite good below Gwinn, with brook trout perhaps predominating. This section requires a full day of fishing and casual paddling. We

made it in eight hours of drifting and fishing with a few stops to cast to especially attractive pools.

The river below the junction of the East Branch is 60-80 feet wide, with depths of one to four and three to six feet, depending on season and dam discharges upstream. The current alternates between very slow and very fast. Immediately below Gwinn, all streamside development disappears, and the river becomes inaccessible and remote. Terrain is largely hilly with upland forests of pines, spruce and hardwoods. The bottom is almost entirely rock and gravel, with some sections of fast water studded with boulders.

There is a stretch of rapids, with boulders to dodge, shortly below Gwinn, but they should present few problems for moderately experienced paddlers, except during very high water. Another set of rapids is just before the junction with the West Branch. These are very characteristic of Escanaba rapids — flowing over smooth bedrock ledges, there are few rocks to create surface disturbance, yet surprisingly large standing waves are created that could easily swamp an open canoe. During high water these waves should be given careful consideration.

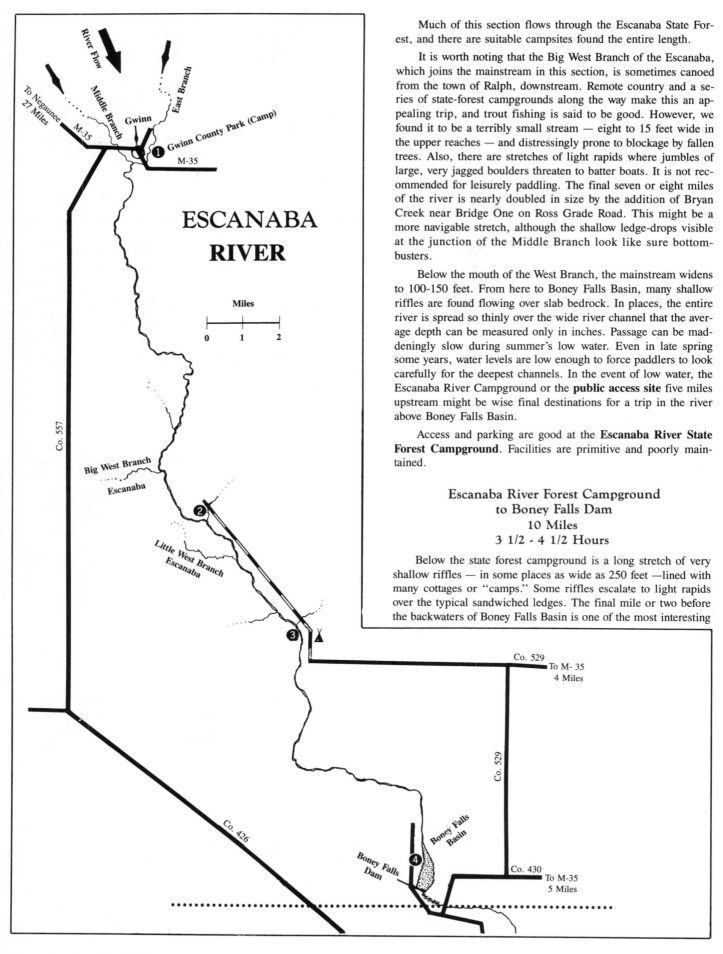

ESCANABA RIVER

Much of this section flows through the Escanaba State Forest, and there are suitable campsites found the entire length.

It is worth noting that the Big West Branch of the Escanaba, which joins the mainstream in this section, is sometimes canoed from the town of Ralph, downstream. Remote country and a series of state-forest campgrounds along the way make this an appealing trip, and trout fishing is said to be good. However, we found it to be a terribly small stream — eight to 15 feet wide in the upper reaches — and distressingly prone to blockage by fallen trees. Also, there are stretches of light rapids where jumbles of large, very jagged boulders threaten to batter boats. It is not recommended for leisurely paddling. The final seven or eight miles of the river is nearly doubled in size by the addition of Bryan Creek near Bridge One on Ross Grade Road. This might be a more navigable stretch, although the shallow ledge-drops visible at the junction of the Middle Branch look like sure bottom-busters.

Below the mouth of the West Branch, the mainstream widens to 100-150 feet. From here to Boney Falls Basin, many shallow riffles are found flowing over slab bedrock. In places, the entire river is spread so thinly over the wide river channel that the average depth can be measured only in inches. Passage can be maddeningly slow during summer's low water. Even in late spring some years, water levels are low enough to force paddlers to look carefully for the deepest channels. In the event of low water, the Escanaba River Campground or the **public access site** five miles upstream might be wise final destinations for a trip in the river above Boney Falls Basin.

Access and parking are good at the **Escanaba River State Forest Campground**. Facilities are primitive and poorly maintained.

Escanaba River Forest Campground
to Boney Falls Dam
10 Miles
3 1/2 - 4 1/2 Hours

Below the state forest campground is a long stretch of very shallow riffles — in some places as wide as 250 feet —lined with many cottages or "camps." Some riffles escalate to light rapids over the typical sandwiched ledges. The final mile or two before the backwaters of Boney Falls Basin is one of the most interesting

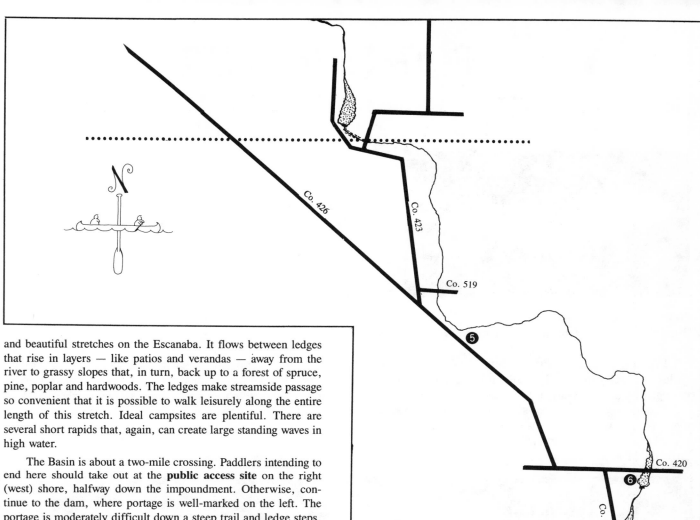

and beautiful stretches on the Escanaba. It flows between ledges that rise in layers — like patios and verandas — away from the river to grassy slopes that, in turn, back up to a forest of spruce, pine, poplar and hardwoods. The ledges make streamside passage so convenient that it is possible to walk leisurely along the entire length of this stretch. Ideal campsites are plentiful. There are several short rapids that, again, can create large standing waves in high water.

The Basin is about a two-mile crossing. Paddlers intending to end here should take out at the **public access site** on the right (west) shore, halfway down the impoundment. Otherwise, continue to the dam, where portage is well-marked on the left. The portage is moderately difficult down a steep trail and ledge steps. Access to the parking area at the right side of Boney Falls Dam is difficult from the river due to eight- to 10-foot-high sheer cliffs.

Boney Falls Dam to Co. Rd. 420 Public Access
17 Miles
5-6 Hours

To begin a trip at Boney Falls it is easier to start at the access site on the west side of Boney Falls Basin and portage the dam rather than attempt to put in down the sheer cliffs below it.

The river immediately below the dam contains a set of potentially dangerous rapids over ledges and some boulders. Even in low water, the standing waves are capable of swamping an open canoe; during high water when all the turbines in the powerhouse are operating, awesome waves are sometimes created. There is also a danger of sudden discharges — which occur at no set schedule — from the dam. A warning horn sounds moments before each release, and the resulting rush of water, we were told, is sufficient to overtake and swamp a canoe. In spite of the hazards, however, this is a breathtaking stretch of river. It flows for almost two miles through a gorge framed by sheer eight-to 20-foot-high rock sides and past numerous waterfalls — some quite spectacular — descending from small creeks and streams. In the event of mishap, rescue would be difficult. Access is virtually impossible at Co. Rd. 430 Bridge, about a mile below the dam. A mile below that bridge, the banks open up and the cliffs dwindle. The river widens to several hundred feet in places, and, again, shallow riffles are a nuisance in summer. Homes and cottages are found along much of the remainder of the river.

Co. Rd. 519 has fair access with roadside parking. Shallow riffles alternate with pools of deep water and little current. Brown trout and fewer brook trout are found from Boney Falls Dam to below here, but their numbers are said to have dwindled in recent years.

A **public access site**, with good access and parking, is located about a mile below Co. Rd. 519. From here, expect more riffles and light rapids alternating with long pools. Some riffles are extremely shallow in summer, but most have a deeper channel where passage is usually possible.

The final take-out is a **public access site** with good access and parking just below the Co. Rd. 420 Bridge, halfway across the backwaters of Dam Three. Further progress through the remaining two dams and backwaters before entering Escanaba on Lake Michigan is blocked at Dam Three with signs announcing "No Portage."

FORD RIVER

County: Delta

Start/End:	Co. Rd. 414 Bridge to M-35 Bridge (mouth of river)
Miles:	14.75
Gradient:	Co. Rd. 414 to US-2 — 7.9 ft/mile
	US-2 to mouth — 10.9 ft/mile
Portages:	None
Rapids/Falls:	Unnamed rapids below US-2 — Class II-III
	Several unnamed rapids below US-2 — Class I-II
Campgrounds:	None
Canoe Liveries:	None

Skill Required: I-II

Topo. Maps: Gladstone, Escanaba (15 min.)

Like many Upper Peninsula rivers, the Ford is quite seasonal, and midsummer paddlers should be prepared to walk through shallow riffles and rock gardens. Generally, it is a quick-spirited, rock- and gravel-bottom river with slightly tea-colored water. Most of it flows through private land with quite limited camping opportunities. Fishing is for smallmouth bass and occasional northern pike.

The most remote section of the Ford is only canoeable during periods of high water. It is reached by a bridge on an unnamed gravel road that runs west of a railroad siding called Woodlawn, on Co. Rd. 426 north of Cornell. The river here flows quickly over gravel and rock, but even by the beginning of June, when we were there, water levels are often insufficient to float a canoe. That, coupled with difficulty of access and parking at the bridge because of private property, caused us to begin our trip 17 miles downstream.

Whitewater on the Presque Isle River.

Co. Rd. 414 to US-2 Bridge
7.5 Miles
2-3 Hours

1   **Access** is fairly good at Co. Rd. 414, with often-used parking areas on both sides of the river. The current is quick over mostly gravel bottom, but it gives way soon to slow water over sand bottom. In the slow stretches, the river meanders through lowland forests punctuated by a few open meadows. Occasional fallen trees and minor logjams create partial obstructions, but the river, at 40-90 feet, is generally wide enough to allow free passage. From Co. Rd. 414 to the mouth of the river, at the town of Ford River, we found no obstructions that required portaging, although it is likely that the long, remote and less-often-floated section above 414 will have some.

Co. Rd. 533, five miles downstream from Co. Rd. 414, has fair parking and access. From here to US-2, expect more or less continuous light rapids and riffles over gravel and bedrock. Stretches flow between flat ledge formations similar to those found in places on the Escanaba River. Homes and cottages are scattered along the entire length of the river, though not in large numbers.

2   At US-2, **access and parking** are upstream on the left and are fairly good, with room to park half a dozen or more vehicles.

US-2 Bridge to M-35 Access Site
7.25 Miles
2-3 Hours

This is the fastest section of the Ford and should not be attempted during high water conditions by beginning paddlers. There are long stretches of nearly continuous light rapids and riffles, and even the intervals of slower water are over rock and gravel bottom. Many of the riffles are shallow but runnable well into June, most years. The rapids are generally straightforward and easily negotiated by paddlers with average whitewater skills. The exception is a short drop of intense water encountered about halfway through the section. This rapids is formed by a pair of ledge-drops at a point where the river narrows between other ledges. It is easily recognized, coming after the river divides around a large island, converges, then bends to the right at the rapids. At least one source lists this unnamed rapids as Class II-III because of the high waves that develop. Even in relatively low water, the waves are substantial and — since they do not look large from above — come as a surprise. Scouting is recommended. Portage either right or left.

After these rapids, light rapids continue for a mile or more, with descent gradually increasing until it is fairly extreme and creates a long Class I-II rapids during high-water periods. During low water, expect to have to pick your way through channels between rocks, scraping and bumping along the way. Ledges and low cliffs are, again, similar to those found on the Escanaba.

The lower end of this section slows and deepens, with stretches of riffles getting shorter and more widely spaced. Houses become more frequent.

3   Access and parking are good at the **public site** just below M-35 near the town of Ford River.

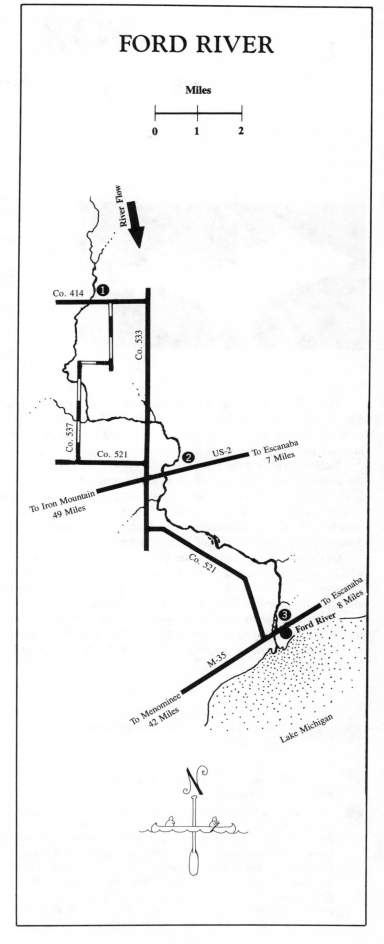

FORD RIVER

FOX RIVER

County:	Schoolcraft
Start/End:	**Wagner Dam Access to M-77 Bridge in Germfask**
Miles:	**32**
Gradient:	**5 ft/mile**
Portages:	**Numerous fallen trees, logjams**
Rapids/Falls:	**None**
Campgrounds:	**Several**
Canoe Liveries:	**One**
Skill Required:	**I**
Topo. Maps:	**Sunken Lake, Seney NW, Seney, Hardwood Island (7.5 min.)**

This slow- to moderate-flowing cold-water river has long been known for its outstanding trout fishing. It has also earned a degree of fame for being the river Ernest Hemingway had in mind when he wrote his famous short story, "Big Two Hearted River." Mounted 18- to 20-inch brook trout on the walls of stores and taverns in Seney and Germfask lend credence to the theory that Hemingway wanted to hide the identity of this great trout stream.

Paddlers will find the Fox to be an interesting and mild-tempered river. Numerous access sites, campgrounds and adjacent roads in the section above Seney tend to diminish the sense of isolation and remoteness that pervades this portion of the Upper Peninsula. Below Seney, a total lack of streamside development preserves the more expected atmosphere. Fallen trees create occasional problems along the entire river. It is best to allow plenty of time and be prepared for frequent short portages and lift-overs. Numerous sunken logs and the remnants of water-control dams are evidence of heavy early 20th-century logging activities. The surrounding plains in the Seney area are dotted with the aged stumps of pines and hemlocks that once covered the entire region.

Of the several tributaries to the Fox, only the East Branch is navigable. Its small size and the frequency of obstructions caused us to decide against including it in this description. Access is possible as far upstream as the East Branch Forest Campground, 8.5 miles north of Seney on M-77, with intermediate access points at M-77 four miles north of Seney and at M-28 just east of Seney. There is a section of "spreads" below M-77 that may hinder passage.

Water levels in the Fox River system do not fluctuate greatly; low water is seldom a problem, even in dry summers. Most of the region is within the Grand Sable and Manistique River state forests. Streamside camping possiblities are quite good in spite of large areas of lowlands and mosquito spawning grounds. High, pine-crested knolls open to the wind are recommended, as are liberal supplies of insect repellent.

Wagner Dam Public Access to Fox River Forest Campground
9 Miles
6-8 Hours

Paddling time for this section is greatly affected by fallen trees and minor logjams.

❶ Access at **Wagner Dam Public Access** is good with good parking. The river here is 25-35 feet wide and one to four feet deep with moderate current over sand bottom. Terrain is lowland forests with mixed hardwoods and conifers and very thick undergrowth of tag alders. Deadfalls begin almost immediately. Some have been partially cleared; others will have to be skirted. Dragging a canoe through damp undergrowth during mosquito season can be unforgettable. Occasional high banks and clearings lead to stump-dotted plains. Campsites directly beside the river are rare.

The Little Fox River joins the Fox about 2.5 miles above the campground and swells the mainstream slightly.

Access at **Fox River State Forest Campground** is fair, down a steep stairway. Look for handrails and stairs on the right, from the river. Facilities are primitive. **❷**

Fox River Campground to M-28 Bridge (Seney)
7 Miles
3-4 Hours

Passage is somewhat clearer below the campground, although recent windfalls will require negotiating. The river is very similar to above, with moderate current and sand bottom consistent throughout. Deep water at the frequent bends makes wading difficult for fishermen.

River Flow

1 Wagner Dam Public Access

N

Co. 450

2

FOX RIVER

Miles

0   1   2

M-28

To Munising
36 Miles

3

To Newberry
23 Miles

Seney

Spreads

M-77

East Branch Fox River

Manistique River

Germfask

4

Co. 498/Ten Curves Road

---

and pines protrude. The sites are not frequent, so it is better to stop at the first or second after the spreads than risk spending the night on low ground.

The East Branch joins the mainstream just before the junction with the Manistique. It enters on the left and is dark and very slow. The Manistique, which also joins from the left, is clouded and has moderate current. From here to the town of Germfask, the Manistique River is 60-80 feet wide and darkly colored and flows generally at a moderate rate. Fishing is for pike, bass, walleyes and occasional trout. Deadfalls and jams are piled at the bends but do not obstruct passage. There are one or two short stretches of quicker water over rocks.

Near Germfask a few houses appear. There is private access at the canoe livery and private campground before Ten Curves Road Bridge (Co. P498). Access at the bridge is poor. There is better access and good parking at the **roadside park** on the left **4** upstream side of the M-77 Bridge.

3   A **municipal campground** is on the right bank three-quarters of a mile above Seney. Access and parking are good both there and at the M-28 Bridge downstream.

M-28 Bridge to
M-77 Bridge in Germfask (Manistique River)
16 Miles
5-7 Hours

This is the most remote and least visited section of the Fox. We completed it after 4 1/2 hours of steady paddling, but it can easily be extended into a full-day or two-day trip.

The river from here is 40-60 feet wide and two to six feet deep. Bottom is almost entirely sand. Most of the terrain is lowland forests, with large silver maples predominating. Tag alders frequently border the water. Fallen trees are common, though many have been partially cleared.

About one mile below Seney is a "spreads" similar to one on the East Branch of the Fox. The river divides and re-divides into channels through a large marshland of grasses and cattails. The prominent channels tend to lead toward the left. Most channels are deep and fairly quick, even when only three to four feet wide, and there is not much chance of getting stranded or lost.

The remainder of the trip is through lowland forests. A few adequate campsites are found on knolls, where large hemlocks

INDIAN RIVER

Counties:	**Alger, Schoolcraft**
Start/End:	**Widewaters Campground to Indian Lake**
Miles:	**36**
Gradient:	**2.4 ft/mile**
Portages:	**Occasional fallen trees**
Rapids/Falls:	**None**
Campgrounds:	**Several**
Canoe Liveries:	**None**
Skill Required:	**I-II**

Because it is small and plagued by obstructions, the Indian River would probably not be navigable except for the efforts of the U.S. Forest Service. Trees that fall due to bank erosion are regularly cleared by forest-service crews. The river lies almost entirely within the Hiawatha National Forest, and numerous access sites and excellent campgrounds are conveniently located for paddlers.

Generally, the river maintains a steady, moderately strong current, is sand-bottomed, and flows through upland forests of hardwoods and pines. Water quality appears to be good and, though slightly tea-colored, the water is much clearer than many Upper Peninsula rivers. It is significant that the Indian maintains quite stable water levels and is therefore an excellent midsummer choice for canoeists.

Fishing is for brown and brook trout and was once considered outstanding. Erosion, however, has caused sand to choke most of the gravel stretches essential for spawning and, as a result, trout populations have suffered. Efforts have been made to halt this erosion, and it is particularly important that canoeists and fishermen avoid walking on the sand banks found at almost every bend in this river.

Widewaters Campground to Thunder Lake Road Bridge
12 Miles
5-7 Hours

1 Put in either at the public access site at **Widewaters USFS Campground** or one-half mile upstream at Fish Lake Public Access. Between Fish Lake and the campground, the river progresses through a series of ponds and small lakes connected by channels with little current. Below the campground the river narrows, and current increases to flow steadily over sand bottom, with some stretches of light riffles over gravel and stone. There are some fairly fast riffles just above FH-13, where there is fair access and roadside parking. The terrain along this section, as along much of the river, is upland forest of low hills and hardwoods with scattered birch, poplar and pines. Some tag alders and cedars line the banks. The river is small — 15-30 feet wide — with depths of one to three feet.

2 One to two hours below Widewaters is **10 Mile Bridge**, on FR-2258, where there is good access but limited roadside parking. By here the river has gained water volume from lake outlets and tributary streams and has increased to 30-50 feet wide, with depths remaining at one to three feet. Shortly before the bridge, a channel allows access to Straights Lake, which in turn leads to several other lakes. Most of the property around the lakes, however, is privately owned, and several cabins line the shores. There are also a few houses and cabins beside the river in this area; otherwise, it is national forest land. Good campsites are abundant. Deadfalls and sweepers are frequent, but most have at least a narrow passage cleared. Basic maneuvering abilities will get most paddlers through with little trouble.

3 **Access** at Thunder Lake Road (Co. Rd. 437) is good with good parking beside the river on the left.

Thunder Lake Road Bridge to Eight Mile Bridge
16 Miles
5-7 Hours

From Thunder Lake Road to beyond the town of Steuben, the river is similar to above. However, several miles of river below Steuben have not been cleared as assiduously as the river above and below, and passage can be difficult. According to local USFS officers, a crew opens this section once a year, but windfalls and logjams are so frequent that 12 or 15 portages are not uncommon. Tricky maneuvering and the hazards presented by obstructions make this section inadvisable for beginners. The bridge at Steuben has poor access and poor parking. Anyone wanting to avoid the difficulties in this area can bypass the entire section from Thunder Lake Road to the **Indian River Picnic Area (USFS)**. There is a campground just downstream from the picnic area. Access — wooden stairs down the steep banks — at both sites is fair. **4**

Below the picnic area and campground, expect a two- to three-hour float to Eight Mile Bridge. At first the river flows through typical terrain, though the banks are steeper and the river slightly faster and narrower. Very tight bends and frequent partially cleared deadfalls call for fairly complex maneuvering. Beginners will have difficulty, although it should be no problem for anyone with intermediate or higher skills. Wooded hills give way gradually to marshlands, and from there to Eight Mile Bridge and beyond to Indian Lake, the river divides into spreads, with narrow channels winding through the marsh grasses. Although a wrong decision can lead to backtracking or portaging, generally, all the stronger channels will lead to clear passage.

At **Eight Mile Bridge**, take out on the pine-wooded point **5** just upstream on the left, where access is good and parking is adequate for three or four vehicles.

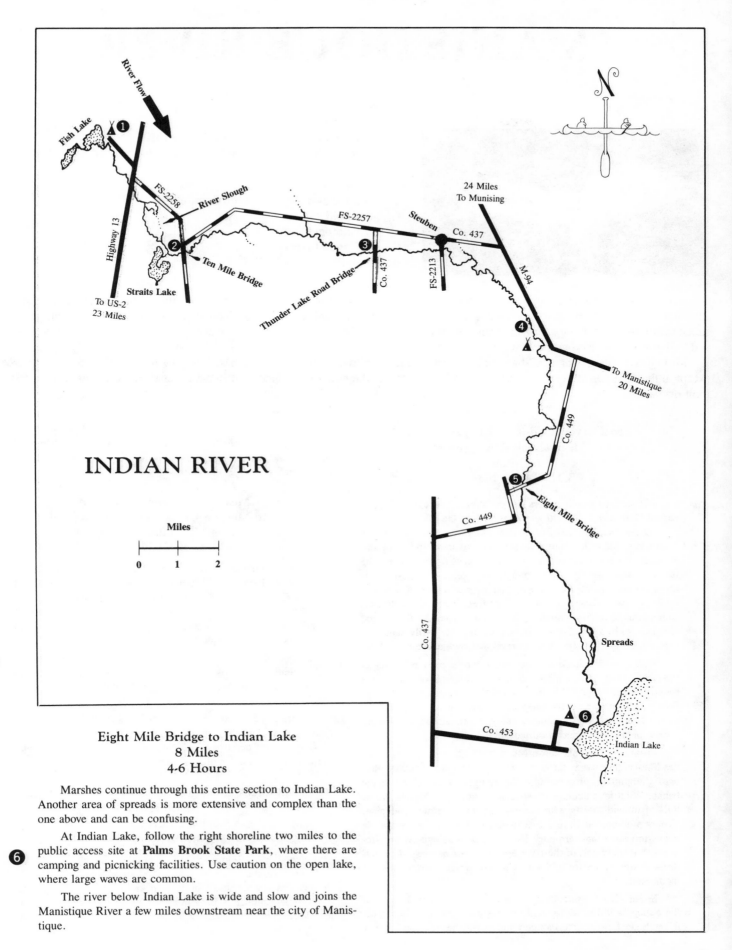

INDIAN RIVER

Miles

0   1   2

Eight Mile Bridge to Indian Lake
8 Miles
4-6 Hours

Marshes continue through this entire section to Indian Lake. Another area of spreads is more extensive and complex than the one above and can be confusing.

❻ At Indian Lake, follow the right shoreline two miles to the public access site at **Palms Brook State Park**, where there are camping and picnicking facilities. Use caution on the open lake, where large waves are common.

The river below Indian Lake is wide and slow and joins the Manistique River a few miles downstream near the city of Manistique.

MANISTIQUE RIVER

Counties:	**Luce, Schoolcraft**
Start/End:	**Ten Curves Road Access to City of Manistique**
Miles:	**67**
Gradient:	**1.5 ft/mile**
Portages:	**One dam, easy**
Rapids/Falls:	**None**
Campgrounds:	**Several**
Canoe Liveries:	**One**
Skill Required:	**I**

Emerging from the west end of Manistique Lake, the Manistique River flows southwest to the city of Manistique, at Lake Michigan. Through most of its length after the junction with the Fox River, the Manistique is wide, with slow current and sand bottom, and is well-suited to combined camping and fishing trips by paddlers of all abilities. Veterans of Fox River trips will be glad to know that fallen trees and logjams do not obstruct the Manistique.

Fishing is primarily for pike, bass and walleyes, with some trout in the upper reaches. Camping possibilities are good to excellent except in the 10 miles of Seney Wildlife Refuge below M-77, where it is prohibited, and in the lower river, where lowland and swamps limit dry access.

Ten Curves Road (Co. Rd. 498) Access
to Mead Creek Campground
16 Miles
3 1/2 - 4 1/2 Hours

❶ Put in at the **public access site** on Ten Curves Road 2.5 miles east of Germfask. This is the Lake Branch of the Manistique, and although it may be possible to start a few miles upstream at Manistique Lake, it is not a large river and may tend to be obstructed above the access site. A short distance downstream is the junction with the Fox River, and from here, the Manistique is always large enough for unobstructed passage. Average width is 60-80 feet with depths of two to eight feet. In the Lake Branch, water tends to be discolored — stained dark from the Fox — and clouded, with almost a milky hue. Bottom is primarily sand, except for a few short stretches of gravel and rock above Germfask.

❷ Access in Germfask is limited to either the private landing at the canoe livery and campground on the north edge of town or the roadside park on M-77 south of town. The bridge at Ten Curves Road has poor access and parking. **Access** down a steep bank at M-77 is only fair and is not a developed site, although there are toilets, picnic tables and good parking.

From M-77 to just above Mead Creek Forest Campground, the Manistique passes through the Seney National Wildlife Refuge. Camping is prohibited in the refuge, as is access to the banks. Wildlife is abundant, especially waterfowl. Terrain is low hills of upland forests with hardwoods, birch, spruce and pine. Cedars predominate in low areas near the river. Some streamside banks are steep and eroding. Fallen trees and logjams are frequent, but the width of the river ensures clear passage. The bottom is almost entirely sand. Current varies from slow to moderate.

❸ **Mead Creek State Forest Campground** marks the end of the Seney Wildlife Refuge and the beginning of the Manistique River State Forest. The campground is on the left bank and is

obvious from the river. There is a developed access site with good parking, and the campground has primitive facilities with toilets and water.

Mead Creek Campground
to Merwin Creek Campground
29 Miles
6 1/2 - 8 1/2 Hours

The river remains virtually unchanged through this section. Topography alters slightly to include abandoned farmlands and lowland forests. Riverside Truck Trail (Co. Rd. P433) and Co. Rd. 436 parallel the river but do not detract from the sense of isolation and quiet. Surrounding lands are almost entirely within the Manistique River State Forest.

❹ Access and parking are good at **Cookson Bridge**. The current is gentle, bottom is sand and width is 90-120 feet — characteristics that remain basically the same through the remainder of the river.

❺ There is good access at **Merwin Creek State Forest Campground**. Facilities are primitive with toilets, water and picnic tables. We ended our trip here, choosing not to continue through the remaining 22 miles of slow water.

Merwin Creek Campground to City of Manistique
22 Miles
5-6 1/2 Hours (est.)
(Not on Map)

Although our information is incomplete for this section, we do know that the river is wide and slow and passes primarily through lowland forests. The most striking feature of this section is the large number of backwaters or sloughs it contains. Many are large enough to warrant names: Klegstad's Slough, Clear Slough, Catfish Slough, Bear Town Slough, Sturgeon Hole

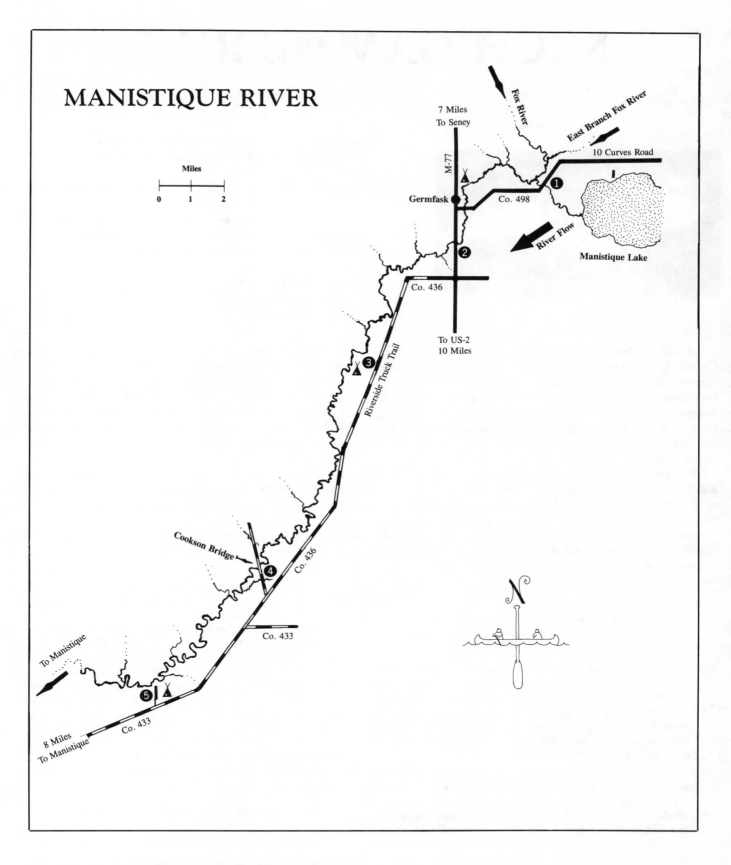

MANISTIQUE RIVER

Fox River

East Branch Fox River

7 Miles
To Seney

10 Curves Road

M-77

❶

Germfask

Co. 498

River Flow

Manistique Lake

❷

Co. 436

To US-2
10 Miles

Riverside Truck Trail

❸

Cookson Bridge

Co. 436

❹

Co. 433

To Manistique

N

❺

Co. 433

8 Miles
To Manistique

Miles
0 1 2

Slough, Island Slough. This area offers interesting possibilities for exploring and fishing. Most of the region is within the state forest, but campsites are limited because of low ground. Be aware that mosquitos, black flies and deer flies can be a major problem in season.

In Manistique, there is a small dam and community park at the north side of the city, where parking and access are good. It is preceded by a series of major backwaters and sloughs that include Jamestown Slough and the junction with the Indian River.

MICHIGAMME RIVER

Counties:	**Marquette, Dickinson, Iron**
Start/End:	**Republic Dam to M-69 Bridge**
Miles:	**40.5**
Gradient:	**Republic Dam to Michigamme Reservoir — 8.6 ft/mile**
	Hemlock Falls Dam to M-69 — 4.4 ft/mile
Portages:	**Two dams, moderately difficult**
Rapids/Falls:	**Witbeck Rapids, above M-95 Bridge — Class I-II**
Campgrounds:	**None**
Canoe Liveries:	**One**
Skill Required:	**I-II**

A major tributary of the Menominee River system, the Michigamme River begins in Lake Michigamme, in western Marquette County. Dams at Lake Michigamme, Republic, Michigamme Reservoir (Way Dam), Hemlock Falls, Peavy Falls and Lower Michigamme Falls interrupt what would otherwise be a fine river for extended expeditions. As it is, paddlers can plan on a several-day trip — with almost half the distance through backwaters — from Lake Michigamme to the junction with the Brule River. Without meaning to discourage such a trip, we must advise that crossings of Michigamme Lake, Michigamme Reservoir and Peavy Reservoir are formidable. Each of these impoundments is a significant wilderness area, with numerous islands, bays and channels that make navigation difficult. The sections of river between the dams are not as isolated and inaccessible as the reservoirs themselves but are interesting and well worth investigating.

It is important to note that the large drainage area of the Michigamme system and the influence of the many dams causes extreme water-level fluctuations. High-water marks are eight to 10 feet above normal summer levels and indicate that this otherwise hospitable river might not be kind to beginners in the spring. Several light rapids and a slightly more difficult stretch at Witbeck Rapids should not be difficult at normal water levels for paddlers with average ability.

Fishing in the river and impoundments is outstanding for walleyes, pike, smallmouth bass and muskies, with occasional trout reported in the river below Hemlock Falls Dam. Unfortunately, recent discoveries of high levels of mercury make the consumption of fish inadvisable.

Republic Dam to Michigamme Reservoir
25 Miles
6 1/2 - 8 1/2 Hours

1 In Republic, put in below **Republic Dam**, in the shadow of the slag heap from Republic Mine. The river above Republic is navigable all the way to Lake Michigamme, but access is so difficult we chose not to include that section in this description. One alternative is to make the difficult crossing of Lake Michigamme from the state park off US-41 west of Marquette, portage the dam, and come down to Republic.

Below Republic Dam, the river is 60-75 feet wide, shallow and rocky with slow to steady current. Water is clear. Terrain alternates open meadows with thickets and woodlots of hardwoods. From Republic to Witbeck Rapids, shallow riffles alternate with long, deep pools, some as large as small lakes. Banks are lightly developed, with only a few houses and farms visible from the river.

2 Halfway to Witbeck Rapids is a **state roadside park** with access, parking and picnic area. The river here spreads out to very wide, is very shallow, and may need to be walked through during low-water periods. It is followed by long stretches of still water to Witbeck.

Witbeck Rapids Public Access has good access and parking **3** just upstream of the rapids. The rapids themselves are a series of dense rock gardens with table-size to automobile-size boulders stacked to form natural reefs. Passage is through channels and short, quick chutes in and among the rocks. At least one short portage is required during low water. Most of the stretch can be tricky — if not treacherous — during high water because of tight corridors, sharp drops and the need for precise maneuvering. Current is only moderately fast during normal water levels but increases dramatically as the levels go up. Rapids extend for over a mile, then the river slows and deepens before the M-95 Bridge south of Witch Lake.

M-95 Bridge has fair access and roadside parking.

Newburg Road Bridge has fair access and limited parking.

Below M-95, generally slow to moderate current gives way to still water as the river widens and deepens entering Michigamme Reservoir. There is a **public access site** with good access and **4** parking at the upper end of the reservoir, off Race Road. Take out here or continue the eight miles across Michigamme Reservoir to Way Dam.

Hemlock Falls Dam to M-69 Bridge
4.5 Miles
1 1/2 - 2 1/2 Hours

⑤   Below Way Dam are three miles of backwaters leading directly to **Hemlock Falls Dam**. Portage this dam on the right and follow the gravel road downhill and to the left. There is access, parking and picnic tables at the end of Stream Road. The river here is 80-125 feet wide, one to two feet deep in the riffles, and three to six feet deep in the slow pools. From the dam to the bridge at M-69 is an easy float through alternating riffles and pools, with light Class I rapids near Old 69 Bridge. Basic paddling skills are sufficient. Bottom is generally gravel and stone. Terrain is hills, some large, of hardwoods. Occasional houses and cabins are visible from the river. There is reported to be excellent fishing for pike, smallmouth bass, muskies, and occasional rainbow and brown trout.

Access and parking are fair at Old M-69 Bridge.

⑥   At **M-69 Bridge**, there is a canoe livery and tackle shop, where access and parking are available with permission.

Below M-69, the backwaters of Peavy Pond begin almost immediately and extend for nine miles to Peavy Falls Dam. Many older county and topographical maps will have "Glidden Rapids" marked just below M-69, but these rapids are now submerged under Peavy backwaters.

Below Peavy Falls Dam is another three miles of backwaters of Michigamme Falls Dam. Immediately below this final dam, the Michigamme River joins with the Brule River to become the Menominee.

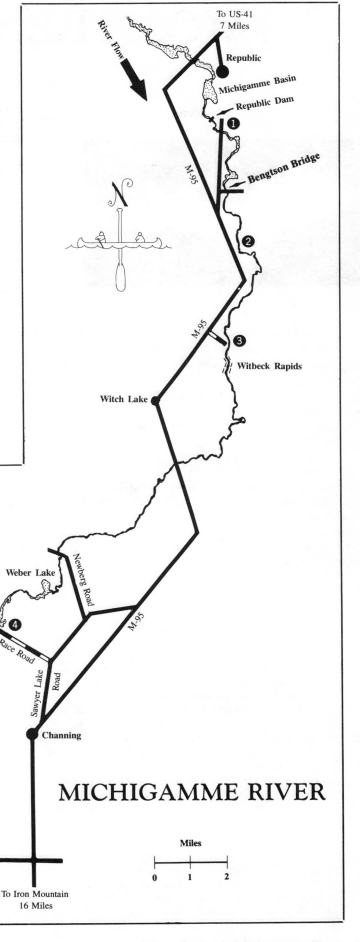

MICHIGAMME RIVER

MONTREAL RIVER

County:	**Gogebic**
Start/End:	**US-2 Bridge (West Branch) to Lake Superior Road Bridge**
Miles:	**16.5**
Gradient:	**US-2 to Saxon Falls Power Dam — 10.8 ft/mile**
	Saxon Falls Dam to Lake Superior Road — 40 ft/mile
Portages:	**Saxon Dam and Falls, difficult**
Campgrounds:	**None**
Canoe Liveries:	**None**
Skill Required:	**II-III**
Topo. Maps:	**Ironwood, Little Girls Point (15 min.)**

Like the Menominee and Brule rivers, the Montreal forms a boundary between Michigan and Wisconsin and is claimed by paddlers from both states. This westernmost Michigan river is also one of the state's loveliest and most spectacular. The final 3.5-mile section above Lake Superior is an unforgettable, nearly continuous run of Class I-III rapids through a deep gorge in remote, seldom-visited country.

Upstream, the Montreal has many Class I rapids and riffles and passes through equally remote, though less spectacular, country. In the cities of Ironwood, Michigan, and Hurley, Wisconsin, the Montreal has been the site of kayak and canoe whitewater competition but is only runnable in this area for short periods each year. We were there in September and again at the beginning of June, and water levels were too low for practical navigating both months.

Generally, only consider the river below the junction with the West Branch to be consistently runnable, with only the lower section below Saxon Falls runnable during very dry seasons. Whitewater fanatics would do well to contact the Ironwood Chamber of Commerce and local DNR and USFS field offices for up-to-the-minute reports on the upper sections that include Ironwood and, below it, Interstate Falls. (See Appendix V, page 131, "Further Information.")

Fishing is for brook and brown trout. Camping facilities are limited, although the river passes through public land and there are abundant riverside campsites. There is a municipal campground in Ironwood, but it is plagued by traffic noise. A much better atmosphere is found at Little Girls Point — five miles northeast of the mouth of the river on Lake Superior Road (Co. Rd. 505) — where camping and picnicking are on a bluff overlooking Lake Superior.

US-2 (West Branch) to Saxon Falls Power Dam
13 Miles
3 1/2 - 5 1/2 Hours

There is no easy access to this remote, seldom-paddled section. During high water, advanced paddlers can get there by putting in on the mainstream in Ironwood. Otherwise, the best approach is to put in on the little West Branch a mile inside the Wisconsin border and paddle down to the junction with the main- ❶ stream. Access is good with roadside parking at the **US-2 Bridge**. The river is 20-30 feet wide, shallow and very rocky. Water is clear and current is fast. During spring or when water is being released from Giles Flowage Dam, upstream, this can be a very challenging little river. During low water, expect to bump and scrape. Tight bends and occasional obstructions require fairly advanced maneuvering skills. Terrain is low hills of hardwoods and mixed conifers with willows common at the banks.

The junction with the mainstream is about one mile downstream. During the summer it is not unusual for the mainstream to be smaller than the West Branch. It also tends to be discolored from red clay and mud. From the junction of the rivers, there are several miles of continuous Class I rapids and rock gardens, some

of which are quite shallow during low-water periods. Rocks vary from grapefruit-size to wheelbarrow-size and are jagged. The river is 30-40 feet wide and generally clear, although the potential for obstruction from fallen trees exists. High-water marks indicate levels five to six feet above early summer levels.

Closer to Saxon Flowage, the current slows, and sections of light riffles alternate with slow water over sand bottom. Some high banks of eroding clay contribute to the river's discoloration. Rock stretches give way entirely to a narrow backwater before Saxon Flowage, where numerous bays and channels can be confusing, especially during heavy fogs that are not unusual off Lake Superior.

Take out at the left of the **dam**, where access and limited ❷ parking are both good. Do not continue downstream. This is the first of two hydroelectric dams, and between them, there is a series of high falls culminating with Saxon Falls. Arrange to shuttle to the lower dam or make a one-mile portage on roads. Access to the river at Saxon Falls Dam, the lower power station, is through power-company property. Permission is required to enter a gate and reach the river down steep metal stairs.

Saxon Falls Dam to
Lake Superior Road (Co. Rd. 505) Bridge
3.5 Miles
2-3 Hours

Access to the river is difficult down the stairway at Saxon Falls, but the trip is well worth the effort. This is one of the most beautiful places in Michigan and one of the finest sections of whitewater. Saxon Falls are immediately upstream from the grassy landing at the bottom of the stairs and make an unforgettable sight. The river from the falls downstream consists of nearly continuous Class I-III rapids for at least three miles, with difficulty dependent on the amount of water coming over Saxon Falls. According to paddlers who have made the trip many times, when there are three "fingers" of water coming over Saxon Falls, expect a wild trip with much Class III and, perhaps, Class IV water. We made the trip when one finger came over the falls and found it to be a wonderful, fairly challenging run through Class I and much Class II-III water. At that level, there were only a few rock gardens and riffles shallow enough to be bottom-draggers and one or two stretches that required short walk-throughs. Even at low levels, however, this is not a section recommended for beginning paddlers or even intermediate paddlers without whitewater experience.

At any water level, numerous chutes with high standing waves and backrollers have the potential to swamp open canoes, and the remoteness of the region and total lack of intermediate access points means that, in the event of mishap, a long and difficult hike is necessary to find assistance. Some drops and chutes require scouting at all water levels, and all require care and attention.

The river is 50-100 feet wide. Water is discolored. Terrain is spectacular, with high, sheer cliffs of conglomerate rock rising 100-200 feet above the river in many places. Forests of pines and hemlocks dominate steep valleys and the low hills that line the river between cliffs. Through the gorge, high rock walls on one side of the river are usually opposed by lower ground on the other side, so that access to shore is possible in most places. Good potential campsites are quite frequent, although many of the lower banks are covered with thick underbrush.

The river slows and widens shortly before the **bridge at Lake Superior Road**. Access is good at the bridge, but parking is limited to the roadside. Further progress to Lake Superior is impeded by a power dam and Superior Falls, just below the bridge.

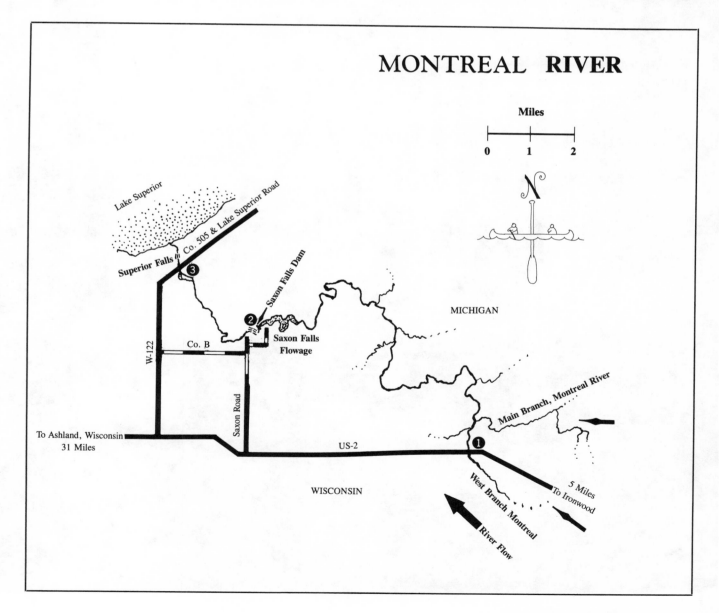

ONTONAGON RIVER, SOUTH BRANCH

County:	Ontonagon
Start/End:	Ewen to Victoria Dam
Miles:	26.5
Gradient:	7.5 ft/mile
Portages:	At least one rapids may require portaging
Rapids/Falls:	Flannigan Rapids, 12 miles below Ewen — Class I-II
	Unnamed rapids 25 miles below Ewen — Class II-III
Campgrounds:	One
Canoe Liveries:	None

Skill Required:	II
Topo. Maps:	Matchwood, Rockland (15 min.)

The South Branch may be the least-known and least-often-paddled of the major branches of the Ontonagon, yet we found it to be the most attractive and challenging. Although in this description we have included only the final section from Ewen to Victoria Dam, the upper river is composed of some unusual features that deserve mention. It begins as the Cisco Branch of the Ontonagon, a small but navigable stream in southwestern Gogebic County, better known for trout fishing than canoeing. About eight miles south of Ewen, in the area of 18 Mile Rapids, it is joined by Sucker Creek, which is the final channel for water diverted from the Middle Branch into the flume at Bond Falls Basin. The addition of this water increases the size and volume of the Cisco Branch significantly, and from there it becomes known as the South Branch. Water levels for the remainder of the river are dependent on flow from the flume and from Sucker Creek, which in turn depends on power-generating needs of the hydroelectric plant at Victoria Dam.

Fishing in the Cisco Branch and South Branch is excellent for brook trout. Most of the surrounding lands downstream from Ewen are in the Ottawa National Forest, and suitable riverside campsites are abundant. With the exception of the rapids in the final 1.5 to two miles before Victoria Dam Basin, paddlers with average ability should not have difficulty on the South Branch. Those final rapids, however, are very heavy and very difficult during medium to high water and should be attempted only by advanced whitewater paddlers.

MAP #1: ONTONAGON

Ewen to Victoria Dam
26.5 Miles
6-8 Hours

❶ Because there are no intermediate access points in this section, paddlers planning to complete the trip in one day are advised to start early. Put in at the public access site at **M-28 Bridge** in Ewen. Here, the river is 40-60 feet wide, slow and muddy. Water is the color of coffee with cream, and current is slow to moderate. Plan on about an hour and a half of steady paddling before the current increases to anything more than moderate. At first, terrain is low hills of hardwoods with lowlands of maples and dead elms near the river. Farther downstream, high, wooded hills predominate, with hardwoods, pines and hemlocks most common.

Flannigan Rapids are the only rapids marked on most county and topographical maps we have seen, and they are shown to be about half a mile long through several tight bends. It is difficult to determine just which are Flannigan Rapids, since rapids of varying length occur for at least 10 miles beginning about 12 miles below Ewen. Most are either riffles or Class I-II rapids with

standing waves and bushel-basket-size boulders to avoid. Channels are clear and easily detected, although during low water, shallow riffles and rock gardens will need picking through. The discolored water makes detecting rocks sometimes difficult, especially in slower water. Rapids alternate with stretches of slow water through much of the section. Two runs of virtually constant Class I-II rapids are several miles long each.

After the junction with the West Branch, the river slows and widens to 80-120 feet. From here the South Branch is technically known as the West Branch, even though the West Branch is the smaller river. The West Branch itself is considered navigable from the M-28 Bridge — just below its outlet from Gogebic Lake at Bergland Dam — but only during high water in spring, when it is said to be a fast, challenging trip.

After the junction of the West Branch and South Branch, a long stretch of slow water leads to a final one-hour run of rapids that culminates in a major rapids about 1.5 miles above Victoria Basin. After a gradual right bend, the river drops out of sight. You will hear the rapids before you see them. Take out on the left and scout carefully. In high water, this rapids is runnable only by advanced paddlers and probably only in covered boats. We ran it during medium-high water with the banks close to overflowing. The initial drop is about four to five feet, with the most intense water and a very large backroller near the left shore. A chute just right of center squeezes between intimidating standing waves and backrollers — easily large enough to swamp an open canoe — and huge partially submerged rocks immediately downstream need to be avoided. We made it through, but barely. Someone who came before us wasn't so fortunate; we found an aluminum canoe wrapped around rocks just below the steepest pitch.

Portaging around this apparently unnamed rapids is difficult over uneven ground and thick underbrush. But it is not nearly as difficult as the walk out — the nearest road, at Victoria Dam, is three miles as the crow flies. About a thousand yards of relatively easy Class I-II rapids follow the first difficult drop, and they are followed by one-quarter mile of still water through a steep, wooded canyon. Around a bend to the left is another rapids down

steep descent. Although shorter and less intense than the water upstream, these are solid Class II rapids with quite high standing waves and should be negotiated with care. They empty directly into Victoria Basin.

Follow the left shore of the reservoir and make the long crossing to the **dam**. Portage on the left at the landing, where access and parking are good. Avoid the right side of the dam and the spillway leading to spectacular Victoria Falls. A small, primitive campground is near the dam.

There is no good access to the river below Victoria Dam. Much of the water is diverted down a flume that follows a gravel service road about 1.5 miles to a generating station and the river. The portage is so long — and the remainder of river before the mainstream of the Ontonagon so short — we recommend taking out at Victoria Dam and shuttling to either the Victoria Falls Road Bridge or Military Bridge on US-45 to continue on the mainstream.

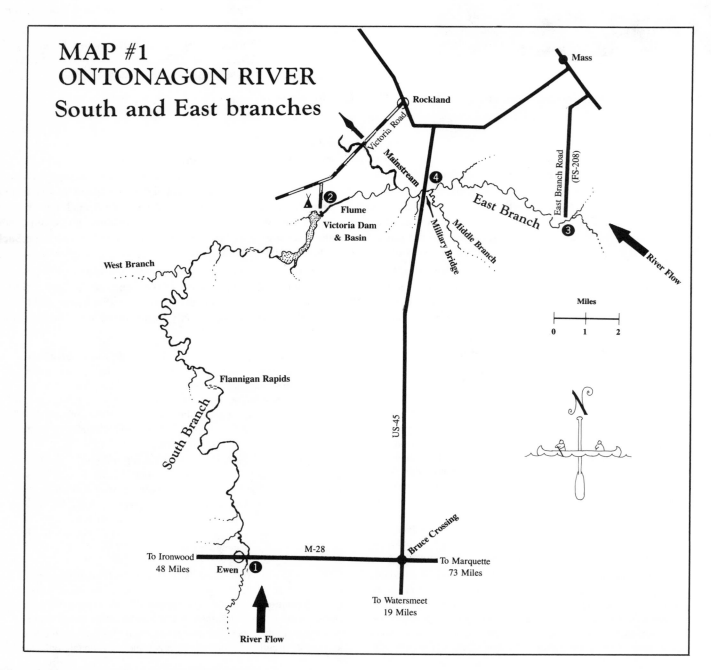

MAP #1
ONTONAGON RIVER
South and East branches

ONTONAGON RIVER, EAST BRANCH

County:	**Ontonagon**
Start/End:	**FS-208 to US-45 Bridge**
Miles:	**7.5**
Gradient:	**24 ft/mile**
Portages:	**Occasional fallen trees**
Rapids/Falls:	**Numerous unnamed rapids — Class I- III**
Campgrounds:	**None**
Canoe	**Liveries: None**
Skill Required:	**II-III**
Topo. Maps:	**Rockland (15 min.)**

This small river is noted for having one of the finest and longest stretches of Class II-III rapids in Michigan. Although access is possible as far upstream as the M-28 Bridge in Kenton, extensive logjams and frequent fallen trees make passage difficult and discouraging in the upper reaches.

We chose to include only the final 7.5 miles above Military Bridge. This remote section of nearly continuous rapids is best run in late spring and early summer, when the rapids rate Class II-III. In summer and fall the rating drops to Class I-II, with passage during very low water difficult and tedious through shallow rock gardens. Only experienced paddlers should attempt this section, especially during high- water periods, when only those with whitewater experience can expect to negotiate it successfully.

MAP #1 — ONTONAGON

**FS-208 Road (East Branch Road)
to US-45 Bridge (Military Bridge)
7.5 Miles
2 1/2 - 4 Hours**

3 Put in at the site of the **washed-out FS-208 Bridge**. This is on private property, and permission must be obtained before access can be attempted. The owner of the property lives in the farmhouse on the right, at the end of East Branch Road. Access is through the gate at the end of the road and leads across cow pastures to the river. The river is 40-80 feet wide and the color of coffee with cream. Current is moderate near the access site but increases quickly downstream. Terrain is mostly low hills of hardwoods with many eroding clay bluffs. Occasional fallen trees partially obstruct the river.

Most of the riverbed is strewn with bushel-basket-size and smaller boulders, many of them quite jagged. The low visibility of the water makes it difficult to detect them, especially during low water, and collisions are inevitable. Passage through the rapids is relatively straightforward. Rock gardens and chutes require some precise maneuvering, but the runs are primarily down steep descent through standing waves. The action is fast and relentless for several miles and demands good whitewater skills.

One note worth mentioning is that, because of the river's nearly due-west course, late-afternoon sun and glare proved a hindrance to us in reading the water. A morning or early afternoon run would be better.

Take out at the **roadside park** on the right, before Military **4** Bridge. Access is fair up a steep bank, parking is good, and there are toilets, water and a picnic area.

ONTONAGON RIVER, MAINSTREAM

County:	Ontonagon
Start/End:	US-45 Bridge to Ontonagon
Miles:	24
Gradient:	2.5 ft/mile
Portages:	None
Rapids/Falls:	Irish Rapids, 4.5 miles below Victoria Road — Class I-II
	Grand Rapids, 7.5 miles below Victoria Road —Class I-II
Campgrounds:	None
Canoe Liveries:	None
Skill Required:	I-II

Topo. Maps: Rockland, Ontonagon (15 min.)

The mainstream of the Ontonagon and its major tributaries — the East Branch, the Middle Branch and the South Branch — make up one of the most interesting and varied river systems in the Upper Peninsula. Remote, undeveloped country, excellent fishing, and many stretches of Class I-III rapids are characteristic of the entire system. Although several dams and waterfalls make extended expeditions difficult, trips of one to several days are possible on each of the branches.

The mainstream begins after the confluence of the East Branch and the Middle Branch at Military Bridge on US-45. This large, generally slow river is the tamest of the major branches, but two rapids may require caution, especially during high water.

Camping possiblities are good on abundant public land along the river. Fishing is excellent for walleyes and other warm-water species and for lake-run trout and salmon in the spring and fall. An extended season from April 1 to December 31 is in effect up to the junctions of the East Branch and Middle Branch.

MAP #2: ONTONAGON

US-45 Bridge (Military Bridge) to City of Ontonagon
24 Miles
7-9 Hours

4 There is a developed **roadside park** — with good parking, a picnic area, toilets and water — on the right upstream side of the river at Military Bridge. Access is only fair down a steep bank. The East Branch and Middle Branch are visible just upstream. The river is 125-200 feet wide and flows over light riffles. Visibility is less than one foot through red-brown water.

One mile below the put-in, the West Branch (already joined by the South Branch) enters on the left and increases water volume noticeably. Levels on the mainstream are usually sufficient for good floating even during dry summers, although some shallow riffles and sand bars may avoid detection in the discolored water and cause bottom-dragging.

Three and a half miles below US-45, there is fair access and good parking on the left upstream side of the **Victoria Road Bridge**. This is the last access before Ontonagon and also an alternative put-in for paddlers wishing to reach Ontonagon in one day without hurrying. We made the trip from here in 5 1/2 hours of steady paddling. Current in the final half of the section is nearly nonexistent and will not aid progress. It is also worth not-

ing that prevailing northwest winds can hinder progress significantly; we fought winds strong enough to blow whitecaps on the river.

There are a few scattered cabins visible from the river, but most of the way is through a deep, wooded valley with few signs of habitation or other development. Banks up to 150 feet high or more are wooded with hardwoods and pines; low valleys and banks have hardwoods, birch, pine and hemlock. Much of the bordering land is in the Ottawa National Forest and the Baraga State Forest. Not far to the west is Porcupine Mountains State Park. Good campsites are abundant on low, wooded banks and frequent large sandbars. The river alternates long stretches of slow water with short, light riffles.

Irish Rapids are eight miles below US-45. During low water, take the right channel around the island at midriver, where most of the water volume is forced — the shallow riffles to the left will probably not float a canoe. Standing waves in the channel may create difficulties for beginners even during low water. During high water they have the capacity to swamp open canoes and should be scouted from the right bank. The length of the rapids is only a few hundred feet, and portaging would not be difficult.

Grand Rapids are three miles below Irish Rapids and are preceded by long stretches of slow water. These several-hundred-yard-long rapids are formed by a series of low rock shelves. The river is wide over them, creating very shallow water in summer with no obvious channels or chutes. During high water, standing waves develop that could be difficult. Light riffles continue downstream, with several islands immediately below the rapids.

The remainder of the river is generally wide and deep with slow to barely noticeable current. Terrain becomes gradually lower with many eroding clay banks. Large sandbars at nearly every bend create ideal campsites at most water levels. Power boats frequently come upriver the final few miles before Ontonagon.

In Ontonagon, there is **public access and parking** at the marina on the left past the railroad trestle. **6**

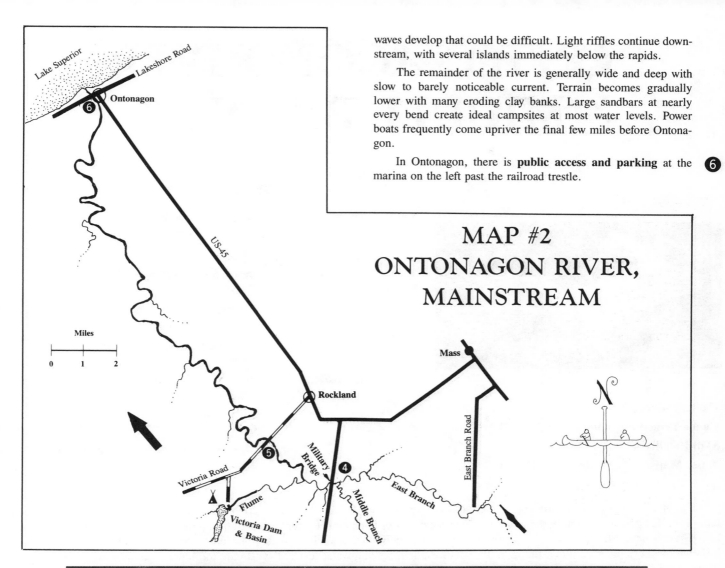

MAP #2
ONTONAGON RIVER,
MAINSTREAM

ONTONAGON RIVER, MIDDLE BRANCH

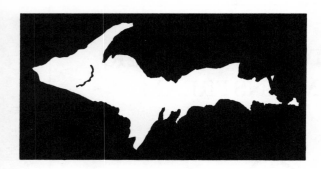

Counties:	Gogebic, Ontonagon
Start/End:	Watersmeet to Bond Falls Flowage
Miles:	20.25
Gradient:	Watersmeet to Burned Dam Campground —2.2 ft/mile
	Burned Dam to Bond Falls Flowage — 7.3 ft/mile
Portages:	2-3 small falls, fairly easy; occasional fallen trees
Rapids/Falls:	Several unnamed rapids below Burned Dam Campground — Class I-II
	Little Falls, just before Bond Falls Flowage — Class II
	Mex-I-Min-E Falls, at Burned Dam Campground

Campgrounds:	One
Canoe Liveries:	One
Skill Required:	II
Topo. Maps:	Watersmeet (15 min.)

This small, clear trout stream begins at Crooked Lake, in the Sylvania Tract Recreation Area, but is not large enough to be navigable until 10 miles downstream near the town of Watersmeet. From Watersmeet, there are about 50 miles of river until the junction with the East Branch near Military Bridge, but only the section to Bond Falls Flowage is considered consistently navigable. At Bond Falls Flowage, water is diverted into a flume to the South Branch, leaving water levels downstream too low for passage except in early spring. Water levels above Bond Falls are consistently high enough for good paddling, even in midsummer. Several short rapids and occasional tight bends require basic paddling skills, especially below Burned Dam Campground. The ledge-drops at Little Falls, before Bond Falls Flowage, should be portaged by all but experienced whitewater paddlers.

Good streamside campsites are available on public land in the Ottawa National Forest and at Burned Dam Campground. Fishing is excellent for brook trout, with browns and rainbows also present.

MAP #3: ONTONAGON RIVER
Watersmeet to Burned Dam USFS Campground
9.25 Miles
4-5 Hours

① There is good access and parking on Russes Road (USFS-378) three miles above Watersmeet, or use the public site at the **US-45 Bridge** in Watersmeet, where access and parking are good. Here, the river is 15-25 feet wide and two to four feet deep over mostly sand bottom. Water is clear, though slightly tea-colored. Current is slow to moderate with several short chutes and drops of fast water that will not be difficult for moderately experienced paddlers. Terrain is generally low hills of hardwoods away from the river, with tag alders and cedars predominant near the water.

At Buck Lake Road Bridge, access is fair with limited parking. Below here are several miles of slow, wide river through marshlands. The river is paralleled by Old US-2 (Co. Rd. 208), and occasional houses and cabins are visible from the river. After a low railroad trestle, the river narrows, and current increases

over mild riffles.

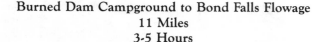

Burned Dam USFS Campground is at Mex-I-Min-E Falls. The falls are a short, furious drop that could be run by advanced paddlers in covered boats but should be portaged by all others. The portage trail is on the right and is about 300 feet long. Camping facilities are primitive.

Burned Dam Campground to Bond Falls Flowage
11 Miles
3-5 Hours

There are several moderately difficult Class I-II rapids in this section. Tight bends, minor logjams and occasional fallen trees combine with the rapids to make this the most difficult section of the river and one that is not recommended for absolute beginners. The longest rapids are 1 1/2 hours below Mex-I-Min-E Falls and are a 300- to 400-foot-long run of steep descent with standing waves and exposed rocks. There is not much maneuvering required — stay to the center but watch for a large rock at midstream at the bottom of the run. Other short rapids follow in succession, alternating with stretches of slow water.

Interior Bridge (USFS-172 Road) has fair access and limited parking. Fairly fast water below the bridge gives way to slower water through lowlands of silver maple, where fallen trees are not uncommon. Several trees and minor jams may require short portages.

About an hour below Interior Bridge, just before the river enters Bond Falls Flowage, are two sets of rapids at Little Falls. The first is runnable but requires scouting. Take out on the right, through heavy underbrush. The zig-zag course through the only clear chute requires precise and skilled maneuvering. The second drop follows almost immediately. A sudden three-foot drop and jagged, exposed rocks make portaging advisable, although the stretch may be runnable by advanced paddlers when high water covers most rocks.

Take out on the left, just as the river opens into Bond Falls

Flowage. A trail leads to a two-track road that runs south to Interior Road. Or, cross the flowage 2.5 miles to the northeast, heading toward the white dam-house. There is good access, parking, camping and supplies near the dam at **Bond Falls Park.**

Bond Falls are immediately below the dam. The river from here is usually not recommended for passage. About half the water of the Middle Branch is diverted into a flume at Bond Falls Flowage, leaving the remainder of the river very rocky and shallow. We have heard that these lower sections can be run in early spring when other rivers are at flood stage. Keep in mind that Agate Falls, at M-28, requires a long and difficult portage. From there to the junction of the East Branch is an estimated 10-hour float — including some fast water — through remote country. In that section, clay banks and tributaries change the clear water of the Middle Branch to the red-brown more characteristic of the Ontonagon system.

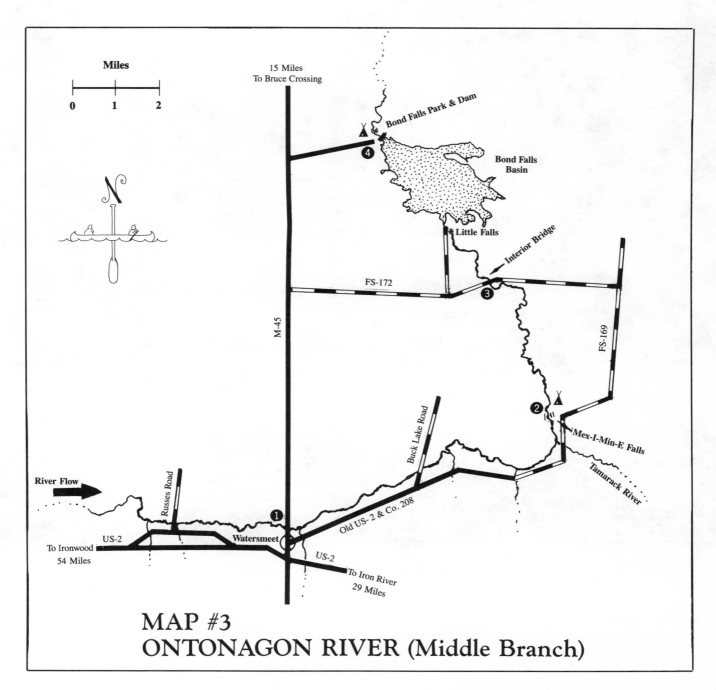

MAP #3
ONTONAGON RIVER (Middle Branch)

Montreal River in the gorge below Saxon Falls.

PAINT RIVER

County:	**Iron**
Start/end:	**Gibbs City to Little Bull Dam**
Miles:	**38**
Gradient:	**4.2 ft/mile**
Portages:	**Possibly two at rapids, fairly difficult; one dam, difficult**
Rapids/Falls:	**Unnamed rapids below the junction with the Net River — Class I-II**
	Hemlock Rapids, Upper and Lower, 13 miles below Gibbs City — Class II-III
	Unnamed rapids immediately below Crystal Falls Dam — Class I-II
	Horserace Rapids, below Little Bull Dam — Not runnable

Campgrounds:	**Several**
Canoe Liveries:	**None**
Skill Required:	**Rapids: III; all other sections — I**
Topo. Maps:	**Gibbs City, Sunset Lake, Amasa, Kelso Junction, Crystal Falls (7.5 min.)**

The Paint is part of the large river system — including the Brule and Michigamme rivers — that comes together in the southeast corner of Iron County to form the Menominee River. Except for Hemlock Rapids (about halfway between Gibbs City and Crystal Falls) and the gorge, rapids and falls at Horserace Rapids (near the end of the river), it is a generally quiet, moderately paced river well-suited to beginning paddlers and families.

Camping potential is good, with several USFS campgrounds as well as abundant streamside sites in the long stretches that run through state and national forest land. The upper reaches support brook, brown and rainbow trout, and the lower reaches hold smallmouth bass and northern pike. Other wildlife is abundant, especially deer and bald eagles, which we saw in numbers greater than anywhere else in Michigan.

Gibbs City to
Bates-Amasa Road Bridge (Co. Rd. 643)
17 Miles
6 1/2 - 8 1/2 Hours

This long section has much slow water but also several sets of rapids, two of which — the Upper and Lower Hemlock — may require portaging. The wide range of canoeing time indicated above is to allow for the portages at Hemlock. We completed the trip in 6 1/2 hours, running all rapids. We spent 30-45 minutes scouting Hemlock Rapids, a delay that is absolutely necessary. Allow at least two hours more for portaging, if necessary, or plan to make it a two-day trip. There are several well-used campsites in the area of the rapids.

❶ A **U.S. Forest Service campground** is located just above the non-existent town of Gibbs City. There are only four campsites and no water facilities, so bring your own water. Put in directly right from the campsites. The river is low by late summer, when some riffles will be too shallow to float through. During periods of higher water, trips can begin on either the North or South Branch well above their junction at Gibbs City.

At Gibbs City, the Paint mainstream is 40-75 feet wide and rocky and flows through high country of mixed forests, with thickets and tag alders frequent. From the beginning, there are sections of very slow water that give way to quick, shallow riffles — a pattern that is repeated all the way to Crystal Falls. There are occasional cabins — or "camps," as most residents of the Upper Peninsula call them — much of the trip, but they affect wildlife

very little and do not detract from the sense of remoteness and wildness that lingers over the Paint. We saw two eagles fly from perches apparently in the front yard of one cabin; deer were bedding down at another.

The second **USFS campground** is about five miles — 1 1/2 **❷** to two hours paddling time — below the first. It has only three sites and no water. Access and parking are good.

The junction with the Net River is two to three hours below Gibbs City. The Net is often mentioned as a canoeable river, but when we saw it, after a week of heavy rains in September, it was still much too shallow to run. Reports are that it is a beautiful river through remote country and well worth investigating during spring or early summer.

After the junction with the Net, slow, deep water becomes more predominant, culminating finally in several miles of still water. Current is nearly imperceptible. Dead elms and cedars are reminiscent of some southern-Michigan rivers. One or two hours of this ends at a sudden, fast chute of whitewater. This 100-foot-long run of standing waves can be taken down the center, but use caution.

One-half to one hour further, there is a similar, though shorter and less-intense, drop out of dead water that should not be difficult for most paddlers.

Upper Hemlock Rapids can be heard not long after the Hemlock River — visible as a cascading stream in a small bay on the left — enters the Paint. The rapids are approximately 13 miles, or

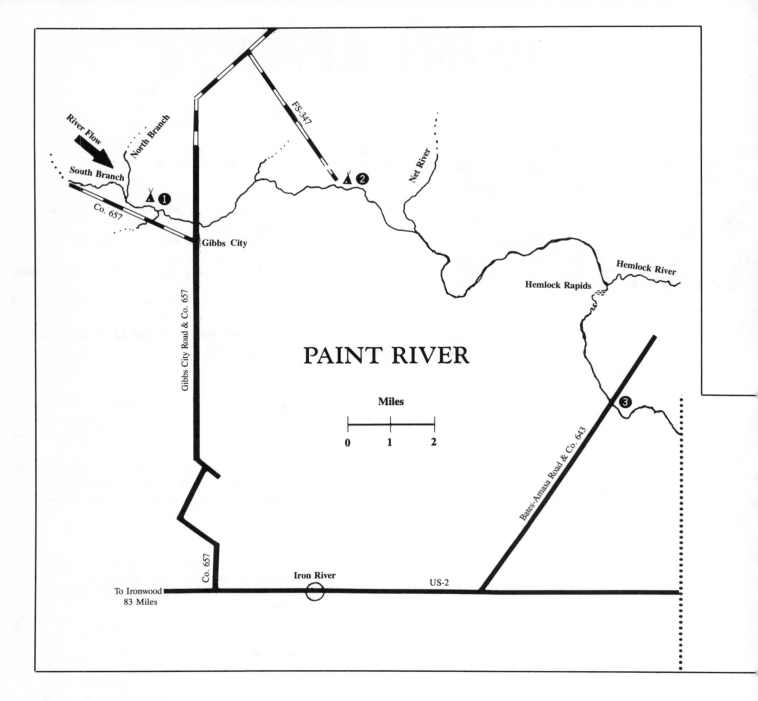

PAINT RIVER

Miles

0   1   2

three to five hours paddling time, from Gibbs City. The first drop is fairly straightforward. Run it down the center and take out on the left in the quiet pool below to scout the remainder of the rapids.

Most references we have encountered consider both Upper and Lower Hemlock Rapids unrunnable and strongly recommend lining through or portaging. We found them to be runnable at medium to low water levels but only by experienced whitewater paddlers. Fairly complex maneuvering is required through chutes and standing waves capable of swamping an open canoe. During high water in spring, these rapids are, as a local resident told us, "awesome" and are perhaps unrunnable in open boats.

The trickiest spot on Upper Hemlock is a 90-degree turn to the left near the beginning of the rapids. Scout carefully and seek out the strongest chute, or V, to run. Backrollers could be a problem in higher water, and standing waves are always present. Total length of the rapids is about 1,400 feet. There is a good trail on

the left, so portage if in doubt.

A quarter-mile stretch of still water follows Upper Hemlock. Lower Hemlock, like the upper rapids, is audible well in advance. Take out on the left and scout carefully. These are more difficult than the upper rapids and require serious consideration. There is one Class III drop of approximately four feet, followed by a potentially dangerous backroller. Total length is about 2,000 feet, with much of it difficult, extremely fast water over bushel-basket-to picnic-table-size boulders. Chutes are narrow and require precise maneuvering. The one-half-mile portage is more difficult than the one on the upper rapids, but don't let it be a deterrent to portaging. These rapids are not suited for canoeists inexperienced in whitewater. Much of the land bordering the rapids is within state forest, and there are several good and often-used campsites near the river.

Three miles below Lower Hemlock Rapids, access and parking are good at the **Bates-Amasa Road Bridge**.

3

Bates-Amasa Road Bridge (Co.Rd. 643) to Crystal Falls Power Dam
13 Miles
4-5 Hours

From Bates-Amasa Road to Crystal Falls, the river is wide (75-125 feet) and alternates shallow riffles with slow, deeper water, most of it over rock and gravel bottom. We found good smallmouth-bass fishing in the slower, deeper water.

Erickson's Landing is a state-maintained access site with good access and parking.

US-141 Bridge has no public access or parking. From here the river slows and widens into the backwaters of Crystal Falls Power Dam. The backwaters are little more than a mile long, but the portage at the dam is difficult. Take out on the left side at the grassy access site about 200 feet before the lower station and carry to the steep bank across the road. The bank is heavily overgrown, and there is no trail that we could discern. Bust your way through and down to the grassy banks below the dam or arrange to shuttle to the public access site at M-69 Bridge, one-half mile downstream. Below the dam is a short, fairly difficult stretch of Class I-II rapids followed by milder riffles that extend beyond the access site and bridge at M-69.

M-69 Bridge to Little Bull Dam
8 Miles
2-3 Hours

Access and parking are good at the public site on the right upstream side of the **M-69 Bridge** in Crystal Falls. From here, riffles diminish quickly, and the river widens and slows considerably. This is some of the most isolated country on the river. We saw only one cabin and much wildlife, especially waterfowl, eagles and deer.

Little Bull Dam might as well be considered the end of the Paint River. Downstream was once several miles of extremely challenging and beautiful water climaxing at Horserace Rapids. However, Wisconsin Electric's Little Bull Diversion Canal now runs much, if not most, of the Paint River's water over to Peavy Pond and the Michigamme River for power-production, leaving the Paint too depleted for good canoeing. Horserace Rapids are virtually unrunnable, except perhaps in spring and then only by the most experienced whitewater experts. The diversion canal is navigable, but somewhat uninspiring, and makes possible a long expedition to Peavy Pond, down the Michigamme and into the Menominee river.

There is good access and parking at **Little Bull Dam**. Camping is permitted, although space is limited, and it is very much like camping in a parking lot. Follow signs off M-69 to Wisconsin Electric Public Recreation Site #22.

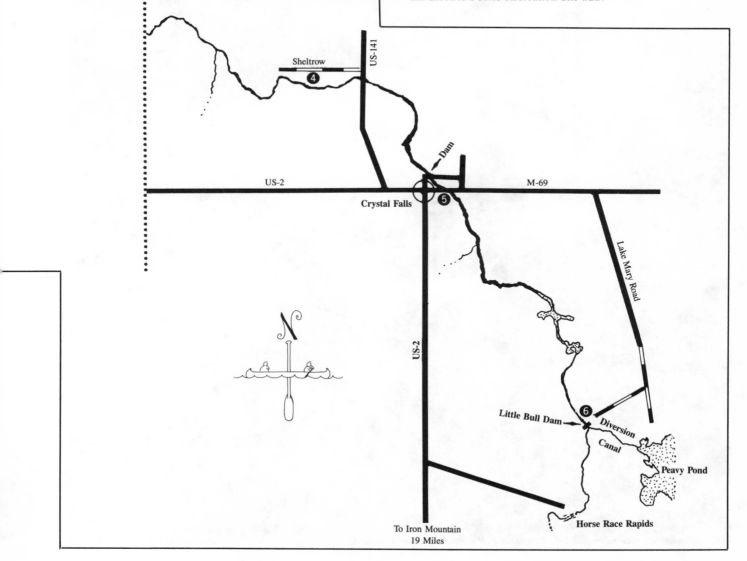

PRESQUE ISLE RIVER

Counties:	**Gogebic, Ontonagon**
Start/End:	**M-28 Bridge to South Boundary Road Bridge**
Miles:	**17.5**
Gradient:	**M-28 to Steiger's Bridge — 17.5 ft/mile**
	Steiger's Bridge to South Boundary Road — 46.5 ft/mile
Portages:	**Several falls and rapids, moderately difficult to very difficult**
Rapids/Falls:	**Many unnamed rapids — Class I-IV**
	Minnewawa, Nimikon, Nakomis, Lepisto, and Iagoo Falls
Campgrounds:	**One**
Canoe Liveries:	**None**

Skill Required: III-IV
Topo. Maps: Thomaston (15 min.)

The Presque Isle below M-28 is the most challenging whitewater river in Michigan, if not the entire Midwest. *Canoe Magazine* (July 1981) listed it as one of the 10 North American rivers "that define the outer edge of contemporary whitewater paddling," and it has a reputation among experienced whitewater paddlers for being a difficult, unpredictable river that tests their abilities. Local DNR, USFS and law-enforcement agencies report having to frequently transport stranded and injured paddlers out of the Presque Isle. The country is wild, access is extremely limited, and it cannot be stressed too strongly that this is a river only for experienced, well-equipped and safety-minded kayakers and canoeists.

Although there is navigable water as far upstream as the West Branch of the Presque Isle — above Presque Isle Flowage in south-central Gogebic County — we decided to include in this description only the 17.5 miles of whitewater from US-28 to above Lake Superior. The section above M-28 contains primarily slow water through lowland forests and tag alders, with light rapids below Presque Isle Flowage and below Yondota Falls, north of Marenisco. Fishing is said to be good in the upper reaches, and canoeing is suitable for paddlers with intermediate ability. Expect occasional logjams and downed trees as well as a quarter-mile portage around Yondota Falls.

To attempt the 17.5 miles of Class II-IV rapids below M-28, it is necessary to divide the trip in half. We have heard of advanced kayakers who know the river well making the entire trip in one long day, but the more usual time required is at least two days. Figure an average of a little more than one mile per hour, which takes into account numerous stops to scout rapids and negotiate several short portages as well as one long one. The river divides conveniently at a bridge known as both Connorsville Bridge and Steiger's Bridge. The catch is that the road and bridge are private, and to gain access it is necessary to get a key to the road gates from Mr. Steiger at Steiger's Hardware and Home Center, on US-2 just east of Bessemer.

Water levels fluctuate greatly on the Presque Isle. In the past, there has been a water gauge located a couple of hundred feet below South Boundary Road Bridge on the right bank. Readings of 7.0 to 7.8 feet are considered optimum, with higher levels too dangerous, and lower levels creating the need for many more portages. Ideal levels are usually found in May and early June. April levels tend to be high, and cold water makes wet suits advisable. USGS water-gauge data indicates a flow-rate range from 1500 cubic feet per second in spring to as low as 40 cubic feet per second in August. It is worth noting that the Presque Isle does not lose navigable water levels as quickly as the nearby Black River, nor does it rise as readily after heavy rains.

M-28 Bridge to Steiger's Bridge
8.5 Miles
7-9 Hours

①   **Access** and parking are good at M-28, where the river is 60-80 feet wide and three to six feet deep with slow current. Water is tea-colored. Terrain is lowland forests with thickets of tag alders and underbrush near the river. Slow water extends for about two miles and can be avoided by putting in at the washed-out bridge on FS-481 one mile west of the M-28 Bridge.

From here to Steiger's Bridge, rapids steadily increase both in intensity and duration. Initially, light rapids over small to medium-size rocks alternate with wide, lake-like pools of still water. Many of the pools have narrow outlets over natural rock

reefs. Some of these outlets are short, fierce chutes of whitewater over two- to four-foot drops. Gradually the pattern alters to include stretches of rapids between pools. Typical rapids consist of stretches of broken water — over small to medium-size jumbled rocks — punctuated by ledge-drops. The ledges generally occur in a series of steps, some as high as four to five feet, and they often stretch across the entire 80- to 100-foot width of the river. Usually one or two chutes will funnel water over the ledges and create a tongue that allows clear passage. At the bottom of these chutes, watch for standing waves, side- curlers and backrollers — many can easily swamp an open canoe, even at lower water levels.

Minnewawa Falls are a difficult but runnable series of ledge-drops and chutes forced between car- and house-size boulders.

Two major Class III drops require precise maneuvering through narrow and not always obvious channels and should be scouted. The second, especially, demands careful consideration, although it is somewhat forgiving in that a large pond-size pool at the bottom makes rescue comparatively easy. There are several cabins on the shore of the pool, with two-track roads available in emergencies.

Class I-II rapids continue downstream less than a mile to Nimikon Falls. This is a 12- to 15-foot drop that should be portaged, although kayakers have been known to run it on the left side during high water. Portage on the right.

From here to Steiger's Bridge are about 3.5 miles of Class I-II rapids, with occasional drops that might require scouting.

② To reach **Steiger's Bridge**, follow the largest of the dirt logging roads reached off Co. Rd. 519 north of Wakefield. The road is labeled "Old Camp Four Grade" on some maps. One or two gates along the six miles of dirt road are likely to be locked and require a key from Steiger's Hardware in Bessemer.

Steiger's Bridge to South Boundary Road Bridge
9 Miles
7 1/2 - 10 Hours

The section below Steiger's Bridge is considerably more difficult than the one above. Beginning just below the bridge are about eight miles of continuous Class II-IV rapids with an average descent of 46.5 feet per mile. Access to the banks is difficult through much of this section, with small eddies often being the only places to rest and scout. Rapids increase in intensity, with drops becoming more frequent and larger as you progress through the first mile of river.

After about one mile, Triple Drop, a trio of small falls and chutes, marks the beginning of the infamous gorge of the Presque Isle — a mile-long pitch of intense Class III-IV rapids (Class V in spring) in which the river descends 140 feet. The gorge is through a steep valley with densely wooded banks 120-150 feet high. Access to the banks from within the canyon is possible but extremely difficult due to fast water near shore, steep banks, and heavy growth of underbrush and trees. Portage is recommended for all but the most advanced paddlers.

Triple Drop can be scouted and run, but the proximity of the gorge directly downstream makes mishaps so hazardous that we recommend portaging the entire stretch. Take out on the left before Triple Drop, where the banks are about 75 feet high, and fight through underbrush to the top of the ridge. The portage is long and exhausting but highly recommended over entering the gorge. The river makes a wide swing to the left (west), and by hiking northwest you can intercept the river below the gorge. There is no portage trail, but one-quarter mile inland is a series of logging trails that makes passage considerably easier than trail-blazing through the woods. Hike at least a mile until the trail descends to the river. Nakomis Falls marks the end of the gorge and is visible just upstream from the point where the trail comes closest to the river. Access is down a 15-foot bank.

From here to Lepisto Falls, rapids continue without let-up. Drops rate Class III, possibly IV, and the rapids between them are a solid Class II. Lepisto Falls is a Class IV drop that should be portaged on the left, although it can be run by experts in covered boats.

Below Lepisto Falls, rapids continue, with several major drops that require scouting and perhaps portaging, but intensity gradually lowers. The final two miles are through Class I-II rapids with some stretches of light riffles and slower water. These final miles are within the Porcupine Mountains State Park and are dominated by enormous virgin pines and hemlocks. Wildlife, including bald eagles, is abundant.

Access is good at **South Boundary Road Bridge** with fair roadside parking. Take out on the left upstream side of the bridge. Nawadaha, Manido and Manabezho falls are directly downstream and make continuing the final mile to Lake Superior inadvisable. There is camping at Presque Isle Campground near the mouth.

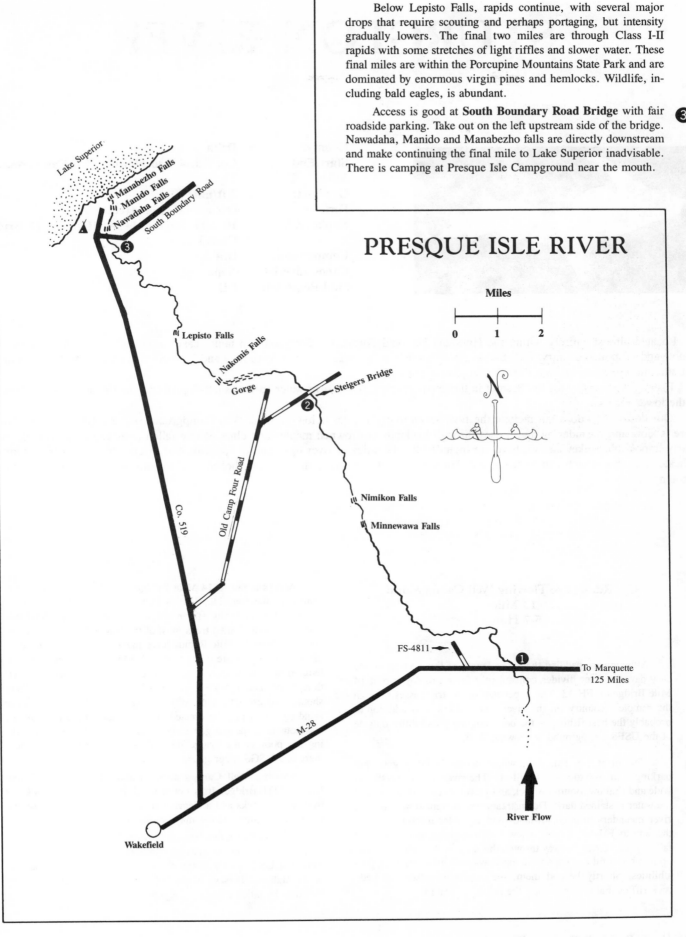

PRESQUE ISLE RIVER

STURGEON RIVER

County:	Delta
Start/End:	Co. Rd. 442 to Flowing Well Campground
Miles:	13
Gradient:	7 ft/mile
Portages:	Occasional fallen trees
Rapids/Falls:	10 Mile Rapids, below Highway 13 Bridge — Class I-II
Campgrounds:	One
Canoe Liveries:	None
Skill Required:	I-II

Located almost entirely within the Hiawatha National Forest, the Sturgeon is a tame, easily accessible river that passes through remote and unspoiled country. Like the nearby Whitefish, it is a seasonal river, with May and June offering ideal water levels, although a wet autumn will bring enough water for enjoyable trips.

Fishing is primarily for brook trout in the upper reaches, with warm-water species such as pike and smallmouth bass predominating in the lower reaches.

Our description does not include the final seven to eight miles below Flowing Well Campground and the US-2 Bridge. The river there is slow and meandering and passes through lowlands of drowned maples and elms, where fallen trees and logjams make passage nearly impossible. Likewise, we have not included the 19 miles of river upstream of Co. Rd. 440 to Co. Rd. 442. USFS information indicates that this stretch can be navigated, but we found it too small, shallow and choked with logjams and fallen trees for enjoyable canoeing.

Co. Rd. 442 to Flowing Well Campground
13 Miles
5-7 Hours

Although we paddled the entire length of this section in one easy day, the river divides conveniently for a two-day trip at 14 Mile Bridge on FH-13. The upper half of the trip passes through the remotest country on the river and offers — in addition to probably the best fishing — the best camping possibilities outside of the USFS campground at Flowing Well.

1 Put in at Co. Rd. 442, where **access** is fairly good but parking is limited to a small pull-off. The river here is 30-40 feet wide and shallow. Bottom is rock and gravel, current is quick, and the water is stained dark. Downstream, the current slows, and the river meanders through lowlands and tag-alder thickets most of the way to FH-13. Expect a few minor logjams and occasional fallen trees. About midway through the section, the country opens up into beautiful and expansive meadows with great camping possibilities. Shortly beyond them, the current increases over bedrock riffles that continue until the bridge at FH-13.

Access is fair at **14 Mile Bridge** on FH-13, and parking is **2** limited to the roadside. Riffles here give way quickly to slow water and meandering streambed that passes through lowlands and hardwoods. Fallen trees most of the way to the public access site just above 10 Mile Rapids force many short but tedious portages. The rapids are composed of a 50-yard-long series of low ledge-drops, with easy passage between minor obstacles. Although not challenging to experienced whitewater paddlers, others should use caution, especially during high water, when large standing waves may be created. Downstream, there are similar, less notable drops and generally quick current. Access and parking are poor at the bridge on USFS-2231 (28th Road), where there is a USGS water gauge.

Flowing Well Campground is about half an hour below **3** USFS- 2231 Bridge. It is not marked from the river; look for trails to the banks and a clearing at the top of a low ridge on the right, where picnic tables may be visible.

US-2 is five miles beyond Flowing Well Campground. Expect slow water and increasing numbers of fallen trees to there. Access at US-2 is only fair, with parking limited to the shoulders of the highway. Passage below US-2 is not recommended due to blockage by fallen trees and logjams.

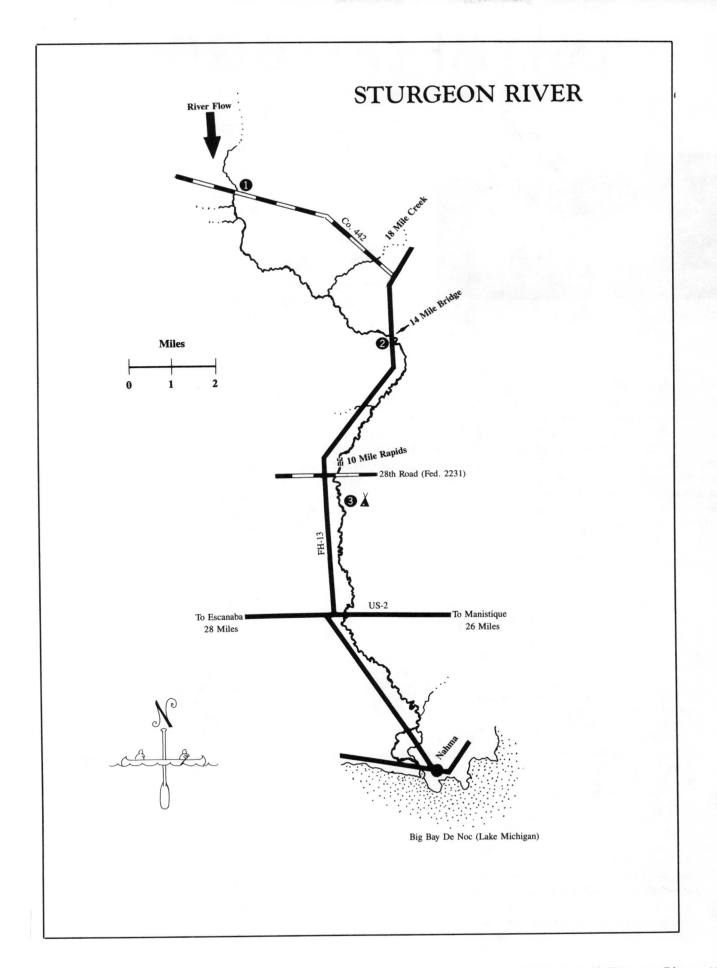

STURGEON RIVER

River Flow

❶

Co. 442

18 Mile Creek

14 Mile Bridge

❷

Miles

0   1   2

10 Mile Rapids

28th Road (Fed. 2231)

❸

FH-13

To Escanaba
28 Miles

US-2

To Manistique
26 Miles

N

Nahma

Big Bay De Noc (Lake Michigan)

TWO HEARTED RIVER

County:	Luce
Start/End:	High Bridge on Co. Rd. 407 to rivermouth
Miles:	20.5
Gradient:	High Bridge to Reed and Green Bridge — 4.2 ft/mile
	Reed and Green Bridge to mouth — 3.6 ft/mile
Portages:	Occasional fallen trees
Rapids/Falls:	None
Campgrounds:	Several
Canoe Liveries:	One
Skill Required:	I
Topo. Maps:	Muskallonge Lake SE, Muskallonge Lake East, Betsy Lake NW (7.5 min.)

If only on the strength of its unforgettable name, the Two Hearted is certainly the best-known river in the Upper Peninsula. Ernest Hemingway contributed greatly to its fame when he used it for the title of his short story about the Fox River, "Big Two Hearted River." For Hemingway the appeal, as he once wrote, was simply that "it's poetry," but fishermen and canoeists have long considered the river to have other appeals as well.

Fishing is excellent for steelhead during spring and fall runs, and for brook trout in the upper reaches and tributaries.

The best canoeing is surprisingly limited on this only Upper Peninsula river to be included in Michigan's Natural Rivers category and the only one in the state to be designated a Wilderness River. While it is possible to navigate a canoe on both the South Branch and East Branch of the Two Hearted, these tributaries are reported to be very small and obstructed. The upper mainstream below High Bridge is also frequently obstructed and is not recommended for a casual trip. Much of the river passes through Lake Superior State Forest, and several state-forest campgrounds are available. Basic paddling skills are sufficient to handle any of the Two Hearted's light riffles, except in early spring when extremely high water creates hazards. Early and midsummer plagues of black flies are legendary and should be prepared for.

High Bridge (Co. Rd. 407) to Reed and Green Bridge (Co. Rd. 410)
9.5 Miles
5-8 Hours

Float time will vary on this section depending on the number of obstructions and ability to bypass them. Expect at least a dozen fallen trees to require lift-over or portaging. The river near High Bridge is small (30-40 feet wide) and quite fast over rocks and gravel. In summer expect to bump rocks in shallow riffles. From here downstream, the current alternates quick over light riffles with sections of slow, deeper water. Depths are one to three feet with some deep holes at the bends. Water is tea-colored. Terrain is hills of hardwoods near the bridge with lowlands of tag alders and marshes downstream.

1 Access is fair, with limited parking, at the **washed-out bridge** just below High Bridge. High Bridge Forest Campground has primitive facilities.

Most of the fallen trees are encountered in the upper three-fourths of the section. A canoe campground at Lone Pine is an alternative overnight stop and has primitive facilities. There is apparently no access to the campground by road.

2 Access and parking are good at **Reed and Green Bridge** (Co. Rd. 410). The state-forest campground just downstream has primitive facilities and fair access to the river.

Reed and Green Bridge (Co. Rd. 410) to Rivermouth
11 Miles
3-4 Hours

This is the most frequently paddled section of the Two Hearted, but it will seldom be crowded. The river is 35-45 feet wide, and depth is two to four feet over a bottom of gravel and scattered large rocks or sand. Low hills of oaks, birch, pines and spruce rise away from the river's occasionally short, steep banks; tag alders are common near the water. Moderate current and fairly deep water alternate with short, light riffles over gravel bars. Occasional fallen trees hinder progress — most can be by-passed, although one or two may need portaging.

Toward the end of this section, dunes appear. The Lake Superior surf can be heard long before the end of the river. Scattered houses and cabins are visible from the river. Numerous sandbars make convenient resting and picnic stops.

Access and parking are good beyond the foot bridge at **Two Hearted River Forest Campground**, just before the mouth. Supplies are available one-quarter mile south on Co. Rd. 423. **3**

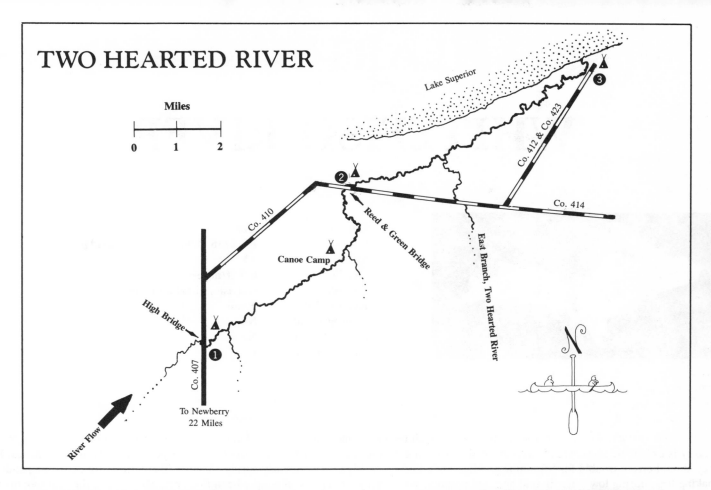

TWO HEARTED RIVER

Miles

0   1   2

Lake Superior

Co. 412 & Co. 423

③

②

Co. 410

Co. 414

Reed & Green Bridge

Canoe Camp

East Branch, Two Hearted River

High Bridge

N

①

Co. 407

To Newberry
22 Miles

River Flow

WHITEFISH RIVER

County:	Delta
Start/End:	FS-2236 Bridge to US-2 Bridge
Miles:	13
Gradient:	6.9 ft/mile
Portages:	Occasional fallen trees
Rapids/Falls:	None
Campgrounds:	None
Canoe Liveries:	None
Skill Required:	I

This short river, with its clear water flowing through remote country, makes a good choice for a one-day float or fishing trip. Water quality is excellent, and current varies from slow to quick. There are many riffles and light rapids, especially in the upper reaches, but they should create trouble for beginning paddlers only during the high water of early spring. A more likely difficulty exists for paddlers making trips during low water in mid and late summer, when many stretches will simply be unfloatable. Most years, the best months for ideal water levels are May and June.

Camping potential is only fair due to private property and thick underbrush in many places. Fishing is for brook trout in the upper reaches and smallmouth bass from near the junctions of the East and West Branches downstream.

FS-2236 on East Branch to US-2
13 Miles
4-6 Hours

According to the U.S. Forest Service, access to the East Branch of the Whitefish is possible as far upstream as Trout Lake, off Co. Rd. 00-3. We found that section too small and congested with fallen trees to be enjoyable, although it would be a challenging trip through remote country for anyone with the energy to take it. Expect much of the river to be fairly quick, flowing over bedrock, and shallow except during the spring.

(1) Access at **FR-2236 Bridge** (38th Road) is fair with very limited roadside parking. The river from here is 30-50 feet wide, quick, shallow and rocky. Mixed hardwoods, conifers, cedars and tag alders line the banks. From here until the junction with the West Branch, shallow riffles alternate with slow, deep boulder-paved pools. Some suitable campsites can be found on state land between stretches of private property. A few houses and cottages are scattered through the section.

After the junction with the West Branch, water volume nearly doubles and is probably sufficient for floats longer into the summer. However, because there are no access sites below the junc-

tion of the two branches, the upper shallow water is a necessary inconvenience. The West Branch is said to be canoeable in early spring, at least from Co. Rd. 444 down to the bridge on FR-2236 (a few miles west of the bridge over the East Branch). Farther upstream are several falls that make passage difficult, and in the section below Co. Rd. 444, we have heard that there are rapids that can be run successfully in April and May. Low water makes the West Branch extremely shallow, and when we were there near the beginning of June, water levels were already too low for sensible paddling. USFS information indicates a float time of one to 1 1/2 hours from CR-444 to FR-2236, with no information available for the stretch from FR-2236 to the junction with the East Branch.

The remainder of the section has long riffles where the widened riverbed creates shallow water, but for the most part, expect easy passage to US-2. The final two to three miles of river slows — with long, pool-like stretches lined with dead trees and drowned logs — before the marshes that characterize the rivermouth region of the Whitefish. The final miles can be tedious in a strong headwind; otherwise, they are a pleasant, quiet trip through meadows and marshes with waterfowl abundant.

Access at US-2 is good downstream, left of the **bridge**. Parking is limited.

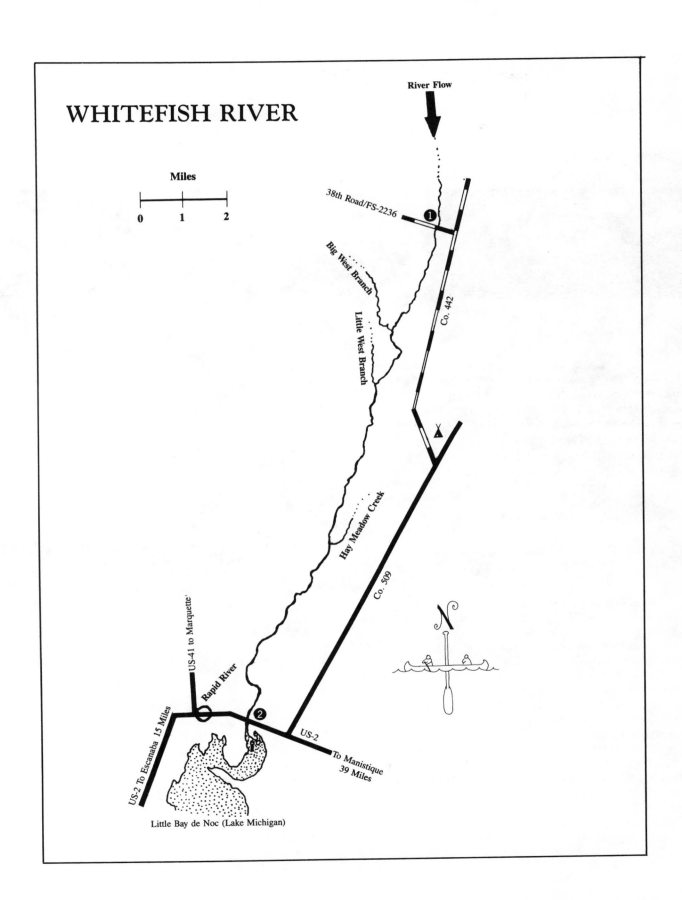

WHITEFISH RIVER

Miles

0   1   2

River Flow

38th Road/FS-2236

1

Co. 442

Big West Branch

Little West Branch

Hay Meadow Creek

Co. 509

US-41 to Marquette

Rapid River

US-2 To Escanaba 15 Miles

2

US-2

To Manistique 39 Miles

Little Bay de Noc (Lake Michigan)

N

APPENDIX I

THE INTERNATIONAL SCALE OF RIVER DIFFICULTY

CLASS I: Moving water with a few riffles and small waves. Few or no obstructions.

CLASS II: Easy rapids with waves up to three feet, and wide, clear channels that are obvious without scouting. Some maneuvering is required.

CLASS III: Rapids with high, irregular waves often capable of swamping an open canoe. Narrow passages that often require complex maneuvering. May require scouting from shore.

CLASS IV: Long, difficult rapids with constricted passages that often require precise maneuvering in very turbulent waters. Scouting from shore is often necessary, and conditions make rescue difficult. Generally not possible for open canoes. Boaters in covered canoes and kayaks should be able to Eskimo roll.

CLASS V: Extremely difficult, long, and very violent rapids with highly congested routes which nearly always must be scouted from shore. Rescue conditions are difficult and there is significant hazard to life in event of mishap. Ability to Eskimo roll is essential for kayaks and canoes.

CLASS VI: Difficulties of Class V carried to the extreme of navigability. Nearly impossible and very dangerous. For teams of experts only, after close study and with all precautions taken.

If rapids on a river generally fit into one of these classifications, but the water temperature is below 50 degrees F., or if the trip is an extended trip in a wilderness area, the river should be considered one class more difficult than normal.

(Thanks to the American Whitewater affiliation for this information. For a copy of the "American Whitewater Safety Code" send a self-addressed, stamped envelope to the American Whitewater Affiliation, P.O. Box 1261, Jefferson City MO 65102.)

APPENDIX II
MICHIGAN RAPIDS

LOWER PENINSULA			
RIVER	NAME OF RAPIDS/LOCATION	DIFFICULTY	PAGE
BLACK	Crocket's Rapids, above South Black River Road Bridge	I	12
BOARDMAN	Beitner Rapids, below Beitner Road Bridge	I-II	15
CHIPPEWA	Unnamed rapids, above Deerfield County Park Unnamed rapids, below Chippewa Road Bridge	I I-II	21 22
FLAT	Unnamed rapids, at old dam site before Ingall's Bridge	I	26
HURON	Unnamed rapids, at Territorial Road Bridge Delhi Rapids, above Delhi Road Bridge	I I-II	30 30
LITTLE MANISTEE	Several unnamed rapids, below Nine Mile Bridge	I-II	39
LITTLE MUSKEGON	Several unnamed rapids, below County Line Road Bridge	I	41
MUSKEGON	Big Rapids, below Baldwin Street Bridge in Big Rapids	I-II	52
OCQUEOC	Numerous unnamed rapids, below County Road 638 Bridge	I-II	54
PERE MARQUETTE	Rainbow Rapids, below Rainbow Rapids Landing	I	58
PIGEON	Numerous unnamed rapids, below Pigeon River Road Bridge Numerous unnamed rapids, below M-68 Bridge	I I-II	60 61
PINE	Numerous unnamed rapids, above and below M-37 Bridge	I-II	62
RIFLE	Overhead Pipeline Rapids, below M-55 Bridge Unnamed rapids, below Greenwood Road Bridge	I-II I	67 67
STURGEON	Numerous unnamed rapids, below Wolverine Park	I-II	73
THORNAPPLE	Unnamed rapids, at Ruehs Park in Alaska	I	75
THUNDER BAY	Speehley Rapids, below M-65 Bridge	I	77

UPPER PENINSULA

RIVER	NAME OF RAPIDS/LOCATION	DIFFICULTY	PAGE
BLACK	Granite Rapids, below County Road 513 Bridge Numerous unnamed rapids, above and below Ramsay Numerous unnamed rapids, below US-2 Bridge	II I-II II-III	83 83 84
BRULE	Several unnamed rapids, below M-189 Bridge Unnamed rapids, below Pentoga La Chapelle Rapids, below US-2 Bridge	I-II II I-II	87 87 88
ESCANABA	Unnamed rapids, below Gwinn Unnamed rapids, before junction with West Branch Escanaba Unnamed rapids, before Boney Falls Basin Unnamed rapids, below Boney Falls Basin	I-II I-II I-II II-III	89 89 91 91
FORD	Several unnamed rapids, below US-2 Bridge	I-III	93
MENOMINEE*	Big Bull Rapids, below Brule River Dam Piers Gorge, below Little Quinnesec Falls Dam	III III-IV	88 88
MICHIGAMME	Witbeck Rapids, above M-95 Bridge	I-II	100
MONTREAL	Numerous unnamed rapids, below US-2 Bridge Numerous unnamed rapids, below Saxon Falls Dam	I-II II-III	102 103
ONTONAGON, SOUTH BRANCH	Flannigan Rapids, below M-28 Bridge Unnamed rapids before Victoria Falls Reservoir	I-II II-III	105
ONTONAGON, EAST BRANCH	Numerous unnamed rapids, below FS-208 Road	II-III	107
ONTONAGON, MAINSTREAM	Irish Rapids, 4.5 miles below US-45 Bridge Grand Rapids, 7.5 miles below US-45 Bridge	I-II I-II	108 108
ONTONAGON, MIDDLE BRANCH	Several unnamed rapids, below Burned Dam Little Falls Rapids, before Bond Falls Flowage	I-II II-III	110 111
PAINT	Unnamed rapids, below junction with Net River Hemlock Rapids, Upper and Lower, below Gibbs City Unnamed rapids, below Crystal Falls Dam Horserace Rapids, below Little Bull Dam	I-II II-III I-II Not Runnable	113 114 115 115
PRESQUE ISLE	Numerous unnamed rapids, below M-28 Bridge Continuous rapids from Steiger's Bridge to Lake Superior	I-III I-IV	117 118
STURGEON	10 Mile Rapids, below Highway 13	I-II	120

*Although we have not included the Menominee River in this book, we have given a brief description of these two notable rapids at the end of the Brule River section, page 88.

APPENDIX III
PERMITS and SPECIAL REGULATIONS

PINE RIVER

Regulated Area: Pine River Corridor. Defined as the land one-quarter mile on each side of the final 26 miles of river (approximately from Lincoln Bridge downstream).

Regulations: 1. No camping except at Peterson Bridge Campground. An exception is made for winter camping, from December 1 through March 31, when camping is permitted in the Pine River Corridor by special permit at designated sites. 2. Watercraft can be launched only at sites listed as developed access sites. 3. Watercraft cannot be left unattended for more than 36 hours. 4. Permits are required to enter or leave the river using national forest land.

Permits: All boats, canoes, innertubes, rafts and inflatables are considered watercraft and require permits during the period May 1 to October 1. There is no charge for permits. Private users who bring canoes (or other watercraft) with them and do their own hauling, launching and retrieval must obtain permits from the Forest Service Permit Station, located one-half mile west of the M-55/M-37 junction on M-55. Canoe-livery customers can obtain permits directly from any six area liveries. Reservations of permits can be arranged by mail, telephone or personal visit.

Mail: Beginning April 1, mail requests are accepted and are honored on a first-come, first-served basis. Address: District Ranger, USDA-Forest Service, Cadillac Ranger District, 1800 W. M-55, Cadillac, MI 49601.

Telephone: Beginning April 1, telephone requests for reservations are accepted Monday through Friday from 8:00 a.m. to 4:30 p.m. Phone: (616) 862-3333.

Reservation Requests must include the following items:
1. Separate reservations for each group of six canoes.
2. Name and address of the applicant.
3. The dates desired, including an alternate date.

Other Conditions: 1. It is advisable to list other names in the party when applying for reservations; the person signing for the permit must be listed on the application.
2. Permits must be claimed in person — they will not be sent through the mail.
3. Permits must be picked up by 10:00 a.m. of departure day, but no sooner than 48 hours before that day.
4. Unclaimed reservations will be given out on a first-come basis after 10:00 a.m. of departure day.

Allocation of Permits:

	Total Private	Total Livery
Monday through Friday	60	140
Saturday and Sunday	100	516

PERE MARQUETTE RIVER

Regulated Area: Forks Public Access to Custer Bridge

Regulations: 1. A permit is required to launch or retrieve a watercraft from national forest land between May 10 and September 20.
2. Watercraft may not be launched or retrieved from national forest land before 9:00 a.m. or after 6:00 p.m. between May 10 and September 20.
3. Possessing or operating a motor is prohibited above Indian Bridge.
4. Watercraft cannot be left unattended more than 36 hours.
5. Camping is prohibited on national forest land except at designated sites.

Permits: Permits are required between May 10 and September 20 to launch or retrieve from national forest land. There is no charge for permits and, at least at the time of this writing, no daily limits. Permits are available at the Ranger Station in Baldwin and from all area canoe liveries.

APPENDIX IV

FURTHER INFORMATION — GENERAL

Canoe Liveries

For an up-to-date list of canoe liveries in Michigan write:
Recreational Canoeing Association, P.O. Box 296, Montague MI 49437

Topographical Maps

Topographical (also known as quadrangle) maps of Michigan are available in 7.5-minute series (1:24,000 scale) or 15- minute series (1:62,500 scale) from:

Branch of Distribution, Eastern Region U.S. Geological Survey, 1200 South Eads St., Arlington VA 22202; U.S. Department of the Interior Geological Survey, 6520 Mercantile Way, Suite 5, Lansing MI 48910; and Michigan United Conservatioin Clubs, Box 30235, Lansing MI 48909.

Recommended Reading

There is an extensive, sometimes baffling, number of canoeing and kayaking books available. The following is nothing like a complete list, but is, rather, a representative sampling that includes some of our favorites.

Getting Started:
Path of the Paddle: An Illustrated Guide to the Art of Canoeing, Bill Mason, Van Nostrand Reinhold, Toronto and New York, 1983.
Sports Illustrated Canoeing, Dave Harrison, Harper and Row, New York, 1981.
The Open Canoe; Bill Riviere; Little, Brown and Company; Boston; 1985

Whitewater:
A Whitewater Handbook for Canoe and Kayak, John T. Urban, Appalachian Mountain Club, Boston, 1974.
Whitewater!; Norman Strung, Sam Curtis and Earl Perry; Macmillan; New York; 1976.

Wilderness Expeditions:
The Complete Wilderness Paddler, James West Davidson and John Rugge, Vintage Books, New York, 1983.
Wilderness Canoeing and Camping, Cliff Jacobson, Dutton, New York, 1977.
One Incredible Journey, Clayton Klein and Verlen Kruger, Wilderness House Books, Fowlerville MI, 1985.

FURTHER INFORMATION — SPECIFIC RIVERS

LOWER PENINSULA

AU SABLE, Mainstream

Grayling Chamber of Commerce
Grayling MI 49738
(517) 348-2921

DNR — Au Sable State Forest
RR #1, Box 146
M-33 North
Mio MI 48647

AU SABLE, South Branch

South Branch Canoe Livery Association
Roscommon MI 48653

DNR—Roscommon Forest Area
8717 N. Roscommon Rd.
P.O. Box 128
Roscommon MI 48653

BETSIE

DNR—Platte River Field Office
15220 Honor Hwy.
Beulah MI 49617
(616) 325-4611

BOARDMAN

DNR—Traverse City Forest Area
404 W. 14th St.
Traverse City MI 49684
(616) 946-4920

FLAT

Michigan Grand River Watershed Council
3322 W. Michigan Ave.
Lansing MI 48917
(517) 489-0552

DNR—Flat River Field Office
RR #2
Belding MI 48809

HURON

Huron-Clinton Metropolitan Authority
3050 Penobscot Bldg.
Detroit MI 48226

JORDAN

DNR—Boyne City Field Office
303 North St.
P.O. Box 120
Boyne City MI 49712
(616) 582-6681

KALAMAZOO

DNR—Allegan Field Office
4590 118th Ave.
Allegan MI 49010
(616) 673-8176

MUSKEGON

Croton-Hardy Chamber of Commerce
Rte. 2
Newaygo MI 49337

OCQUEOC

Rogers City Chamber of Commerce
P.O. Box 55C
Rogers City MI 49779
(517) 734-2535

PERE MARQUETTE

USFS—Manistee National Forest
Baldwin Ranger District
Baldwin MI 49304
(616) 745-4613

PIGEON

DNR—Pigeon River Forest Area
RR #1, Box 179
Vanderbilt MI 49795
(517) 983-4101

PINE

USDA-Forest Service
Cadillac Ranger District
1800 W. 'M-55
Cadillac, MI 49601

PLATTE

See *Betsie River*

STURGEON

DNR—Indian River Forest Area
6984 M-68
Indian River MI 49749
(616) 238-9313

THORNAPPLE

Michigan Grand River Watershed Council
3322 W. Michigan Ave.
Lansing MI 48917
(517) 489-0552

THUNDER BAY

Alpena Area Chamber of Commerce
P.O. Box 65
Alpena MI 49707
1-800-582-1906

DNR—Alpena Field Office
4343 M-32
Alpena MI 48707
(517) 354-2209

UPPER PENINSULA

BLACK

Bessemer Chamber of Commerce
Bessemer MI 49911
(906) 667-0832

Ironwood Chamber of Commerce
P.O. Box 400
Ironwood MI 49801
(906) 932-1122

Wakefield Chamber of Commerce
Wakefield MI 49968

DNR—Wakefield Field Office
US-2
Wakefield MI 49968
(906) 224-2771

USFS—Bessemer Ranger District
Bessemer MI 49911
(906) 667-0261

BRULE

Iron County Chamber of Commerce
Iron River MI 49935
(906) 265-3822

Iron County Chamber of Commerce
Crystal Falls MI 49920

DNR—Crystal Falls Forest Area
US-2 West
P.O. Box 300
Crystal Falls MI 49920
(906) 875-6622

USFS—Iron River Ranger District
Iron River MI 49935
(906) 265-5139

(continued on following page)

ESCANABA

Delta County Area Chamber of Commerce
Escanaba MI 49829
(906) 786-2192

DNR—Escanaba River State Forest
1126 N. Lincoln Rd.
P.O. Box 495
Escanaba MI 49829
(906) 786-2351

DNR-Gwinn Forest Area
Gwinn MI 49851
(906) 346-9201

FORD

See *Escanaba River*

FOX

DNR—Seney Field Office
M-28
Seney MI 49883
(906) 449-3346

INDIAN

Manistique Chamber of Commerce
Manistique MI 49854
(906) 341-5010

USFS—U.S. Dept. of Agriculture
2727 N. Lincoln Rd.
Escanaba MI 49829

USFS—Rapid River Ranger District
US-2
Rapid River MI 49878

USFS— Manistique Ranger District
US-2
Manistique MI 49854

MANISTIQUE

Manistique Chamber of Commerce
Manistique MI 49854
(906) 341-5010

DNR—Thompson Field Office
RR #1, P.O. Box 335
Manistique MI 49854
(906) 341-6917

MICHIGAMME

Marquette Area Chamber of Commerce
Marquette MI 49855
(906) 226-6591

MONTREAL

For current water-flow information call the
Saxon Falls Power Dam at (715) 893-2213.

For other information see *Black River*

ONTONAGON

Ontonagon Chamber of Commerce
P.O. Box 266
Ontonagon MI 49953
(906) 884-4735

Watersmeet Chamber of Commerce
Watersmeet MI 49969
(906) 358-4390 or 358-4522

USFS—Bergland Ranger District
Bergland MI 49910
(906) 575-3441

USFS—Kenton Ranger District
Kenton MI 49943
(906) 852-3501

USFS—Ontonagon Ranger District
Ontonagon MI 49953
(906) 884-2411

USFS— Watersmeet Ranger District
Watersmeet MI 49969
(906) 358-4551

PAINT

See *Brule River*

PRESQUE ISLE

See *Black River*

STURGEON

See *Indian River*

TWO HEARTED

Newberry Chamber of Commerce
P.O. Box 308
Newberry MI 49868
(906) 293-5562

DNR—Newberry Forest Area
309 W. McMillan Ave.
P.O. Box 445
Newberry MI 49868
(906) 293-5131

WHITEFISH

See *Indian River*

APPENDIX VI

MICHIGAN NATURAL RIVERS PROGRAM

Michigan's Natural Rivers Act (Act 231) was initiated in 1970 for the purpose of protecting certain rivers from unwise development and use. The objectives of the program are:

1. *General*: To preserve and protect the ecologic, aesthetic and historic values and enhance the many recreational values of the river and adjacent lands.
2. *Water Quality*: To maintain or improve water quality consistent with the designated classification of the river and adhere to the concept of non-degradation of water quality.
3. *Free-Flowing Condition*: To maintain existing free- flowing conditions where they presently exist for the purpose of preserving this part of the natural environment of the river.
4. *Fish and Wildlife Resource*: To maintain, protect and enhance desirable fish and wildlife populations and plant communities.
5. *River Environment*: To protect riverbanks, the floodplain and other adjacent river areas essential to the perpetuation of the total environment of the river system.

There are three categories of Natural Rivers in Michigan's program. They are:

Wilderness: A free-flowing river, with essentially primitive, undeveloped adjacent lands.

Wild-Scenic: A river with wild, forested borders that is near developed lands and is moderately accessible.

Country-Scenic: A river in an agricultural setting — with pastoral borders and some homes — that is readily accessible.

Designated Michigan Natural Rivers are:

Wilderness River: Two Hearted
Wild-Scenic Rivers: Betsie, Boardman, Jordan, Kalamazoo, Pere Marquette, Pigeon, Rifle and White
Country-Scenic: Boardman*, Flat, Huron, Rogue** and White*

*The Boardman and the White rivers have sections designated Wild-Scenic and sections designated Country-Scenic.
**The Rogue River is not included in this guide.

NATIONAL WILD and SCENIC RIVERS PROGRAM

The National Wild and Scenic Act, like the Michigan Natural Rivers Act, is intended to preserve and protect rivers with outstanding aesthetic, scenic, historic and other features. Rivers are designated as Wild, Scenic or Recreational. At this time, there are 66 rivers, or portions of rivers, so designated in the nation. In Michigan, the Pere Marquette and the portion of the Au Sable mainstream from Mio to Alcona Dam are designated as National Scenic Rivers. In addition, other sections of the Au Sable, the South Branch of the Au Sable, the Manistee and the Pine rivers are being studied for possible inclusion in the national designation.

Further information about the natural rivers programs of Michigan and the U.S. can be obtained from:

Michigan Department of Natural Resources
Division of Land Resources Programs
7th Floor Stevens T. Mason Building
P.O. Box 30028
Lansing, Michigan 48909
(517) 373-1170

THE AUTHORS

Jerry Dennis (L) and Craig Date (R)

Craig Date and Jerry Dennis began canoeing together 10 years ago when they joined a group of Traverse City paddlers who were making annual winter trips down northern-Michigan rivers. Since then they have paddled together all over the state.

When he's not canoeing or catching bragging-size bass, Craig Date is a freelance photographer and also an illustrator and musician. He has been a social worker, a carpenter and a long-haul truck driver and is currently studying applied music.

Jerry Dennis is a freelance writer who has had articles and stories appear in several state and national publications including *Canoe* magazine, *The Flyfisher* and the *Michigan* magazine of the *Detroit News*. When not canoeing or working as a carpenter, he enjoys fishing for trout on many of the rivers described in this book.

Saxon Falls, Montreal River